THE
PRACTICAL
SAILOR

THE PRACTICAL SAILOR

ROGER F. DUNCAN

Editor

CHARLES SCRIBNER'S SONS • NEW YORK

Library of Congress Cataloging in Publication Data

Main entry under title:

The Practical sailor.

Selected articles originally published in The practical sailor, 1975–1979.
Includes index.
1. Yachts and yachting. 2. Seamanship.
3. Navigation. I. Duncan, Roger F.
VM331.P68   623.8′223   80-22515
ISBN 0-684-1662-6

1 3 5 7 9 11 13 15 17 19   V/C   20 18 16 14 12 10 8 6 4 2

Printed in the United States of America

Contents

Preface

Simple, clear, concise, and practical information for yachtsmen of more or less limited means was the conception of William Bean of Warren, Gorham & Lamont in Boston. Under the editorship of the author of this book, *The Practical Sailor* was launched in February 1975.

Consistent with its title and purpose, this periodical was above all practical. Unhampered by advertising, it was concerned with advice proven by practical and personal experience. Where the books and popular magazines advise jibing at once to pick up a man overboard, the *Sailor* tried it under varying conditions and offered advice based on experience. Where the authorities recommend anchoring with scope of six times the depth of water, the *Sailor* found that in no popular harbor is this possible and a reassessment of the whole anchoring problem was necessary.

Soon a widening circle of practical readers began to add ideas either in formal articles or in letters, telephone calls, or conversations. The present volume is a selection from these. Unsigned articles were written by the editor.

In the summer of 1976 *The Practical Sailor* was purchased by Robert Englander of Englander Communications and the same policy continued. If a certain old-fashioned, down-east, gaff-rigged attitude began to be more apparent, perhaps it was because the editor and others too had discovered that many of the old-time ways were efficient, easy, and

inexpensive. Yet new products and new methods were discussed and evaluated. Radar, LORAN-C, diesel engines, and inflatable dinghies provoked comment and discussion.

With the October 1979 issue, *The Practical Sailor* was taken over by Jeff Spranger on a full-time basis, expanded, and modernized. He wanted it to be of increased interest and value to the modern yachtsman. This volume is a selection of some of the most interesting, useful, or provocative articles from the *Sailor's* first four years. Limitations of space made it necessary to omit many equally good articles, especially a series by Susan P. Howell on celestial navigation. Her *Practical Celestial Navigation,* available through Mystic Seaport, is written clearly and fully. In the tradition in which the articles in this book were written, the editor hopes that any reader with comment, criticism, or useful experience to add will write him.

Acknowledgment must be made to William Bean and Robert Englander for fostering the publication and to the latter for permission to publish the articles herein. My wife, Mary, is also largely responsible for the creation of the *Sailor* and this book. She kept files, clipped innumerable publications, cleared away obstructions to progress, and typed almost every issue. My colleague Hugh Williams, who joined the staff in March 1979 to do four pages of "Along Shore" in each issue and who contributed numerous earlier articles, was an encouragement and an inspiration. Robert Barry and Robert Petrilli, the men responsible for the production of *The Practical Sailor,* are to be thanked for its neat and attractive appearance. Mr. Jean Koefoed is responsible for the conception of this book and Michael Pietsch for its publication. Finally, our thanks go to our widening circle of subscribers, readers, and contributors.

Roger F. Duncan
EAST BOOTHBAY, MAINE

1

Design and Construction

Cruising Rigs

The cruising boat must meet all kinds of conditions of sea and wind in protected waters and at sea, at anchor, under way, and hove to. She must be handy enough to navigate intricate passages and crowded harbors, able enough for an offshore passage, and fast enough to get where she is going to the satisfaction of her skipper. Let us leave until later the matter of hull form, deck plan, and cabin layout and consider her rig.

The masthead sloop, the rig adopted by most racing boats, is probably the most efficient. If we remember that a sail is simply a

wing on end, an airfoil, it will be clear that the longer the luff or leading edge of the sail and the faster the wind passes the lee side of the sail, the greater is the drive. In the masthead sloop we have a long luff on each sail and the overlapping jib funnels the wind behind the mainsail most effectively. In order to extend the luffs of the sails without unduly increasing the area of the mainsail, the mast is built as tall as possible and the boom shortened. With the mainsail trimmed very flat and the jib pulled aft hard with a winch, the racing sloop can point high and still foot fast, a winning combination to windward. Considering that the largest part of a race is spent getting to the weather mark, speed to windward is essential. Off the wind, speed is achieved with the spinnaker, which makes up for the tall, narrow mainsail and loose-footed jib, neither very efficient with the wind aft.

The cruising man, however, spends much less time beating to windward and is unlikely to carry a muscular and well-trained spinnaker crew. He may go with one or two companions, perhaps with only his wife or daughter, neither of whom is prepared to wrestle with a thrashing #1 Genoa on a spray-slashed foredeck. Without losing a fair turn of speed, he needs a rig useful both on the wind and off it and one easily reduced or extended. To what extent must he compromise with the efficient racing rig?

In boats under thirty feet, he need compromise very little. The jib, even the #1 Genoa on such a boat, is small enough for one man to subdue, especially if the boat is run off before the wind to provide a lee for it behind the mainsail. By using a staysail with a boom or even a smaller jib with less overlap, the boat can be tacked in close quarters by one man alone or by a "man and a boy." * By extending the main boom enough to make the mainsail effective off the wind, and either moving the mast forward or adding a short bowsprit to preserve proper balance, the advantages of a sloop rig for a boat under thirty feet can be retained. A schooner, ketch, or yawl under thirty feet would lose the efficiency of the single large mainsail, and the mizzen or foresail would be so small as to be quite ineffective.

In larger boats, however, consider seriously the ketch or schooner with a divided fore triangle. Granted, we lose efficiency to windward as we increase the number of sails. The farther forward we go, the slacker each sail must be trimmed in order not to backwind the sail behind it and to provide a proper slot through which the wind is funneled. However, if we are willing to sail 4½–5 points off the wind instead of 3½–4 points, we gain a great deal with a ketch or schooner.

First, on a ketch we divide the area of what would be a rather large mainsail for one man to handle. Second, we move it all inboard and amidships where it is much easier to reef or furl. Third, we have introduced a great deal of flexibility so that in an increasing breeze we need not reef or change jibs but can simply drop one sail or another. First to go would be the jib. Set it on a roller so it can be zipped up like a window shade. If then the ketch carries too much weather helm, ease the mizzen sheet a grind. If it continues to breeze up, take in the mizzen and make a sloop of her. If this is still too much, you can take in the mainsail and sail her under staysail and mizzen. Many ketches will work to windward quite well under this rig. If even this rig is too much, run for shelter or heave to under trysail and storm jib.

With two masts instead of one, neither need be very tall, so they may be more strongly stayed and need not be tuned so

---

*Yachtspersons, Now Hear This

It may appear that *The Practical Sailor* is addressing a male audience exclusively. Such is not the case. The English language has failed to keep up with the quickstep of progress. No pronoun adequately replaces the awkward "his or her." There is no graceful way of saying "helmsman or woman." Helmsperson is a clumsy solution, as is leadsperson, oarsperson, or watchperson. We need more words like *skipper, mate,* and *navigator,* which bear no discriminatory overtones.

tightly, putting less thrust on the masts and less strain on the hull. Also, in light airs, which prevail much of the cruising season, a ketch can spread a magnificent mizzen staysail as well as a variety of spinnakers, drifters, balloon jibs, or whatever the skipper finds appropriate for the strength and training of his crew.

The divided fore triangle, while it clearly prevents pointing as high as with the single head rig, has advantages for the short-handed. Only the jib requires a winch, and that need not be as big as the big sloop's, for the mast is farther forward and the jib smaller. Second, in narrow waters the jib can be furled and the boat tacked by one man, for with the staysail rigged on a traveler like the main and mizzen, no sheet need be tended. In coming to an anchor, picking up a mooring, or coming alongside a float, the jib and mizzen sheets can be manipulated to turn a ketch in her own length or to permit her to lie to a mooring head to wind with the mizzen sheeted flat and the other sheets slack. She can even be sailed straight backward and then cast on either tack by backing the staysail and slacking the mizzen sheet.

A ketch need not be slow, although many are, on the assumption that an underrigged boat is safe. Such is far from the case. Not only is she unresponsive in anything less than a reefing breeze but she is not much fun to sail, hence useless. With a ketch, one can safely carry what might be considered a large press of sail because sail may be quickly and easily reduced.

The schooner has advantages over the ketch in this respect, for the mainsail of the schooner can be larger than that of the ketch

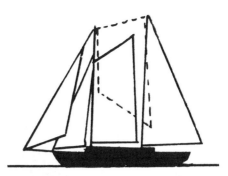

and the foresail fully as large as the mizzen, yet the same flexibility remains. A schooner can be designed to do very well under foresail alone or foresail-and-staysail or mainsail-and-staysail. Off the wind, a schooner sails wing-and-wing and balances well, although it may be well to rig boom tackles to prevent jibes as the commercial vessels used to do.

In light airs a schooner can set a variety of sails between the masts from a fisherman staysail above the foresail to a huge "golliwobbler," a balloon fisherman from the top of the mainmast to the top of the foremast, tacked down to the foot of the foremast and sheeted either to the taffrail or the end of the main boom.

When it comes on to blow, a schooner can be progressively shortened down. First drop the foresail. Next, drop the jib and reef the main after resetting the foresail. Some schooners will do very well, especially off the wind, under foresail and staysail. *In extremis,* a schooner under double-reefed foresail can take almost anything she is likely to meet.

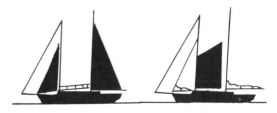

In close quarters a schooner is handy under mainsail, foresail, and staysail and will lie at anchor with mainsail set. Reefing the schooner's mainsail is more difficult than reefing the mainsail of a ketch, but it may seldom be necessary in either case. With her larger mainsail, the schooner may be faster than a ketch, but that is a hard line to draw.

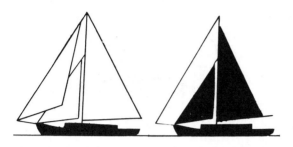

The other possible answer is the cutter, a sloop with the mast well aft and a divided fore triangle. For yachts under forty feet, this is a popular rig, for the mainsail may be reduced in size and the staysail increased. A big jib adds liveliness in light air, yet under mainsail and staysail the cutter does well to windward in a breeze. Off the wind, the staysail can be poled out, but the combination is probably less efficient than in a ketch or schooner. A spinnaker may be almost necessary for a cutter in moderate weather. For the man who wants to pile on the light sail, a gaff-headed cutter with a topmast is a possibility. While this involves a maze of running rigging, it gets a topsail and jib topsail high off the water, yet sail can be quickly reduced.

The yawl rig has its advocates, yet its advantages over the ketch for cruising are few and the limitations it puts on the cutter rig are serious. The staysail schooner is another possibility, and while this is perhaps a faster rig to windward than the conventional schooner, it cannot sail wing-and-wing downwind, hence requires a spinnaker. In yachts under forty feet most yachtsmen prefer the ketch or conventional schooner.

With the flexibility of a divided rig a cruising boat can be easily handled by a small or inexperienced crew.

Rethink the Watertight Cockpit

Either you have a watertight self-bailing cockpit or you do not. If you really need one, you cannot compromise on it; if you do not, why not abandon the concept and plan a cockpit that fits your use of the boat?

Who needs one? If you are going to sea in a small boat with little freeboard and low bulwarks, you need a place to hide. You need a place to brace your feet when you are at the wheel. When you are trimming sails, you need a place to stand so your work can come nearly waist high. Offshore you may run into a gale with breaking seas; therefore you cannot afford a big hole in your deck. The cockpit must be watertight so no water can get below, and it must be as small as possible so that if it is filled, its weight will not bear the stern down and leave you cold turkey for the next breaking sea. Therefore you will have something like a small shallow fiberglass tub with a wide lip that can sit in a hole in the deck, the only break in its complete integrity being a scupper in the bottom leading overboard through a sea cock. Many oceangoing yachts are so rigged and the ocean-racing rules practically require such design.

However, if you are sailing coastwise and never get out where the great seas crest up and break in half an acre of white water, you will no doubt find it convenient to have a small hatch in the cockpit floor so you can get at the engine, which usually lives underneath. The space between the cockpit and the side of the boat, too narrow for a quarterberth and too high for gas and water tanks, is a convenient place to keep stops, a plastic bucket, even life preservers and spare sails. This means hatches in the seat or locker doors in the sides of the ''tub.'' Holes for ventilation of the counter and side decks may be bored just under the deck. A clutch lever may be led up through the floor through a less-than-watertight connection. To make the cabin larger and more accessible, the house is carried aft, the bridge deck eliminated, and the companionway carried down to within perhaps six inches of the cockpit floor.

Convenience and comfort are improved, but the concept of protection against breaking seas has been tacitly abandoned. True, rain water will run out through the scupper, but even just the top of a heavy chop will soon find its way into the bilge. Yet the cockpit is still narrow, shallow, and uncomfortable.

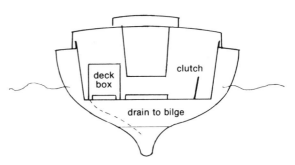

Comfortable coastwise

Cutter Adventure *in trials for Whitbread Round-the-World Race. Note small cockpit. Only compromise is watertight hatch in top of seat.*

If you are not going to sea—and many yachtsmen never do—why not rethink the cockpit completely, as the racing people have done? Make it wide enough and deep enough so people can sit in it comfortably or winch and tail sheets without being in each other's way. Let there be a *big* hatch in the floor so the engine is easily accessible and can be hoisted out conveniently. Let there be deck boxes for storage with cushioned tops. Let us admit that with a floor below the water line, rain and spray will get into the bilge; pipe them there and provide a powerful pump. With the cockpit floor wider and lower, one will not feel as if he were falling off the boat when she heels; for he will be not *on* it but *in* it.

It is interesting to note that commercial sailing vessels seldom had watertight cockpits. The larger ones were flush decked except for deckhouses, and the helmsman stood up to his work. Smaller vessels like long-shore fishermen had wide, deep, open cockpits draining into bilge and narrow side decks so a man could stand close to the side and conveniently haul aboard lobster traps or heavy fish. Seldom did we hear of a Cape Cod catboat's being swamped by breaking seas, and even a Block Islander could run for shelter before it got too rough.

If you are an offshore man, then keep your cockpit small, tight, and uncompromised; if not, make it as comfortable and useful as possible, accept your limitations, and run for shelter before the gale builds up.

When his sloop leaked around the centerboard, the old man dumped sawdust into the top of the trunk. The suction pulled it into the seams and plugged them for a while. It still works.

Quality in Fiberglass

It is very difficult to judge the quality of a finished fiberglass boat without doing it considerable damage. About the only way to tell what goes into a glass boat is to see one being built. An index of quality in a boat, as in anything else, is the reputation of the builder. Therefore *The Practical Sailor* visited the yard of Henry R. Hinckley in Manset, Maine, to observe and discuss quality fiberglass construction.

The *Sailor* found men laying alternate layers of fiberglass cloth, mat, and roving in huge female molds of hulls. Of course, before the process began, the molds were waxed and coated with gel coat. Then eight to twelve layers were laid on, but only one at a time, with drying time between. Each layer must be smoothly laid with care that joints in successive layers are staggered. Enough resin must be used to soak the fiberglass, and it must be rolled and worked to drive out air bubbles. Layer by layer it is cured, for resin gives off heat when it hardens and the heat must be allowed to dissipate before more resin is added. Resin gels in about forty minutes and in twenty-four hours is 90 percent cured. The shell of the boat lies in the mold for about two weeks as successive layers are built up. The finished hull is ½–¾ of an inch thick.

Some builders use chopped fiberglass fibers and resin mixed in a gun and blown into the mold. If mixture and thickness are carefully controlled, this method is acceptable in some parts of the boat, but the chopped fibers are only ½–2 inches long and do not form as strong a shell as mat and roving. Often a gun is used in conjunction with mat and roving.

The deck is built in a separate mold in the same way as the hull. You will note that all vertical parts like the sides of a house slope slightly inward to permit the deck to be popped out of the mold. Corners should be rounded, not only for looks but for strength, for fiberglass is likely to crack at sharp corners where strain is concentrated. Hatch coamings should be properly gasketed and precisely built to prevent leaks.

Take a close look at the way the deck is attached to the hull. One common way is to form a lip in both deck and hull, fasten the two parts together with "pop rivets," and slap a vinyl and aluminum rub rail over the seam. Such a joint is likely to leak or even disintegrate under continued pressure and the working of the boat in a seaway. It may not even withstand a hard slam against a wharf pilling.

A stronger method is to form the lip on the inside of the hull, coat it with thiokol, and bolt the deck and toe rail to it in one operation. The Hinckley yard sets the deck on a lip inside the edge of the hull and bolts the toe rail on top of the seam, thus achieving a water-tight seal with structural strength not dependent entirely on the fastenings.

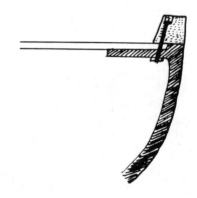

Notice the way the bulkheads are attached to the hull. The deck and bulkheads are what give the hull its rigidity. Sometimes in a finished boat this fastening can be seen inside a hanging locker or head, but usually it is covered up. The bulkhead should fit accurately against the hull. It is usually fastened with fiberglass tape. The tape should fit smoothly, without wrinkles on either the bulkhead or the side of the boat, and the joint should be built up with several layers with wide bearing on both bulkhead and hull. Check the outside of the boat too. If the bulkhead does not fit properly, there may be a "hard spot." You can find it by sighting along the side of the boat and watching the reflections in the shiny gel coat. Sometimes you can even feel it with your fingers.

Notice the way tanks are built in. Here it is most important that taped joints be smooth, accurate, and wide. One boat developed a leak in a gasoline tank which saturated the foam flotation material and rendered the boat useless, an undamaged total loss. Resin used in water tanks should be "sanitary," that is, odorless.

Examine the way the mast and rigging are attached to the hull. The mast should be stepped in such a way as to spread its heavy downward thrust over the length of the boat; it should not just be stood on the center of the bilge. Chain plates should be solidly bolted to a heavy bulkhead or to a big fillet braced against both hull and deck and supported against both by generous reinforcement. Chain plates simply bolted to the hull and glassed over are not going to withstand hard going.

Before the interior cabinetwork goes in and the deck is put on, you can see that the rigging and engine are properly grounded and that ground connections are available for deck pipes and accessories. Also you can inspect the deck's underside to see that it is properly stiffened to prevent flex and that there are strong and wide reinforcements for mast partners and stanchion bases.

Look at all holes in the hull. Are they fitted with proper seacocks firmly fastened down and accessibly situated? Gate valves of good quality are acceptable if well installed, but a gate valve may stick or be hard to turn or may leak around the stem. Globe valves, which do not provide a straight and unobstructed passage, are not acceptable.

Take a walk through the carpentry shop and see how the cabinetwork is put together. Joints merely stapled and glued will not hold their shapes. Drawers, drawer runs, sink supports, and locker doors will all be in the process of construction and you can see whether joints are merely butted, nailed, and glued or are properly mortised.

The rigging loft can't hide its work anyway, but little matters like the proper insulation of cleats and winches on an aluminum mast and the fastening of the sail track and mast tangs can be inspected with the spars laid out on horses.

Beyond question, a first-class fiberglass yacht is expensive, and one who shops for a boat with too sharp an eye on the price is likely to get no more than he pays for. It is easy to hide cut corners and shoddy work behind beading and sheathing. Yet every expensive boat is not necessarily a sound one. A visit to the yard, especially if you can persuade a competent and disinterested authority to go with you, is well worthwhile.

Fer-a-Lite: A New Ferro Construction

Ferro-cement construction offers great advantages for the amateur builder in its comparative simplicity of molding a form of flexible wire into fair compound curves. Bending wire and troweling cement is much easier than steam-bending oak timbers, cutting a rabbet, or scribing plank. It is also less expensive in both time and material. Yet ferro-cement has its disadvantages. It must be plastered all at once, because cement does not bond well to itself. Also, the finished boat, while strong enough to resist ordinary strains, is not very flexible. If water penetrates the cement either through tiny cracks or through its pores, the wire rusts and strength deteriorates, for much of the strength is in the wire.

Platt Monfort of Westport, Maine, has developed Fer-a-Lite wire plank construction to maintain the advantages and overcome the weaknesses of ferro-cement. Fer-a-Lite maintains the simplicity of using a wire foundation to negotiate compound curves, but it produces a lighter, stronger, more resilient hull.

Construction techniques are still being developed experimentally, but the principles are established and easily understood. The basic idea is that overlapping layers of wire plank are troweled with Fer-a-Lite. Wire plank consists of eight parallel strands of 14 or 16 gauge wire, held parallel and 7/16 inches apart by light transverse wires at intervals. The plank comes on a 500-foot roll 3½ inches wide and can be cut to the required length so it need not be butted. Also, because it is so narrow and flexible, it can be bent to compound curves.

Fer-a-Lite is a mixture of reinforced cement with fiberglass resin and hardener. With wire plank support, it sets up into a light, strong structure with about the weight and flexibility of aluminum. Without the wire plank, it is light enough to float, has five times the bending strength of Portland cement, about the same compression strength, and weighs less than half as much. In addition, it is waterproof and thus protects the wire from rust.

Fer-a-Lite construction has been applied to

dinghies, small sailing craft, and to vessels up to sixty-five feet.

To build a dinghy, one first bends a stem and keel out of steel rod and sets up a transom on it, either using an existing hull for a mold or lofting the shape from lines in the usual way. Transverse wire "ribs" are then bent in and fastened to the keel. Longitudinal rods are fastened to stem and transom and to each transverse rod. Next the frame is covered with wire plank, starting at the gunwale rods at an angle of about 45° and running entirely around the bottom of the boat and up the other side. The ends of the plank are wrapped around the gunwale rods and the plank is laced with wire to each member of the frame it crosses. The process is continued forward and aft until the whole frame is covered. Then the method is repeated with a second layer at right angles to the first and all wire intersections are spot welded. Because the plank is narrow and flexible, it can be fitted to tight curves quite easily, although in some places the transverse wires must be crimped to narrow the plank or cut to allow the main wires to spread a little. The result is a surprisingly rigid wire basket in the shape of a boat.

The basket is next covered on the outside with a light fiberglass mat, and when this has hardened, the inside is plastered with Fer-a-Lite. While Fer-a-Lite is wet, it can be smoothed by covering it with newspaper and smoothing it down with a block of wood before the paper soaks through. After it has hardened, the paper can be painted over with further coats of resin. The boat is then smoothed up and finished out in the usual manner.

While this seems like an easy but tedious way to build a dinghy, the application of the principle to larger boats is even more interesting. Monfort is currently finishing up a forty-five-foot ketch on the lines of *Mobjack* by Francis Herreshoff.

The keel is a hollow steel truss of welded rod lined with steel plate and poured full of lead into which the lower ends of the wire plank are cast.

The wooden molds were made an inch narrower on each side than the inside of the hull and one-inch wooden ribbands were bent

Two layers of wire plank in place on bow of dinghy

around the molds. The wire plank was stapled directly to these ribbands with a staple gun. Four crisscrossing layers of wire plank were used instead of two as in the dinghy. Wooden sleepers were bolted to steel-pipe stem and stern and the wire plank fastened to these. In the stern, a hole was drilled for each individual

Stern of Mobjack *ready to plaster*

8

Note battens covered with fiberglass.

wire so it could be bent over and tucked in neatly. The top of the rail is an angle iron to which three layers of plank are welded and the fourth is carried over it and bent down hard on the inside. A wooden rail cap will cover it eventually.

Floors are heavy galvanized steel welded to the keel truss and bolted through the ribbands. Mast steps and engine beds bridge several floors. One great advantage of Fer-a-Lite is that it bonds firmly to itself, so the whole hull does not have to be plastered all at once but can be done in stages as construction progresses and time permits. Once plastered, the hull is covered inside and out with a light fiberglass cloth, the cloth running right over the ribbands on the inside to protect them from water and rot and to bond them firmly to the hull. The outside is then smoothed and faired with a compound like auto body putty and is finished as smooth as ice.

Costs are difficult to estimate. Still, for material alone the dinghy could probably be built for a modest sum. She contains wire plank and Fer-a-Lite plus five gallons of resin, now rising in price while you look at it. Wood for seats, gunwales, knees, foot braces, etc., hardware, paint, and varnish would be the same as for a wooden boat. Labor cost is difficult to estimate but surely would be greater than for a fiberglass dinghy if one already had the mold. If one simply wants a dinghy, he

would do better to buy one than to build it for other than recreational or experimental reasons.

The forty-five-foot ketch is another story. At this time her hull is complete except for final finishing. Deck framing is largely completed. Poured ballast and engine are installed and mahogany plywood for bulkheads is in the shop. Monfort says he now has $9,200 in the boat including $2,200 for the engine and $2,800 in hired labor. That leaves $4,200 for materials, a very reasonable price for a forty-five-foot hull. He has kept no record of his own time because much of the work has been done in short stretches and much of it has been experimental.

A number of large boats have been built of Fer-a-Lite in lengths between forty and sixty-seven feet. Dr. Harry Quick of Wiscasset, Maine, is now building a Friendship sloop in Round Pond with the advice and counsel of Phil Nichols, a builder of wooden boats for over half a century. Any new method of boatbuilding that convinces Phil Nichols *must* be all right.

Platt Monfort is a sailor of long experience as well as a carpenter, machinist, chemist, and engineer of lively imagination and extraordinary good-humored tolerance for the inquisitive visitor or correspondent. He has written a lucid and attractive pamphlet describing Fer-a-Lite wire plank construction including much engineering data as well as many hints on technique. He has admirable photographs of *Mobjack* in progressive stages of construction. Further inquiries should be addressed to him c/o Aladdin Products, Inc., RFD #2, Wiscasset, Maine 04578.

NOTE: *This article was written in January 1976.*

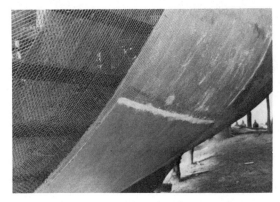

Battens, Fer-a-Lite, and wire plank as seen from outside

Wood and Epoxy

The advantages of wood as a construction material have never been seriously disputed. It is readily available, easily worked, and has a high strength-to-weight ratio. Furthermore, it takes an attractive finish and has a pleasant feel to it. Its disadvantages have been recently overemphasized by mass merchandisers of other materials. Nevertheless, it cannot be denied that wood is subject to swelling and shrinking and to rot. If these objections can be overcome, wood will doubtless regain much of its popularity as the cost of other materials increases.

The WEST system of epoxy penetration may be the answer. WEST is an acronym for Wood Epoxy Saturation Technique developed by the Gougeon Brothers. Both of wood's weaknesses are the result of water penetration of the cells, either as liquid or vapor. Wood is composed of cells of cellulose, each about 100 times as long as it is thick. These lie vertically in the standing tree, hence along the grain of

the wood, and are bound together by an adhesive substance called lignin. The tree is further strengthened by horizontal cells called wood rays extending from the core of the tree toward the bark. All of these wood cells contain water, some of it within and between the cells, some within the cell walls.

When the green wood is dried, the free water in the pores and within cells is the first to dry out. This does not cause much, if any, shrinkage or change of shape in the wood, but it does make it lighter. As the water in the cell walls dries out, however, the wood shrinks noticeably across the grain and gains in strength and stiffness. This is "seasoned" wood.

However, wood does not stay seasoned. The cell walls very easily pick up moisture from water vapor in the air and therefore wood is sensitive to the relative humidity of its surroundings. Everyone knows what happens when a tight boat is hauled and exposed to the sun and wind in the warm dry days of early fall and late spring. A cat could crawl out through her. Yet a foggy spell will close her up quite a bit and forty-eight hours in the water in 100 percent humidity will make her tight as a cup again. This propensity of wooden boats to open up is one of wood's principal disadvantages. Attempts to control it with fiberglass coverings are largely unsuccessful because fiberglass is unaffected by water and does not come and go with the wood; consequently, the bond between the two materials breaks down. Also, fiberglass itself is not absolutely airtight and can be penetrated by air carrying water vapor as an invisible gas. Any crack or nick in the gel coat exposes fiberglass fibers, which draw water into the fiberglass by capillary action and lead to the expansion of the wood within. Even if the fiberglass were airtight, the inside of the planking is exposed to bilge water, condensation, and air at 100 percent humidity, all of which fill the cell walls of the wood and cause swelling.

Wood's other weakness, rot, is also partly the result of the presence of water. Rot is a fungus infection which feeds on wood. To live, it needs oxygen, a temperature above 50°, food, and water. Wood kept under water and away from air will last almost indefinitely. Wood buried in glaciers or tundra or immured with the mummies of pharaohs lasts millennia, but every farmer knows that "three foggy mornings and one rainy day will rot the best birch fence a man can build."

Therefore, if not only water but also air charged with water vapor can be kept away from wood, the wood will not swell, shrink, or rot and it will still retain its positive characteristics as a material for boat construction. In response to this need, Gougeon Brothers in Bay City, Michigan, have developed a low-viscosity epoxy resin which appears to be a successful penetrant and sealer. It is better than paint or varnish because it has no volatile solvents. These leave microscopic pinholes which admit air carrying water vapor under the film. The epoxy is also better than cuprinol and other preparations which prevent rot by poisoning the wood which supports the fungus, because these do not prevent swelling and shrinking.

The wooden member—plank or timber—is cut to shape of well-seasoned wood and given at least two coats of epoxy—treated with hardener, of course. This penetrates the outer fibers of the wood and, when cured, renders it totally impervious not only to water but to water vapor in the air.

Because epoxy is also a good adhesive, it makes an excellent binder for the layers of a cold-molded hull. The successive strips of veneer or plywood are coated with epoxy and set in it, thus making the entire structure impervious to moisture so there is no uneven swelling and shrinking, hence no delamination. Epoxy as an adhesive is hard and strong, requires less clamping pressure than resorcinol glue, and does not require a perfect joint, as it will fill small voids and has considerable strength of its own. It may be thickened with asbestos fibers to make a filler with structural strength, with collodial silica to make a very hard filler, or with "microballoons" to make a softer, more easily sanded filler with less structural strength.

This miracle material, however, is not entirely without its weaknesses. It comes in two parts: epoxy resin, and hardener, which must be mixed in exact proportions. This is a fussy and messy business. If any great amount is to be used, order the Gougeon Brothers' mixer, which dispenses simultaneously from separate containers an accurate mixture of resin and hardener. All you have to do is stir.

Beware of the hardener. It can cause serious skin inflammation, especially in its unmixed state. Continual exposure can sensitize a person to it so that he cannot come near the stuff. Wear rubber gloves and use it only where ventilation is good. When mixing it with asbestos fibers to form a putty, there is little danger, but one must avoid breathing the sanding dust after the putty is dry, for the tiny asbestos fibers are damaging to the lungs.

The "pot life" of the mixed solution is only about twenty minutes, so it must be mixed in small batches and used quickly. Lower temperatures increase pot life, but at low temperatures the resin thickens up and will not penetrate the wood. It should be used at about 70° if possible.

The hardened product is sensitive to ultraviolet light and will therefore break down under exposure to strong sunlight. One compensates for this partly by adding pigment to successive coats after the first and partly by painting or varnishing the finished product. Alkyd enamels and Z-Spar 1015 Captains Varnish are recommended. If the epoxy does begin to break down, it must be removed by sanding, for paint removers will not touch it. Because the epoxy sets very hard, this can be a tedious job.

The Gougeons have built a number of boats using WEST over the last eight years and report that so far it has held up very well. One of these is *Golden Dazy*, a forty-one-foot sloop that successfully defended the Canada's Cup. The Apprentice Shop in Bath, Maine, has used the preparation, principally as an adhesive, and reports good results. One of the shop's alumni is now working for Gougeon and is enthusiastic about the system.

Anyone putting in the time and money to build a wooden boat would be well advised to look into this method of protecting his investment. Write to Meade Gougeon, 706 Martin St., Bay City, Michigan 48706.

Gasoline Is Dynamite

Most yachtsmen treat gasoline with the greatest respect. This attitude, however, must extend below the deck to the tank and its connections. The installation illustrated here combines many of the best practices, practices often short-cut by builders in a hurry.

1. There is no opening whatever in the bottom of the tank. If the engine is installed below the level of the gasoline in the tank, gasoline could siphon through a loose connection into the bilge.

2. To prevent this, there is a positive shut-off valve close to the tank and well away from the engine. It should be closed whenever the engine is not running.

3. The line from tank to engine opens about an inch above the bottom of the tank, ensuring clean fuel for the engine. If water and sludge collect in the bottom of the tank, the stuff can be pumped out before it reaches the bottom of the pipe.

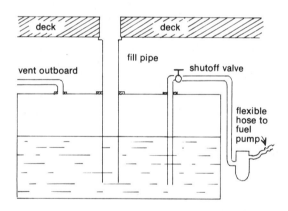

4. The fill pipe is firmly and rigidly attached to the deck plate. This pipe, too, extends to within an inch of the bottom of the tank. Thus, when fuel is being added the vapor in the tank above the gasoline is forced out through the vent and does not rise through the fill pipe. In the event of a static electricity spark at the deck plate, the vapor in the pipe would burn, but the whole tank would not explode.

Such a tank should be fashioned of monel or stainless steel. If it is bigger than twenty gallons, it should have one or more baffles in it to prevent the fuel from heavily sloshing around inside it. It should be very solidly supported in the boat, and of course in accordance with Coast Guard regulations the compartment should be thoroughly ventilated. Even though the tank is grounded to the engine through the fuel line, many builders provide another ground as well.

The fuel line should be rigidly supported to prevent vibration and subsequent metal fatigue and should be connected to the fuel pump with a short piece of flexible metal hose to take up vibration between engine and hull. Finally, every connection should be lightly doped with gasket shellac or white lead and set up firmly. Be careful with the dope. If it gets into the fuel line, it will cause a severe case of sticky valves! With an efficient blower, a sharp eye, and a nose for leaks, you should get by.

A Convenient Bomb

A recent article in *Motor Boating and Sailing* describes a method for installing a rainproof passage for electric and fuel lines through a bulkhead into a compartment where presumably the battery and portable gas tank for the outboard were to be kept. This avoids the necessity of lifting the tank in and out of the boat to fill it. Also, you can lock up the compartment.

However, unless you are *very* careful to ventilate that compartment thoroughly, you might better carry a cargo of nitroglycerine. When you fill the tank, the vapor displaced by the fuel will sink to the bottom of the compartment and lie there waiting for the slightest spark from the battery. Hydrogen given off by the battery will add to the explosion, but you will never notice it.

Any tank in an enclosed space must by law be vented outboard and the compartment must have positive ventilation. Better yet, fill the tank on the float and keep it in the open air.

Beware Galvanic Corrosion

I nearly broke my neck when early in the spring I put my weight on a galvanized shroud to climb aboard. The shroud parted in my hand where a copper clip had been used as a radio lead-in. I have seen half-inch iron keel bolts in a lead keel reduced to the size of pencil lead in two seasons.

Galvanic action develops where dissimilar metals are immersed in a solution that will conduct electricity. The more active metal is rapidly wasted away as its molecules are ionized by the solution and attracted to the less active metal. If the two metals are connected, an electric current will flow from the more active to the less active with sufficient voltage to light a flashlight bulb.

Suppose we take a vessel with a bronze propeller and an iron keel. If the engine is grounded to the keel, as it often is, we have an active metal, iron, and an inactive metal, bronze, immersed in an electrolyte, salt water. The iron will give up electrons, which will run through the ground wire, down the shaft, and out to the propeller. The iron ions, charged positively, will go into solution in the salt water and will leave the iron pitted and corroded.

In the following list, a metal near the top will waste away in contact with one lower down.

1.	Aluminum	6.	Lead
2.	Zinc	7.	Copper
3.	Iron	8.	Mercury
4.	Nickel	9.	Silver
5.	Tin	10.	Gold

Stainless steel, monel, and bronze are alloys combined in various proportions for various uses and are quite inactive. They would appear near the bottom of the list.

If it is necessary to have dissimilar metals in contact with each other in saltwater, the more active one can be protected by putting an even more active one in contact with the less active metal. For instance, in the case of the vessel with a bronze propeller and an iron keel, a piece of zinc, high in the list, can be attached to a strut or a stern bearing bolt. This will occupy the attractive force of the bronze and waste away the zinc instead of the iron.

Galvanic action can be a serious problem in rigging. A bronze turnbuckle on a galvanized shroud will weaken the wire quickly because there is enough salt and dampness present to provide an electrolyte. Slow galvanic action will often take place between two different alloys of stainless steel used in rigging wire and snap shackles. This situation is particularly dangerous when the less noble metal, higher on the scale, is the smaller piece. Then it is even more rapidly weakened.

Galvanic action can take place even within metals. Cheap brass, for example, is composed of copper and zinc, often with the zinc unevenly distributed through the copper. In the presence of saltwater, current flows from zinc to copper, the zinc is consumed, and it leaves the brass pitted, honey-combed, and crumbly because the zinc has been corroded away.

For the same reason an aluminum boat represents serious problems. Aluminum is a very active metal. In the presence of iron or copper, it corrodes rapidly. Zincs will not help, because aluminum is even more active than zinc. The usual practice is to paint the aluminum thoroughly with a nonmetallic insulating primer to insulate the aluminum from electric contact with a bronze shaft, a lead keel, or the copper in the antifouling paint. Another method of solving the problem is to drive the current in the electrical contact from the less active *toward* the more active metal, thus preventing the ionization of the more active molecules and discouraging migration toward the less active. This must be worked out by an engineer, because electrical fields in the water around the boat can lead to complications worse than the original problem.

Be suspicious of all dissimilar metals in contact. Test whether there is current—hence corrosion—between them by touching the two metals with your tongue. A sour, vinegary taste suggests the flow of electricity.

Living Aboard: Water Tanks

The question is not whether to carry fresh water but how to carry it and how much to carry. If we are cruising coastwise, the quantity is a matter of convenience. How often do you want to go alongside a wharf to fill her up? A party of four, drinking milk, soda, beer, and other beverages, eating a considerable amount of fruit, and using water for tea, coffee, cooking, dishwashing, and washing up, can go five days on a sixteen-gallon tank without hardship—without having to think about it. If one is going offshore or is cruising in areas where water may be either unhealthy or unavailable, a great deal more is necessary. One family carried 120 gallons for a party of four on a cruise from England to Patagonia. Their longest passage was forty-five days. The standard allowance of a gallon per man per day for all purposes is more than enough when supplemented with other beverages and fruit.

Stowage of water varies widely from glass gallon jugs to plastic jerry cans upward to glass-lined tanks. We used to carry water in two ten-gallon oak kegs lashed to the sides of the house. It looked picturesque, and it was so hard to get a drink from one that the water lasted very well. It tasted a little woody, but no one minded. Glass jugs keep the water well and are easily taken ashore and filled. However, they are difficult to stow. Plastic jerry cans are easier to stow, but some of them impart a nasty plastic taste to the water. The best answer is probably a tank.

It is well to keep the tanks comparatively small, for water is heavy and slams around hard in a half-filled tank. A twenty-gallon tank weighs about 175 pounds and occupies about 2¾ cubic feet, counting the tank. That is a big tank to put under the cabin sole. If it were three feet long and two feet wide, it would have to average a little less than six inches deep. Of course, it would be deeper in the middle and shallower on the sides to fit the shape of the bilge. One hundred pounds of water slamming around in a tank that size in a seaway would exert considerable pressure on the joints of the tank and on its fastenings. Any bigger tank should be fitted with baffles, an expensive procedure.

Especially in fiberglass boats, some tanks are built right into the boat, the outer wall of the tank being the side of the boat. An eminent authority on the subject, Dan Strohmeier, writes cautiously, "An integral tank in a fiberglass hull may represent a structural hard spot and cause flexure cracks, an undesirable feature where one's water supply is involved. Good design may obviate that trouble but the record of flexure cracks in fiberglass suggests caution." Integral tanks in steel and aluminum boats are not unusual.

One thing to be said for a separate tank, however, is that it can be taken ashore, inspected, repaired, and steam cleaned. A six-inch hole, big enough to admit a hand and a swab, is an important fixture. The lid must be greased before it is screwed down, and it must be provided with some means of getting a wrench on it. Otherwise you have no clean-out hole.

A water tank in the bilge can be filled most simply by bringing the hose down the hatch and shoving it into the fill-hole. Be sure to let the water run a while before you bring the hose below, and taste the water before it goes into the tank. The first couple of gallons out of a plastic hose that has been lying in the sun for an hour can taste foul. With a fill hole in the top of the tank, one can easily sound the tank with a stick. There is only one reliable way to graduate the stick. Pour in water, two gallons at a time, and mark the stick for every two gallons. It is tedious, but the solid geometry involved in calculating the change in level for two gallons of water in an irregularly shaped tank is worse than tedious.

One can arrange a means of filling such a tank from the deck, but it is complex, expensive, and involves a deck plate that may leak, and unless you are to make another hole in the tank, prevents sounding it with a stick. Of course, a handy little electric gauge is no doubt available and expensive, but it, too, requires a hole in the tank.

Every tank must be vented to let air in as the water is used. If the tank is in the bilge, the vent must run far enough up the side of the boat to keep bilge water out and to prevent spillage when the boat is heeled.

It goes without saying that wherever your tank is located, it must be solidly fastened down, so that no matter what the angle of heel, it will stay put.

Once the water is in the tank, how is it to be made available in galley and head? An electrically operated pressure system is the usual answer. This has several drawbacks, however. It is subject to leaks and it is also, because of the complexity of its plumbing and electrical components, subject to Murphy's Law, which states that if something can go wrong, it will do so at the worst possible moment. A simpler and less expensive system is a hand pump. This has the advantage of conserving water, for no one can go off and leave it running; and if one must pump a basin full, it is likely to be a scant basin.

The simplest system is to install the tank right under the deck with a straight fill pipe through which one can drop a sounding stick. The vent can simply protrude through the top of the tank, as no bilge water can get into it. The delivery tube can run direct to the galley and be fitted with faucet or stopcock. A valve under the tank which can be reached through a cockpit locker will prevent loss of the tankful if a leak develops in the line. The drawback here, of course, is the location of weight high up in the boat. Two fifteen-gallon tanks weigh about 150 pounds each with all the plumbing, and that is significant, even though they can be set to balance each other on opposite sides of the boat.

It is wise, especially on ocean-going vessels, to divide the water supply in case of leakage. A **T** fitting can be used where the line from the pump divides to go to each tank. However, there should be a valve on each arm of the **T** and only one should be open at a time. Thus, the two tanks will not be interconnected. Water cannot run from the windward one to the leeward one, overflowing into the bilge through the vent, and if one tank is punctured, the whole supply will not be lost.

Opinions differ on the best material of which to make water tanks. I have used oak (which tastes pretty shippy), monel, stainless steel, and tin-lined copper. All these metallic tanks are tasteless and can be strongly built. One owner used galvanized iron and found no trouble with it. After some years, though, rust

might develop. Rusty water is probably therapeutic, but it is unpleasant to look at. Especially if the tanks must be made to fit the boat at a high cost in labor, the material should be the strongest and longest lasting obtainable.

Whatever the arrangement you choose, carry a three-gallon plastic jug of water in a cockpit locker where it can be easily reached from the deck. This can be quickly put in the dinghy or life raft in case of emergency when you do not have time to stop and fill anything else.

Algae in the Water Tank

If cloudy, green water comes out of your fresh-water tank and it gets progressively worse, the problem may be algae. Buy a handful of copper sulfate at the drugstore. Dissolve the crystals in water and mix up the solution thoroughly in the tank. Fill the tank full and let it stand overnight. Drain and rinse thoroughly. Copper sulfate in small concentrations will not hurt you, but the taste is not attractive, so a thorough rinse is important.

Protect Your Boat from Theft
Roger L. Woods

Neatly furled sails, an outboard hanging over the transom, an anchor on deck ready for use—these are open invitation for the theft of a boat. With the number of boats stolen steadily increasing and the admitted failure of the FBI and other federal agencies—the Coast Guard included—to do more than list the boat data in a computer, a few precautions are in order.

"Sailboats were my game, because they were so easy to steal," one convicted boat thief admitted recently. "Most people left the mainsail on the boom and bagged the jib but left it on the shroud. If the boat had an outboard, they left the gas tank attached to it. All

I had to do was step aboard, cast off, and split!''

Standard Operating Procedure should be:

1. Never leave sails on board.

2. Never leave an outboard on board. An inboard engine should have a hidden switch in the starter or ignition circuit. One owner put it in the pantry behind the cornflakes and coffee.

3. Remove the tiller. A thief might bring his own outboard, sails, and anchor, but it is unlikely that he will fool with a boat with no tiller. I have found removing the distributor rotor to be effective also.

Depending on a cabin lock is a mistake. If a thief is determined to steal a boat, a small lock is not going to stop him—assuming the sails, motor, anchor, and tiller are aboard. If a boat has a skylight, the screws are easily removed to gain access to the interior.

Alarm Systems

The most commonly sold alarm system is triggered by intrusion into the cabin. Therein lies a fatal defect. Some boat owners, following the instructions of naive alarm system manufacturers, plaster a big, bright decal on the cockpit wall: WARNING! ALARM SYSTEM. The thief who spots the decal, if the boat with sails, anchor, and outboard is an offer he cannot refuse, will cast off the lines, put out from the harbor, and when in the channel or across the bay will open the cabin and the alarm be damned!

Are Private Marinas Safe?

They used to be, but with today's unprecedented demand for dockage, it is a seller's market, and the night watchman has become an expendable luxury.

In the Annapolis, Maryland, area there are several large boat dealers and brokers. Almost all the major yards along the waterways are unguarded. Each of the yards insures its own boats heavily, but the private owner who rents dock space must carry his own insurance. The yard owners prefer slightly higher insurance rates to the expense of a night watchman.

Other Alternatives

As boat thefts increase and complaints pour in to police departments, patrols are increased. These seldom continue long, however, before criminal activity elsewhere demands attention. Therefore, each owner should call the local police department—its public relations department if there is one—and ask what precautions are being taken against boat theft. All dock areas should be visited by police on an irregular schedule. With rising complaints of police harassment, officers are reluctant to accost people in dock areas and ask for identification. Sailors are often legitimately afoot in the wee hours of the morning. They should make clear to the police that they are glad to identify themselves. Thus sailors become known to the police, making it easier for them to identify interlopers.

Private security agencies have been used less than they should, primarily because group action in hiring them is difficult to arrange. There is little incentive among boat yard and marina owners to do so, because security cuts profits. One group of boat owners in the Maryland area, tired of being ripped off, formed a protective association and paid for a private security agency to patrol their marinas. Theft not only fell off, but several would-be thieves are behind bars.

Offshore Mooring

Lying to an offshore mooring protects a boat from shore-bound crooks. Unfortunately, low-cost portable dinghies make thefts of moored boats easy. In many cases moored boats are actually easier to steal because no one ashore pays much attention to them. Unless there are regular marine patrols, and few communities provide such night patrols, there is little that can be done to protect moored boats except—as mentioned before—to take off sails, anchor, motor, and tiller. One method that worked for one sailor, until some thief thought to bring a pair of bolt cutters, was mooring with a stainless steel chain encased in garden hose. One end of the chain was bolted to the mooring and the other end locked to an eye installed in the bow for the purpose. The owner was confident that his boat was safe, so he left his sails hanked, etc. One day the boat was gone. The lock had been cut off. See "Beware the Ripoff" *(below)* for some suggestions of how to avoid this problem.

Boat Identification

A boat should always have registration numbers *painted* on the bows. Don't use the plastic kind that can be pulled off. The name of the boat should be painted in big letters on the transom, with the name of the home port painted there too. It helps the Coast Guard or the police to find a mass-produced boat with no particular distinguishing characteristics. A boat stolen and taken out of state would be conspicuous in some states.

Tracing a Stolen Boat

Only about 15 percent of the boats stolen are ever found. Often the only way to trace a stolen boat is for the owner to do it himself. He should make copies of the boat date and description, attach a photo to it, and mail it to all marinas in the area and to marine police departments in as many states as possible.

Preventive measures are always best. Once a boat is taken from its dock, it is difficult to find and recover. In the absence of a night watchman no sailboat is safe from theft. Make the boat as difficult to steal as possible.

Beware the Ripoff
Fred N. Schwend

The last few years have seen an alarming increase in the rate of both boat break-ins and boat thefts. For instance, boat thefts in Long Island, New York, increased by 39 percent, boat break-ins by 60 percent, and stolen outboard motors by 26 percent. According to the FBI National Crime Information Center, about 12,000 boats were stolen. This increase is probably due to the fact that most boats are left unattended for considerable periods of time and are likely to contain such valuable and easily sold items as radios, direction finders, and the like, which can be easily car-

ried off once the thief gains entrance to the boat.

Although most marinas provide security measures of some sort, even the best cannot be expected to be 100 percent safe. In some, security consists of merely providing lights and locks on various gates, which is of some help. Some marinas are lucky enough to get local police to send in patrols, but usually this type of patrol is only sporadic. The best protection appears to be the maintaining of private security guards on a night-time basis. Of course, this is expensive, and the cost must be passed on to the boat owners in the form of higher slip fees.

Most boat owners secure their valuables and lock their boats when they leave, but they fail to realize that a smart, or even a not-so-smart, thief armed with a pry-bar, bolt cutter, or master key can gain entrance to a boat cabin in short order. Not only that, but the intruder is not likely to be too gentle in how he opens the cabin door or hatch, so the owner may face both the loss of valuables and a costly repair bill. Although insurance may cover the loss, the owner probably will not recover the full replacement value, since most yacht policies include a "deductible" clause. Besides, there is the inconvenience and the loss of time until the boat can again be ready for use.

Obviously preventive measures are most desirable. Many boats have notoriously poor cabin door locks, which may be easily picked, or the doors may be sprung or jimmied. The addition of a good hasp lock may be in order. Also, hatches are often secured by light hasps or hooks. Install rugged latches that cannot easily be pried loose. The best protection for a hatch is a bar extending across the hatch opening below the hatch, with a long bolt passed through the hatch and the bar set up with a wing nut below. Most portholes and windows are small enough to prevent entrance even if the intruder should break the glass, but where a large window exists, two or three bars could be secured across the glass. Drawing the curtains also helps. There is no need of tempting a potential thief with a view of valuables he may think his for the taking.

Burglar alarms are, of course, a means of deterring a thief. Besides the more complicated and costly forms of alarm systems such as photoelectric and ultrasonic alarms, there are the standard perimeter and interior types. The perimeter alarm comprises a circuit including switches connected to various exterior cabin doors, hatches, and windows, so as to sound an alarm when any of these is opened. An advantage of the perimeter system is that it will sound an alarm before the intruder gains entrance. The perimeter system may also be connected to one or more floor-mat switches placed on deck where an intruder would step on boarding, sounding an alarm before he does any damage at all. The owner should use his ingenuity in providing the best possible system for his individual boat. One trick is to provide an alarm-triggering switch near an entrance, the switch being held open by a box or other obstruction which must be removed to get to the entrance, thus sounding the alarm.

An interior alarm circuit includes switches connected to different items within or even on the outside of the boat, such as television sets, radios, cabinet drawers, and lockers. When any of these is moved, the alarm will be triggered. An advantage of the interior alarm system is that it need not be armed and disarmed every time the owner leaves or enters his boat. Preferably, such alarms should be self-contained so that they cannot be disarmed by disconnecting or cutting the battery leads. As a further protection, bilge-water sensing systems, engine condition switches, smoke-fire detecting switches, and the like may be connected to an interior alarm system, thus calling the watchman's attention to problems other than theft. Both perimeter and interior systems have their advantages, and an ideal arrangement would be a combination of the two.

One burglar alarm system, manufactured by Electro-Guard Co. (1336 North Santa Anita Ave., Arcadia, California 91006), is especially suited for boats, many of the switches being hermetically sealed in glass containers to preclude corrosion of switch contacts. This is a relatively inexpensive system and includes a six-inch gong unit, three magnetic switches, two trigger switches, a panic switch, and a motor switch plus wire, connectors for solderless connections, etc. Additional items such as key switches, floor-mat switches, and the like may be obtained to adapt the system to practically any individual boat. There is no limit to the number of switches that can be included in the circuit. Also, the system may be used for either a perimeter or interior alarm or a combination of both. Any local electrician can install the system, and any one familiar with basic electricity could do it by following the instructions.

Owners of outboard motor boats should be particularly concerned with protection against theft of the motor as well as of the boat itself. Here, a good chain and padlock are essential. The chain should have welded and case-hardened links and the padlock a case hardened shackle to withstand attack by bolt cutters or a hacksaw. Pass the chain through the tow ring on the boat and around the frame yoke on the trailer. Pass another chain around the trailer frame and a post or piling. Boats on trailers are particularly enticing to thieves. If the boat is kept afloat, pass the chain through the tow ring and around a piling or well-secured dock cleat. Another chain should be passed around a basic part of the motor and a permanent part of the boat, such as a seat or stay, in such a manner that it can be released only by opening the padlock.

Finally, to aid in identifying and returning a boat or her equipment if it should be stolen and later recovered, photographs should be taken and identifying marks should be engraved or fiberglassed in an inconspicuous place. Also, pieces of equipment can be marked with the owner's name by using an invisible ink that can be detected by police using an ultraviolet light.

Lightning

You can't make your boat absolutely lightning-proof, but you must do the best you can. The problem is to conduct safely to the water a heavy charge of static electricity built up in a cloud. The charge seeks the easiest path to the water. If your tall aluminum mast comes below it, nothing will prevent an enormous electrical discharge from rushing through your boat. However, there are a number of sensible precautions you can take which will discharge the air near the boat and thus provide a sort of umbrella of neutralized air over you, and you can provide a safe discharge route for surges of static electricity less violent than a full-scale lightning bolt.

1. Ground your rigging. Run heavy copper cables from your chain-plate bolts to your keel bolts or to one of the bolts holding down the engine. Thus, any charge coming down the shrouds, forestay, or backstay can easily find its way to the water without bursting out through the side of the boat. Many boats with outside chain plates run them right down below the waterline

2. Ground the foot of your mast to a keel bolt, especially if you have a metal mast.

3. If your boat is rigged with dead-eyes, attach a chain to the shroud above the dead-eye long enough to go four feet under water. Do this before a threatening cloud gets close. The most dangerous time is just before the rain begins while fiberglass and wood are dry and hence nonconductors.

4. Disconnect antennae. A surge coming down a lead-in wire will blow your radio to pieces.

5. Keep your crew as far away from the mast, standing rigging, and heavy metal objects as you can.

6. Keep up your courage. Vessels have been struck by lightning and survived.

Zero-based Budget

A yacht lay alongside the boatyard float, returned by her new owner after two days because he couldn't get a drink of water. The tanks in the bilge were full, but the electric pump that ran the pressure system did not work because someone had left a light on in the head all night and run the batteries down. He had tried to start the engine with the low battery and blown the diode on the alternator. He had tried to trace the water pipe back from the hand pump to find the valve to turn it on, but the bilge was so complicated with wires, water pipes, and fuel pipes that he could not find the right valve. So he brought his new boat back to have the yard fix her up so he could get a drink.

The yard's solution: bring down a battery charger to recharge the battery. Replace the diode and start the engine. Press the reset button on the electric pump. Install a converter so shore current at 110 volts could be used to recharge batteries or run lights. Write out an astronomical bill.

How much in a new boat is there because you need it there? If what you want is comfortable cruising at bearable prices, consider stripping your boat to the bare hull and putting back what you really need for a month's cruise. Pressure water is convenient, but would not a hand pump be more reliable and less expensive? How important are electric cabin lights? Would kerosene do as well? If you really need a good reading light, could you get by with just one over the chart table? Do you really need electric running lights? (If you sail where there is night-time traffic, you do.) What is the simplest and most reliable stove you can buy? Do you really need an elaborate gimbaled range? You may decide to have some of these, but it will be *your* choice.

What about instruments? For centuries men have navigated without depth finders, radar, anemometers, apparent wind indicators, electric logs to show speed and distance run, and LORAN. How many of these do you really need? For which of them would you spend a day alongside a wharf making repairs instead of sailing? You will probably decide in favor of some of these instruments; with others you may raise doubts.

Assess the total electric drain for a day's cruising. How much does electric refrigeration, electric hot water, an electric head, and an electric anchor winch pull down the batteries? How long must your engine run to restore them? Do you find that you are running the engine to get in and out of harbors and whenever the wind comes ahead, explaining to your crew that we might just as well run it now when it will do us some good because we have to run it three hours a day anyway so we can have showers and ice?

Doubtless, few of us will decide to go back to rowing in a calm, cooking over a wood fire in a black iron stove, using a cedar bucket for a head, and heaving the lead in a fog. Still, a careful assessment of what we are willing to pay for in terms both of available cash and of sailing time might help us to use more wisely our expensive yachts and short vacations.

The Practical Sailor at the Boat Show (1976)

The Sailor paid his $2.50 and walked through the door, to be staggered by a blaze of light, a flutter of fan-blown flags, and a glare of waxed plastic and polished chrome. He was interested this year in the thirty-foot auxiliaries, so made his way resolutely by all temptation to the Tartan exhibit. Reverently removing his shoes in obedience to a neatly lettered sign, he climbed carpeted stairs and stepped aboard.

He reports that he could tell little about the construction of the hull, for it was all sheathed in. However, a salesman described how the deck was fastened to the hull, a critical point in a fiberglass boat. A shelf was molded inside the top of the hull. The deck was set on this in a bedding of thiokol. The seam was covered with a teak toe rail and bolted down through rail, deck, thiokol, and hull to nuts set up under the shelf. A search disclosed the nuts with the thiokol squeezed out by their pressure. Bulkheads were glassed in with full-length fiberglass tape, which fitted snugly despite sharp angles and compound curves. The engine stood in the middle of the cabin, set a little off-center to port to compensate for the spin of the wheel. It had a neat cover over it, but the cover easily lifted off to give complete "walk around" access, a convenience that makes up for any and all inconveniences. The whole accommodation plan was neat and well planned with handholds where useful, a handy galley, a small chart table, and the necessary bunks, lockers, and head. The Sailor admired the mast step and chain plate fastenings, weight and strength where it counted.

However, a tour of several other thirty to thirty-three-foot boats showed such a combination of bad planning, shoddy construction, and cheap showmanship as even that cynical old downeaster had not expected. Here are his notes, scarcely legible from indignation and not clear as to which vessel each item referred to:

Item: Stanchions very light and far too low. The top life line appears designed to tip the off-balance sailor over the rail. The after end of the ¼ inch vinyl-covered wire was toggled to a tiny ⅛ inch weldment on the stern pulpit. The salesman expressed confidence in the fitting, but the Sailor was not prepared to bet his life on it.

Item: Cockpit scuppers with no valve or sea cock to shut them off and no through-hull fittings—just pipes glassed into the hull. The hose connections were visible but utterly inaccessible.

Item: Sink drain Y 'ed into scupper pipes and running through bottom of boat in a place completely invisible and with no shut-off down to the length of his arm.

Item: V-drive engine beneath the cockpit. A small scuttle in the companion ladder exposed a view of two spark plugs and part of the block. Another offered a view of the V transmission. The other end of the engine where carburetor, alternator, and distributor lived was reached through a tiny hatch in the side of the quarterberth. Blacker than the Egyptian darkness!

Item: Pretty interior cloth covering extending from cabin floor to deck where it met covering under house top. Away forward in the forepeak, stinking of uncured resin, the joint between deck and hull had been left exposed and daylight was visible through it.

Item: Massive pieces of teak held chain plates to bulkhead by a dozen husky bolts, but tape holding bulkhead did not lie snugly against either hull or bulkhead.

Item: Pedestal steering with cables and quadrant visible under cockpit floor but totally inaccessible. Top of rudder post squared to take emergency tiller but no way to get tiller through cockpit floor.

20

Item: No place whatever, on deck or below, to stow a thirty to fifty-pound anchor and 200 feet of roding. The *only* choice seemed to be to pass it through the fore hatch into the forward cabin, where the mud and wet would spoil the upholstery.

Item: Drawers and cabinets stapled together, not properly fitted and fastened.

Item: Bilge pump in cockpit locker. To pump, one kneels on the helmsman's feet, faces aft, lifts the locker lid with one hand, and pumps with the other, moving the pump handle athwartships.

The design was all of the same piece—exposed propellers and unsupported rudders arranged to catch lobster traps when afloat and to break off when aground, too many bunks, insufficient stowage, huge empty bins under cockpit seats into which sails and gear were to be stuffed, the gear sifting to the bottom out of reach, and all the sails but the top one buried and intertwined.

The Sailor left the scene, dismayed, to wander among the stalls where photographers, woodcarvers, marine hardware dealers, electronics salesmen, et cetera, et cetera were hard-selling their wares. He did find an old friend in one stall who confided that he should buy the cheapest bottom paint that weighed fourteen pounds to the gallon pail and skip the high-priced article. He found a stall selling really beautiful handcarved scrimshaw on real whale ivory, ivory predating the embargo on whale products. (Write Bill Feeney and Bob Rayno, Tara Road, Mattapoisett, Massachusetts 02739.) He found a sailmaker, a purveyor of old photographs, a number of former shipmates and old students grown as gray as he . . . .

There *was* a pretty little sailing gig by Cape Dory and another sold by the Graves yard in Marblehead. And right by the exit was the same lobster boat from Passamaquoddy that was there last year.

The *Sailor* tacked across the street and rounded to in the Oyster House to restore his jaded spirits with a hooker of New England rum. He admitted that here was a lot of good stuff at that show if you could find it, but it was harder work than winter lobstering.

Check the diameter and pitch of your propeller with the engine manufacturer. You may be asking too much or too little of your engine. A heavy boat needs a big propeller with a low pitch. Pitch is the distance the wheel would screw its way through the water in one revolution if it did not slip at all. A heavy load calls for a pitch of less than the diameter. A light boat needs a high pitch in order to give the engine enough of a load to work on. A high pitch on a heavy boat produces excess load, slip, and cavitation.

The Practical Sailor at the Boat Show (1975)

Just inside the door we came slap up against a twenty-foot lobster boat complete with a shelter over the cockpit open on the starboard side, a davit with a snatch block for the pot warp and with slats along the side to protect her from being slammed by traps coming aboard. In the cockpit sat a lady from Eastport who said that a Deer Island, New Brunswick, lobster boat was used as a plug, that the boats were laid up and finished in Eastport, and that the project was proving so successful that a twenty-four-foot model was planned.

The boat was rough and commercial looking. She was quite full in the shoulders, as lobster boats are, and there were small unevennesses in her, reflecting the exact form of the plug. There was no teak on her but a varnished oak rub rail. Her power would be either outboard or inboard-outboard. Of course, she could be finished in any way the owner wanted, but as a rough, able means of marine transportation with no pretense at "yachtiness" she looked good to us. Passamaquoddy Boat Works, in Eastport, Maine, is the builder. The price is near $2,400.

Cape "25" by Cape Dory Yachts

After threading our way through acres of little plastic runabouts and kettle-bottomed "cruiser-racers" that slept five with full headroom in an overall length less than twenty-four feet and had all the easy grace of a brick powerhouse, we came across the Cape Dory 25. She attracted our attention at once with her graceful sheer, modest freeboard, and neat, conventional counter. She had a long keel and rather slack bilges, making for stability and easy motion, especially in a following sea. Her cockpit was long enough so the tiller did not monopolize it, leaving room for guests to be comfortable. Her house was low and not highly crowned, but the hatch was large so that although one might have to scrooch a bit to move around under the house, the cook by the galley aft could stand up with his head in the open air. She had four bunks, which seemed to be crowding it a bit. For two people, using the fore peak for stowage of duffel bags, sleeping bags, and oil clothes, she would make a fast, able, and comfortable cruising boat. She is built by Cape Dory Yachts, West Bridgewater, Massachusetts. With the extras important for cruising, she would cost just under $10,000.

Another boat that stood out from the fleet was the E-22 racing sloop. She is frankly a racing boat and pretends to be nothing else. Thirty feet long, slim and sharp, she is stripped for action inside, with no teak, no seats except for the helmsman's, no pretense of cruising accommodations. With sails, she would cost about $10,000.

We were much interested in the Avon inflatable dinghies, a possible solution to the skiff problem for small cruising boats that cannot take aboard anything bigger than an eggshell and are slowed too much by towing a dinghy. A dinghy you can put in a duffel bag is very handy if it doesn't take too long to blow up, is not too clumsy to row, and will stand being bumped alongside a barnacled wharf piling or being pulled up on a beach. A current owner claims these are no problems.

The well-known Herreshoff Doughdish was there in foam sandwich fiberglass construction, built exactly to Captain Nat's original design and the equal of the wooden model in weight, stability, ballast ratio, and gaff rig. The boat is available with a Bermuda rig. Bill Harding, who makes the sails for these boats, tells us that the Bermuda rig balances about the same as the gaff rig and that hard on the wind in light going is faster. In other conditions, the gaff rig is fully as fast and in strong breezes is faster than the Bermuda rig on every point of sailing.

For further information, write Doughdish Inc., Marion, Massachusetts 02738. With sails, spars, spinnaker, and sail covers, a Doughdish costs in the neighborhood of $5,000.

With no intention of buying one, but just to see how the other half lives, we boarded Uniflite's forty-two-foot Double Cabin Sedan in the Crosby exhibit and were given a guided tour by Brad Woods, who did the electrical work on her. We saw a cockpit and pilot house beautifully carpeted, a steering station with gauges and controls to please an airplane pilot. Fresh-water windshield washers were the ultimate. Below, forward, was a palace of hand-rubbed teak, wall-to-wall carpet, and lovely upholstery. A dinette that changes to a double bed, a wide forward stateroom, a bathroom (not what we would call a head) with hot and cold running water and a shower, a galley with electric stove and oven that operates either on shore current or on the ship's batteries, a refrigerator *cum* icemaker—the list is endless—graced the living space. Air conditioning, stereo sound, and forced ventilation added to the crushing weight of luxury. Amidships, under the cockpit was an engine room with two huge diesels and a 6.5 kw Onan generator to supply the extensive power requirements. Aft was the owner's cabin, if possible more luxurious than the main salon. We idly wondered why anyone with these amenities ashore would want to take them to sea—but *de gustibus*. We departed in awe, thinking about our article on yacht financing.

Take it from stem to gudgeon and from truck to keel, the show was an interesting summary of the directions yachting is taking. True, there are a good many sea monsters that purport to be fast, comfortable, inexpensive, economical to maintain, to have full headroom and accommodate the whole family—and at the same time to be safe and seaworthy. There is a superfluity of shoddy hardware, shaky life-line stanchions, teak veneer, and sleazy rigging. In among it, however, is clearly discernible some honest effort to provide for a discriminating yachtsman a boat in which he can go to sea or cruise along shore in comfort and safety, under sail or power, and whose lines he can admire.

2

Equipment

The Insoluble Dinghy Problem

A perfect dinghy should have four characteristics:

• It should be seaworthy enough to carry the entire crew at sea in the event of fire or other disaster on the yacht.

• It should be suitable for harbor transportation from float to mooring.

• It should be capable of being taken aboard the yacht or of being towed easily.

• It should be available at a reasonable price.

No small boat meets all these characteristics for a yacht of thirty-five feet or less. A boat big enough and buoyant enough to serve as a lifeboat—a small dory or peapod would be ideal—is excellent for harbor transportation but would be too big to take aboard the yacht, and under any but the mildest conditions would drag hard on the painter. However, if the lifeboat factor is sufficiently important to you and you are going to accept the drag on the painter as necessary, include a sailing rig that can be stowed in the dinghy and thus vastly increase the pleasure in owning such a tender. The price in dollars will run high in fiberglass. If you can find a man who builds good light wooden boats, you may be able to do much better.

However, if you do not want to tow a boat

nearly one-third the length of your yacht, you can solve the lifeboat problem with an inflatable life raft. This can be carried either in a plastic box or in a plastic valise. It can be lashed on deck in an easily accessible place but must be kept away from the compass. It has a steel pressure cylinder in it that is strongly magnetic. This is strictly emergency gear, of no use for harbor transportation, and quite expensive. A six-man life raft with a cover, not Coast Guard inspected, unballasted, hard to get into, and which may blow away in a gale as it inflates before it can be controlled, will cost almost one thousand dollars. A proper life raft, Coast Guard inspected, built to ballast itself with water, and properly equipped, will cost twice as much and will make quite a bulky package on the deck of a small yacht.

With the lifeboat problem thus solved, however, the problem of harbor transportation can be taken care of with a Dyer Dink, or any little plywood or fiberglass shell. It must be about eight feet long to provide freeboard enough to keep dry an oarsman, a guest, and a bag of groceries in a harbor chop or in the wake of a passing power boat. To do this, it will be wide and more or less square-ended, thus being very difficult to row at better than a very gentle pace. A small outboard motor appears at first glance to improve the boat's usefulness in smooth water, but the motor must be stored aboard the yacht, provided with oil

Harbor transportation only

and gasoline, and kept clean and dry. Also, it must be rigged anew in every port. Furthermore, it is an expensive item and a temptation to thieves afloat and ashore. A sailing rig is as expensive as a motor and more fun, but it too must be carried aboard the yacht, rigged in every port, and on such a small, light craft is not very efficient.

Then the little dinghy must be hoisted aboard or towed. Many yachts have main booms rigged high enough so that the dinghy can be carried in chocks on top of the house, unless the life raft is occupying the space. By judicious use of fenders, two men can launch or lift aboard a light dinghy, and it is possible to rig a sling on the main halyard so the small boat can be winched aboard. Some power boats have elaborate little davits and some carry the dinghy lashed across the counter—fair enough in smooth water, but potentially a

bit perilous. If you cannot stow the dinghy aboard, however, you must tow it. At slow speeds—four knots or less—the little light boat will float along astern like a bubble, but as the speed increases, it squats its little stern down in its own wake, braces its feet, and rears back hard on the painter, producing a pull entirely disproportionate to its weight. If you find yourself towing a dinghy with a life raft on deck, you find yourself with all the disadvantages of owning a dory or peapod and without the advantages. And you have paid a heavy price in dollars, too.

Another solution is the inflatable dinghy in combination with a proper life raft. The inflatable dinghy can be stowed in a duffel bag and carried on deck or below. It is not dangerously magnetic. It can be inflated with a foot pump in twenty minutes and be deflated and stowed in ten. An eight- or ten-foot boat can

Overpowered Whitehall *and sailing dinghy*

The peapod tows with slack painter

Good lifeboat, fun to sail, but tows hard

the owner does not wish to spend a half hour daily on a coastal cruise inflating and deflating the boat, he will try to tow it. On a long painter the inflatable is tossed about by every wave and in a strong breeze may very well flip over. Of course, it won't sink, but it may yank and twist on its painter hard enough to pull the pad out of the fabric despite powerful reinforcement at this point. The usual way of preventing this is to tow the inflatable on a very short painter, often with its bow right up on the yacht's counter. This is a clumsy and unseamanlike solution, may produce excessive chafe, and spoils the appearance of the yacht to every passing observer.

carry four people and a grocery order quite safely and comfortably in a small chop. The boat rows reluctantly but is little worse than a dinghy. It can be driven by a small outboard motor. Made of heavily treated fabric, it is tough enough to resist ordinary abrasion, although it will not stand sharp nails, continued chafing alongside a float, or being hauled up a beach repeatedly. Even with good care it will not last as long as a fiberglass dinghy.

However, the inflatable's chief drawback appears to be that it cannot be towed easily. If

Other solutions to the dinghy problem have been tried. One can carry a light canoe aboard, lashed along the rail or on top of the house. This is light, easily launched or lifted aboard, has adequate capacity, and is fast and handy for harbor transportation in the hands of an expert. However, a canoe is a tiddly affair and can be easily upset by the inexperienced guest.

A lightly built round-bottomed rowboat like a Whitehall is elegant, steady, easily rowed, and, although it cannot be taken aboard, tows well at low speeds. In a steep following sea it can easily yaw, run its fine bows under, and take the big drink. The same is true of a peapod but less so of a dory.

Diversity—no solution

So there is no ideal solution to the dinghy problem. One must simply resolve either to have a big one, seaworthy enough to be a lifeboat, tough enough to haul on a beach, big enough to sail well and row well, and designed to tow without too much reluctance, or one goes the other way, buys a life raft and an inflatable dinghy or a boat small enough to take aboard.

> Tie several seine floats to your dinghy painter so on a quiet night the weight of the nylon painter won't pull her alongside to bump you awake.

The Perfect (?) Dinghy
William H. Ashbaugh

In addition to the previously given four characteristics of a perfect dinghy, I would add: *It should be soft.*

Dinghies are required to live very close to larger craft. Often they must be pulled aboard the larger boat. Despite careful handling and adequate equipment such as davit tackles on the boom, bringing the dinghy aboard is almost certain to result in nicks and scratches to both boats if the dinghy is made of wood or fiberglass. Even while lying at anchor with the dinghy tied astern, you may wake up some morning to find that the dinghy has bumped and scratched the larger boat during the night. This is because the dinghy's shallow draft and reduced windage mean that she answers different forces of wind and sea than the larger boat does. The dinghy will often therefore not stay astern while at anchor.

There are other times when a dinghy constructed of a hard material can be a real danger. When running before a heavy following sea, the skipper who is towing a dinghy is faced with a real dilemma. If he follows the old rule of "let her run down the second wave," he is likely to find that the dinghy yaws badly; she is threatening sometimes to pull her painter from its eye bolt or worse. If he

shortens the painter, he will frequently look aft to see 150 pounds of plywood or fiberglass poised above his head ready to come crashing down on him should the larger boat bury her bow in the next wave and slow down abruptly. Even when this does not occur, it is not a comforting sight.

So—let's add softness to the desirable qualities of a dinghy and see what we come up with as the ideal dinghy. It is, of course, possible to make the gunwale of even a fiberglass or wooden dinghy softer with rubber hose or the commercially available Dink Guard, but this does not prevent her from chafing under the counter and still leaving you with the 150-pound missile poised over your head in a following sea. Yes—you guessed it—we are talking about an inflatable—but not just the store-bought model, rather one with some additions, which make her closer to the ideal.

In terms of the potential dangers described, inflatables have obvious advantages over plywood or fiberglass dinghies, and some models are quite inexpensive. The one on page 28 (825-pound capacity) was recently purchased for about $50 on sale at a discount house (Two Guys). While a model such as this should not be considered a true life raft, it is relatively well made of neoprene-coated nylon and there have been no leaks or other problems in two years of use.

The inflatable's chief drawbacks are:

1. It tows poorly. Lacking a skeg and having very shallow draft, it lacks directional stability and yaws badly. Its lightness can also allow it actually to flip over in some wind and sea conditions.

2. Inflatables are not hard to row, because their shallow draft offers little resistance, but they are *very* hard to row in a straight line. The lack of directional stability means that an inflatable is just as willing to go sideways as forward, and the oarsman must constantly countersteer or he will find himself proceeding in circles. The lumpy bottom caused by yours and the passengers' bottoms also creates some additional turbulence as the inflatable is rowed through the water.

3. It is difficult to inflate a large dinghy by

hand. The hand pumps that come with these boats are practically useless except for individuals who want to develop extremely strong pectoral muscles as a result of seemingly endless exercise.

4. In an emergency, hand pumping would be far too time consuming, and reliance on such a procedure could be dangerous. Instead of fiddling while Rome burns, you could be pumping while you all go down.

5. Moving around in inflatables is a little like trying to walk through a large pillow. The nonrigid floor gives, and the boat seems to fold up around you. Inflatables last longer and are safer from puncture if not overinflated. Rigidity should not be attempted through hard inflation of the sides.

The dinghy shown here is an attempt to produce an inflatable without the inflatable's problems.

Problem number one, poor towing, is dealt with by adding a skeg. Many inflatables come with motor mounts that make excellent supports for the rear of the skeg. A piece of three-eighth-inch marine plywood held to the motor mount with a strut made of three-quarter-inch plywood is grooved to accept the skeg. The forward support for the skeg is a piece of three-quarter-inch plywood grooved to accept the forward end of the skeg, which is bolted to this support. The support is attached to the floor of the inflatable with contact cement. As the floor is not inflated, this support can also be attached with bolts through it and the floor—washers and additional fabric around the hole will provide added support.

The plywood floor that has been added to this inflatable allows some weight to be carried while this dinghy is being towed. The weight and skeg produce greater vertical and longitudinal stability facilitating towing. Problem number two, difficult rowing in a straight line, has also been ameliorated with the skeg. Even though there is some increased drag because of the skeg, this is more than compensated by the floor board, which smooths out the normally lumpy bottom of an inflatable.

Problem number three, difficult inflation, can be solved in a number of ways, three of which are noted here. For smaller inflatables it is possible to buy a foot pump, which is a great improvement over the hand model you will probably get with such a boat. For larger inflatables such as the one shown, even foot pumping may seem a bit arduous, and an elegant solution is a car or boat vacuum cleaner fitted with a nozzle, a funnel, or anything else that will fit over its exhaust so that the exhaust of the vacuum cleaner can be used to inflate the dinghy. The low pressure, high volume of the vacuum cleaner is just what an inflatable needs. Don't get the electric tire inflater sold by some auto stores—its low volume will take forever to inflate your dinghy, and if left on, its higher pressure could injure the boat. Even the vacuum cleaner should not be left on too long.

If you have a small inflatable and want to carry emergency gas inflation capability, you will find that the systems designed for them are expensive. Auto stores sell compressed gas in cans that also contain a sealant. These cans are designed to seal and inflate flat tires. The tops of these cans are made so that they can be screwed down onto the valve stem of a tire. By picking up a used tubeless tire valve stem at your local garage, you can have a compressed gas system for your small inflatable. Just insert the rubber end of the stem into the inflatable's valve and screw the valve stem onto the top of the can until the gas and sealant enter the inflatable. It will take several cans and the sealant might not be desirable inside your dinghy when it is stored, but as a cheap emergency inflation and sealant system, you may decide it is worth carrying. And so we have at least one answer to the problem of emergency inflation, problem number four.

Problem number five, difficulty in moving around, is greatly lessened by the use of a floor board. This is equipment often used on the more expensive inflatables such as Avon. The floor board makes your dinghy much more of a boat and much less like an inner tube.

And so *voilà*—The Perfect Dinghy—well, almost.

Notes from the Sailmaker: Used Sails

Nathaniel S. Wilson

Secondhand sails are secondhand for a reason, but if you know what you want and what to look for in a sail when you find it, the chances are that you will make out well.

Today with the large numbers of production boats on the market, you are likely, if your boat is of this type, to find a used sail to fill your needs. There is no sense in buying a used sail unless it fits your boat. Alterations can be costly, as much as half the price of a new sail, but there are occasions when a used sail can be a welcome addition to your boat's sail locker.

What are some points to be considered in buying a used sail? The first and most obvious is: Does the sail fit your sail plan? Should minor alterations be required, an estimate from a sailmaker should be in hand before the purchase is final. If it is possible, try the sail on your boat so you are able to see how it sets.

The weight of the sail cloth is critical. A fellow bought a sail meeting the sail dimensions for his boat's spitfire jib; but when it arrived, it was far too light and could have better been used on a fifteen-foot sailing skiff.

A close inspection must be made of the sail when you find what you want. Lay the sail out as flat as possible and check the edges for any irregular shapes. Should you see any distortion it is reason enough to forget the sail. Next check all the corners for wear and broken stitching. If there is stitching gone in the reinforcing patches, see if you can get your finger under the edge of the patch and pull. If it breaks away easily, it is rotten and you are sure to find more rot in the sail. Check all the grommets and slides. On a jib, check the hanks for wear from the stay and for distortion, which will make them hard to open. Note the condition of the bolt rope or tape that lines the edge of the sail. If the sail has a wire luff, check for bleeding rust or wear on the luff tape from the wire. Make sure all the seizings on the hanks and slides are good. Any broken threads should be checked for strength and the stitching marked for renewal if found wanting. An aluminum headboard may be weakened by oxidation, evidenced by a white powder of aluminum oxide on and around it. Today many headboards are external, made in two pieces with the sail sandwiched between them and fastened with rivets. This type will not last nearly as long as the internal headboards, which are sewn into the sail. Many times the external boards are bent and badly worn by the halyard shackle. Check internal boards for wear on the bolt rope where the shackle is attached. Finally, "walk" the seams; that is, inspect the full length of each seam, and mark any broken threads or worn fabric. Look for signs of wear around the batten pockets. It pays to do a complete job.

It is very important in buying a used sail to know first exactly what you want before you begin the hunt and then to know what to look for before you accept the sail. A little extra time spent on detail can save you money and keep you sailing longer.

When the Wind Hauls Aft

Hugh G. Williams

Many of us who have engaged in coastwise cruising, especially in Bermuda-rigged boats, and short-handed, have given much thought over the years to a down-wind sail that would

29

be both suitable for our situation and really effective in increasing boat speed. A full-size parachute spinnaker is certainly the most efficient, provided at least three fairly seasoned hands are aboard—two to set, jibe, or douse the sail, and one to steer and to handle sheets and guys. Even so, however, the spinnaker requires a net on the forestay to prevent hourglassing, and it will also lose much of its ability to draw when the ocean becomes bumpy from a tidal slop, a sudden calm, or passage across a narrow bay with a groundswell setting into it. Moreover, a high proportion of the courses sailed in longshore cruising are only a few miles long, and it's often a question whether the effort of manning a spinnaker for such a short time is really worthwhile. Especially during the flukey days of late July and early August, when the afternoon southwester can so easily die out with no warning whatever and be replaced with a gentle easterly!

What other options are there?

Probably we have all thought fondly of a huge squaresail, perhaps on a yard that could be raised and lowered. Usually, however, the shrouds and spreaders necessary for a tall mast reach outboard so far that the yard couldn't be effectively trimmed as the wind moved around to the quarter or the beam. Also, a spar that was really long enough would be awkward to stow on deck, especially with a sail of the necessary size bent onto it. And carried up the mast on its lift, it would certainly cause an unacceptable amount of windage, no matter how salty it looked.

Twin genoas are probably fine, but the rigging may well be financially unjustifiable to the average coastal sailor. Moreover, like the spinnaker, they might not be worth setting except on a passage expected to last many hours.

Eric Hiscock, in *Voyaging Under Sail*, suggests something like the old-fashioned spinnaker, cut considerably flatter than today's parachute and with less measurable area but boomed out in similar fashion so that the sail can be let well forward when the wind itself starts to move that way. Such a sail can be carried with the wind practically abeam. Still, here also the boom is necessary and, for crews consisting of one couple, awkward to handle, especially in a seaway, and also not suited to rapidly changing conditions.

Certainly the modern yacht, with her stubby little main boom and with so much of her area in headsail, needs something to make her go down-wind; and for many cruising sailors a conventional parachute—the obvious complement to a high-aspect rig—just isn't practical. Or comfortable—which, for my wife and me, is synonymous.

We decided last spring that an effort was finally in order to bring new life to our thirty-seven-foot sloop—slippery enough on all points except with the wind dead aft—especially on those up-the-bay runs before the light summer southerlies so common along the Maine and New Brunswick coasts.

The new sail should be easily manageable by one person on the foredeck, as versatile as possible in order to meet suddenly changing conditions, and quick to set or take in when the wind grew uncertain or flukey.

Several sailmakers of national reputation were advertising a new type of headsail, under various trade names, which seemed to offer just the characteristics we were seeking. It was, in essence, a large, full genoa with a radially cut head (like a spinnaker), with leech- and foot-lines to control the shape, and construction from rip-stop nylon spinnaker cloth. Some had hanks along the luff; others were set loose and could be tacked down either at the stem of the boat or at the outboard end of a pole.

We liked the headsail idea for several reasons. Riding up and down on the genoa halyard, it could be easily flown or doused. Hanked to the forestay, it would be less likely to hourglass. Trimming would be easily managed as the wind shifted or as the course was changed. The genoa sheets, already laid out in place, could be used for this sail—the leeward one for trimming and the weather one, when so needed, for a foreguy. With the number of hanks limited to three, it could be quickly bent on or unbent, or bunched very low on the forestay and left in place, with another headsail set on top of it.

These thoughts were communicated to a local sail loft of very high reputation with the added suggestion that, as a cruising sail, it might be built of slightly heavier material than was usual for summer finery. The completed Kite was of 1.5 oz. rip-stop nylon. Area was just over 600 square feet (at least 20 percent of it in the roaches); the measurable area of a full-size spinnaker would have been about 1,000.

A season's use may not offer sufficient basis for passing judgment, especially for a crew possessed of a magical affinity to attract headwinds. It is, however, fair to say that most of the time this new sail has equaled or surpassed expectations. For one thing, it can be carried with the wind well forward of the beam—up to within about six points—and is therefore a marvelously effective light-weather reaching-sail. Dead before it—and dead she used to be—the radial head and the great bulging shoulder high in the leech cause the Kite to stand surprisingly firmly with no pole whatever. (In very light going, and especially with something of a chop, it is indeed helpful to rig the pole and to set up the inboard sheet rather snug, led as a foreguy through a snatch block up in the stem.) A beam reach is absolutely delightful.

My estimate is that, under all of those conditions, boat speed has been raised, on the average, by at least a full knot—enough to make a very substantial difference in a day's run.

There are serious flaws in the Kite's performance, however, the most serious being evident on any course with a quartering breeze, and especially with the wind within twenty to thirty degrees of dead aft. On this point of sailing, with all sheets paid well off, the wind curls around the upper leech of the mainsail directly onto the leech of the Kite, breaking down the whole upper body and rendering it useless. Taking up the foot-line seems to help; this adds some draft to the sail without curling the leech inboard so the draft from the main doesn't strike it even more directly and harmfully. In addition, it is well to slack the leech line so as to help further in avoiding that inboard curl. The most effective measure of all is to change the lead of the sheet by rigging a snatch block almost directly under the clew of the sail, and then strap the clew right down. Rerouting the sheet lead to a more forward position adds considerably to the draft and also tends to move the sail forward away from the main.

Or try anything else that seems to work. Every downhill run we make, the rules seem to be different!

Light weather compounds the problems as it would with a regular parachute, and unfortunately the Kite does hourglass—though not in so tight a weave that it can't be gotten down and straightened out.

We don't claim the Kite as a complete answer; but, at the end of one season, we see far more pluses than minuses in its performance, and we hope other cruisers who've used similar sails will share their experience with us. All of us would probably agree that, with a Kite aboard, down-wind sailing is far more interesting than it used to be.

Notes from the Sailmaker: Jeni Wings
Nathaniel S. Wilson

Many modern cruising boats are not well adapted to down-wind sailing. The main booms are very short and the fore triangle is greatly enlarged. Unless you have the crew to set a spinnaker, your down-wind performance is somewhat reduced. Winging out a jib with a boathook is at best a jury rig.

In 1963 Wright Britton developed the Roller Jeni Wings. He was dissatisfied with the conventional spinnaker, poling out a jib, or hanking on twin running jibs. The Jeni Wings, unlike other methods, can be set by one person. They are inherently safe and balanced and have the versatility the cruising sailor needs to enjoy sailing down-wind.

Jeni Wings, also known as Twin Wings, consist of two genoas sewn on one 1 x 19 luff wire. They set from the stem head in the same position as your normal roller furling genoa. For down-wind use the Wings are held out by two poles that have on their outboard ends special fittings to take the sheets. The inboard ends are attached to a vertical track on the mast, which permits them to be run up the mast and stowed out of the way, parallel to the mast and close to it.

The Wings are easily set by one person. He goes forward and pulls down the track slide carrying the inboard ends of the poles. The outboard ends, supported by previously set topping lifts, thus raise the poles to a horizontal position forward of the shrouds. The sheets lead through the fittings on the ends of the poles to the clews of the sails rolled up in the usual way. The roller furling trip line is released and the sheets hauled aft, one on each side. The mainsail may now be furled, thus eliminating the danger of a jibe. Since the Wings are set on a roller furling gear, they may be reefed while running down-wind, a decided advantage.

By tying the sheets through the clews of both Wings, they lie on top of each other and

Wings set as a genoa jib

can be used as a conventional roller furling genoa jib.

The Brittons have logged many thousands of miles under Jeni Wings alone in their forty-foot *Delight*. They have made two Atlantic crossings and have cruised extensively on the coasts of Maine, Nova Scotia, Newfoundland, Labrador, Greenland, Scotland, Ireland, Norway, and Iceland. Over two hundred and fifty other yachts from twenty five to seventy feet in length are now using Jeni Wings, and while many have been used for trade-wind passages, the majority have been used for coastwise cruising.

The Jeni Wings are the best solution to the down-wind problem since the full-rigged ship. The poles and hardware are made by Britton of Southport, Inc., West Southport, Maine.

Notes from the Sailmaker: Storm Sails

Nathaniel S. Wilson

Among the most important items for a yacht going offshore are storm sails. It is often con-

Delight *with wings spread*

sidered that adding a third reef makes the mainsail into a storm sail. Most mainsails are much too light, and even when reefed down are cut improperly for storm sails. During the age of deep-water sail when getting home by wind alone meant a man's bread and butter, sails were cut far differently than they are today. There was good reason for this. The Scotch cut, as it is called, has the cloth running with the leech and foot, leaving them free from seams that can split from chafing or excessive strain. Should a cloth split at the leech, the tear is likely to stop at the first seam it comes to. On a modern cross-cut mainsail, the cloths end on the leech and foot. It is easy to split the sail from leech to luff.

There are only two proper ways to secure a storm trysail to the mast. A very quick and strong method is the lanyard-and-toggle method. Many masts today may not accept this method if they have a lot of hardware, such as spinnaker pole fittings, above the boom. On boats where the mast is clear above the goose neck, this method can be used. Through each luff hole a rope is passed. The end is passed through a lay in the rope, forming a tight figure-eight around the bolt rope. On this rope are lignum vitae parral beads that allow the sail to move up the mast freely. Into one end of the rope a toggle is spliced and into the other an eye splice only large enough to pass the toggle. When rigging the sail, it is easy to pass the toggles through the splices, attach the halyard, tie down the tack, and rig the sheet. You are ready to set the sail.

The second method is to use the existing track. To do this, you need a switch in the track above the furled mainsail so that you will not have to unbend it to set the trysail. Do not bend a trysail on a mast that accepts plastic slides. They don't have the strength to withstand heavy gusts. A man came into the loft once holding a handful of plastic internal slides off his thirty-five-foot sloop. He had jibed in only a moderate breeze and snapped almost all the slides from the sail. Use only metal slides on your trysail, and better yet, the cast bronze type.

Some think that rigging the trysail sheet to the boom would make available the main sheet

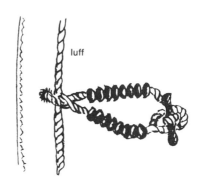

luff

Lanyard and toggle

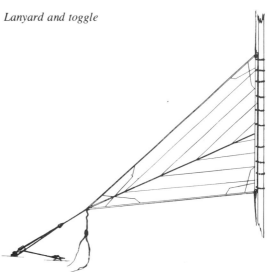

for trimming. It is better to house the boom and secure the mainsail well. The trysail sheet is better under control when sheeted to quarter bitts or pad eyes through-bolted on deck. The clew of the sail should have a sheet pennant attached to a single block. With a snatch block on the pad eye, the sheet can be roved for a two to one mechanical advantage and can be led to a nearby winch or cleat. With two sheet pennants, each with its block, you have a sheet for each tack with the weather one slack and ready when needed.

Before heading out, make sure that all leads have been determined and that you have actually tried them out. Check the fastenings of your sail track where the head of the trysail comes. It should be bolted. Stow all blocks, sheets, and extra lines needed in setting the storm sails in the bags with their sails, and hope they won't be needed.

Storm sails can never be too heavy. They should be roped all around. A taped storm sail is no good for really heavy going. As a rough rule of thumb, the trysail should be about one-third the size of the mainsail and the storm jib one-quarter of the fore triangle. This may vary in individual boats. Consult your sailmaker or the designer of your boat.

Send Your Expenses Out for Bid

Mr. Burnham Chapman of Hamilton, Massachusetts, wanted to move up to a bigger boat. Accordingly, he sold his Cheoy Lee 28 complete with all her cruising gear, including compass, RDF, and even galley equipment. He believes that selling her in this way considerably improved the boat's competitive position in the market. He then ordered a Fantasia 35.

Instead of buying equipment for the new boat piece by piece, he listed every item he would need, right down to fenders and deck bucket. The list included also a number of expensive items like weather instruments, anchors and rode, outboard motor, and galley stove—everything he had left aboard the old boat plus whatever new equipment he needed for the larger one.

Opposite each item were two columns marked "Have" and "Please Bid." Having checked the items he owned, he Xeroxed the list and sent it to a number of suppliers, including E. B. Marine, J. Stuart Haft, Unimetrics, Graves, Handy Boat Service, Sea Track, Robert E. White, Defender, Harbor Electronics, Ocean Marine, Alco, Clark Marine, and various others.

Some of these failed to answer his letter. Others sent catalogs or wrote inviting a visit. Still others bid on such of the items as they could supply. Mr. Chapman thought that Defender Industries in New Rochelle, New York, offered the best deal. Some of the items were the same as the catalog price and some were less. However, Defender's prices are usually below list prices, because they operate out of a warehouse with very little overhead devoted to salesroom and retail expense. Mr. Chapman estimates that on a $9,000 inventory he saved about $2,000 by these means.

The Seacock

A good bronze seacock is an expensive item of yacht equipment, but it is cheap insurance. A seacock should guard every one of the holes in a boat's side or bottom except those occupied by the propeller shaft or rudder post with their accompanying stuffing boxes. The seacock provides a strong, quick, and positive means of closing off the hole.

The first photograph shows how the seacock is installed. The threaded through-hull fitting fits so closely into the hole in the hull that as it is screwed in, its threaded shank cuts threads in the plank and in the wooden backing block, not shown. Then the valve itself is turned down on top of the through-hull fitting into a layer of bedding compound, thus forming a tight seal. Finally the flange of the valve is drilled and screwed down snugly to the backing block. The hose inside the boat is slipped over the tailpipe and tightened down with two stainless-steel hose clamps.

The second photograph shows the seacock disassembled. Note that the core is tapered to fit precisely the taper in the body of the valve and is drilled transversely with a hole the size of the inside diameter of the tailpipe and the through-hull fitting. With the core in place, the washer and the tension nut are put on and the nut tightened enough to make the core water-tight but still leave it loose enough to turn freely. A *thin* application of

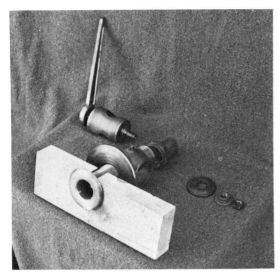

The seacock disassembled

grease will help to achieve this balance. The locknut is then put on, the tension nut held with one wrench, and the locknut set down hard on it with another.

The designer of the boat should·see that holes in the boat are so located that seacocks can be reached by a man with a wrench without the services of a contortionist. Inaccessible seacocks will not be turned off when the boat is left and hence are useless. They will also "freeze up," stick from lack of use, so that when needed they will not turn.

Before the boat goes overboard in the spring, test each seacock to be sure that it turns freely. If it does not, remove the locknut, the tension nut, and the washer. Set a punch or a nail set on the depression in the middle of the shaft, just visible in the second photograph, and tap gently with a hammer to start the core back out of its seat. Take the core out and clean it off. A fine wire brush used very gently will do it, but because the bronze is soft and the machining precise, rough treatment will cause the valve to leak. Grease the core lightly, wipe out the inside of the valve carefully, and reassemble.

Never hit the end of the shaft directly with a hammer. You will destroy the threads at the first blow. Never use a stillson wrench, pliers, or a vise-grip on the tension nut or the locknut, or you will surely round off the corners of the soft bronze.

In the fall, shut off the seacock, remove the tailpipe, and wipe out any water remaining on top of the core. Take out the plugs in the front and back, shown just over the trademark in the first photo, and drain any water left in the hole in the core. Grease the plugs and replace them.

If you notice that despite a stiff tension on the tension nut the water seeps around the core, there are three remedies. The first is an emergency measure, to be taken if the leak is severe. Remove the tailpipe and tap a pine plug into the top of the valve. Provident skippers have plugs prepared in advance. The second alternative is more spectacular. Disassemble the seacock and knock out the core. At once a geyser will spurt into the boat. A sock rammed down the hole will slow it up some, but make haste to grease the core more heavily than before, and reassemble. The third and ultimate solution is to remove the core when the boat is hauled and have a machinist recut the taper to fit exactly the taper on the valve. If it still is not quite right, grind it in gently with a little valve-grinding compound. You will probably have to put a shim under the tension nut or washer if you take off much bronze.

A 1½ inch seacock, complete with through-hull fitting, costs under one hundred dollars from the catalogs. There is another type with a "Buna-N" expanding core for a little less and one of lighter construction with an integral tailpipe for use with hose only for about fifty dollars with through-hull fitting and handle.

There are less expensive shut-off valves used in other parts of the boat and by plumbers ashore, but a seacock is the proper valve for a hole in the boat. It can be solidly attached to the hull with a watertight seal, has a full-diameter hole when open, cannot be held open by small bits of dirt or sediment, and is all of the same metal so is unlikely to corrode unless placed near a more noble metal. (See "Beware Galvanic Corrosion," page 13.) The seacock is the most durable and reliable way to keep the water out of your boat.

The Bilge Pump

No wise sailor ever signed on a vessel with a shiny pump handle, for he knew she leaked and that he would have to pump half an ocean through her before he made port. Modern yachts all have rusty pump handles. What little water gathers in the bilge from condensation or minor leaks is quickly disposed of.

However, a seacock may suffer from electrolysis and break. A hose may overheat and burn. A floating log may spring a plank or butt, or the propeller may strike something solid and start a leak in the stuffing box. A playful whale may swat you or you may run ashore. You may badly need a high-capacity pump quickly.

Because a power-driven pump does not wear out the crew, your first line of defense against rising water will probably be either an electric pump or one geared to the engine. Because the latter may be difficult to install, the electric pump is the most common solution.

There are two common types of electric pumps. One is submersible, lives at the bottom of the bilge where the water is, and discharges just below the surface. A switch will be located on the control board or there will be an automatic switch to start the pump when the water reaches a level in the bilge high enough to make pumping worthwhile. There is a considerable range in both price and capacity in electric pumps. One of the most popular is Bilge King. It will pump seventeen gallons per minute to a height of three feet at a cost of 4.9 amperes. This comes to over 1,000 gallons per hour, a weight of over four tons—enough to sink most small boats. This pump, without an automatic switch, can be purchased through Goldberg's at 202 Market Street, Philadelphia, Pa. 19106. Other discount houses offer it too. Watch for sales, which often reduce prices by as much as another 25 percent.

The Rule No. 1400 pump sold by James Bliss & Co. (Dedham, Massachusetts 02026) throws 1,400 gallons per hour.

Automatic switches for these pumps are of two kinds. One works by means of air pressure conducted through a tube to a switch in a high-and-dry location. The other lifts a float that tilts a mercury switch. The entire mechanism is submersible and sells for under twenty dollars.

Several pumps that deliver about half as much water are also available. The Lovett automatic pump with built-in automatic switch delivers 550 gph, is listed by the Yacht Safety Bureau, and costs in the neighborhood of fifty dollars. The Mini-King, a smaller Bilge King, delivers 360 gph and is still cheaper at Goldberg's and Bliss. An automatic switch is extra. The Rule 500, delivering 500 gph, available from Bliss, and the Rule-Mate delivering 250 gph at only .7 amps, are both modestly priced.

All these pumps work through impellers; that is, the motor turns a little rubber paddlewheel inside a housing, sucking water up from the bilge, carrying it around on the blades, and shooting it out through the outlet. Most water-circulating pumps on engines work the same way. In time, the blades lose their resiliency and the impeller must be replaced. Also, if the pump remains inactive for a long time and dries out, the impeller may stick to the edge of the housing and tear itself to pieces when it starts up. It is well to install a check valve in the outlet line or to run it through a vented loop, for it is possible, although unlikely, for something to clog the pump, causing it to stop with the exhaust line full of water. When the obstruction comes clear, the water can siphon back if it has enough weight to turn the blades of the impeller backward. It has happened in at least one case.

An impeller pump will pass sand, rust, and small particles of foreign matter right through it, but it will choke on anything bigger like a bottle cap or the label from a can. Therefore, a strainer is necessary on the intake and it must be frequently checked to be sure it is clean. If the pump runs dry for any length of time, it may heat up and destroy the rubber impeller, although several brands such as the Rule pumps advertise that they can safely run dry.

Most of these pumps are built primarily of plastic, and their electrical connections are sealed so there can be no short circuit and no electrolytic action through the bilge water.

When the pump is new and as long as it remains undamaged by shifting ballast or beer bottles or whatever else may slam about in the bilge, it is all right; but even though the electrical line to the pump has a fuse in it, there is always a chance of disaster. Anyone who leaves a boat on a mooring untended for more than a day or two has undue confidence in modern technology.

One way of reducing the risk is to raise the pump out of the bilge to a dry location and lift the water to the pump. Jabsco makes an impeller-type pump that delivers 330 gph and uses only 6.5 amps at 12 volts. With a bronze housing this costs under fifty dollars, less with a plastic housing. PAR makes one that delivers 510 gph and a smaller one delivering 270 gph. The latter sells for less than fifty dollars through "Boat U.S.," Boat Owners Association of the United States, 880 South Pickett Street, Alexandria, Virginia 22034. To receive their price, you must join the association, well worth the nominal fee. James Bliss and Goldberg both sell Sea-Gulp, which delivers 480 gph, drawing 7.7 amps, for less than one hundred dollars, and Sea-Gulp Junior, which delivers 300 gph at four amps is much cheaper. None of these is automatic, but with the air pressure-type switch they can be made automatic with all wiring out of the water and in an area where, even if the switch should throw a spark, no damage could be done.

If your engine is running, the drain of four to seven amps is no great problem, for the alternators on most engines will deliver a steady 15 amps if necessary. However, if your engine is not running and you run your pump an hour a day, you will have to run your engine about half an hour a day to keep the battery up. If she lies at a mooring from Sunday night to Saturday morning, the battery will need a good booster.

Many a yachtsman, unwilling to buy an expensive electric pump and equally unwilling to exercise on the hand pump, simply shoves the intake of the water pump on his engine into the bilge and pumps the bilge through the block, manifold, and muffler, and out the exhaust. However, the least obstruction in the narrow passages of the cooling system may lead to serious engine trouble.

To have one's pumps dependent on the complexities of a marine engine is perilous. In addition to an electric pump that can hold its own with a major leak, there should be an accessible hand pump of large capacity. For coastal cruising, it should be on deck. The operator should be able to use it for a considerable period in a comfortable and protected position without undue fatigue.

The simplest solution to this problem is the common fisherman's "guinea pump." It is simply a piece of four-inch galvanized pipe with a foot valve in the bottom and a spout near the top. The piston is a stick with a cone of leather, open at the top. It is a man killer to use, but four strokes fills a bucket.

For many years the piston-type pump in a corner of the cockpit was standard equipment on yachts. PAR makes two good ones: a short-stroke model delivering about three gallons per minute and a larger one delivering about seven gallons. This is 180 and 420 gph respectively, which compares favorably with the smaller electric pumps. However, few crews are going to maintain 50 strokes per minute for an hour. The motion of lifting with the arms and shoulders is very hard on the back, especially if the feet cannot straddle the barrel of the pump. There is a tendency to pull up and back instead of straight up, which materially increases the friction and may bend the pump rod. Furthermore, if any small obstruction catches under the foot valve, the suction is lost. If it catches between the piston and barrel or in the upper valve, the pump works very hard and major surgery is necessary. The PAR pumps are built of brass and rubber and come apart comparatively easily, but clearing one is still quite a project. Each of the PAR models costs about twenty-five dollars.

The diaphragm pump is much to be preferred over the piston type. This amounts simply to a heavy rubber cover that fits tightly over a bowl. When the cover is stretched upward, a simple flapper valve opens, sucking water in from the bilge. When the cover is squeezed downward, the inlet valve is slapped shut and the exhaust valve is pushed open, expelling water on its way overboard. This pump can be mounted in any position, even upside down. It can be mounted below deck with the handle projecting through the deck or on a bulkhead, or cockpit side. The handle should be arranged to work back and forth, not up and down. Pushing and pulling is a much easier motion than lifting; it can be done sitting, kneeling, or standing, and can be kept up without undue fatigue for half an hour.

The diaphragm pump is unlikely to clog, for the ports are about an inch in diameter. You can pump a sock through one with a little luck. An inspection plate gives access to the bowl so a jam can be easily cleared.

A common diaphragm pump is the Guzzler 400. It delivers 11.4 gpm, as much as the medium-sized electrical pumps, and costs about twenty-five dollars. The Guzzler 500, slightly more expensive, delivers 15 gpm, and the Guzzler 600, a real bull of a pump, delivers 30 gpm, 1,800 gph. Three strokes will fill a gallon jug. Naturally, the cost in human effort is proportionately high.

The Whale pumps, made in Ireland, come in sizes delivering 8, 18, and 30 gpm at varying prices. The Henderson pump, made in England and available from Gibb Yachting Equipment (2308 Clement Street, San Francisco, California 94121) or Gibb-Henderson, Inc. (82 Border Street, Cohasset, Massachusetts 02025), is a double-action diaphragm pump with a chamber on each side of the diaphragm. It delivers 25 gpm maximum and sells for about seventy-five dollars. This writer has used one for about ten years with outstanding success.

Offshore yachts should certainly have at least two pumps. One should operate through the engine, either belt driven or electrically powered, and the other should be a hand pump. Some recommend two hand pumps, one of which can be operated from on deck and one from below.

If all else fails, a frightened man with a bucket can move a great deal of water very rapidly.

A Flagstaff

Mr. Douglas Erickson of Coconut Grove, Florida writes: "I suggest the following as being a light flagstaff, sensitive to light wind and easy to make.

"First, use a bamboo stick four to five feet long, cutting both ends so as to leave the fully enlarged knobs at both top and bottom. The in-between knobs keep the two clove hitches in the halyard from slipping.

"Second, use an eight-inch aluminum clothesline wire about three feet long. Make a bottom loop to fit loosely over the bamboo stick, say one to one, and one-half inches inside diameter and cover with 'spaghetti' to prevent chafing. Make another loop for the top only large enough for a #8 or #10 round-head screw or bolt. This top loop rests on top of the stick and is held in place by the screw plus a washer left slack. To hold the burgee,

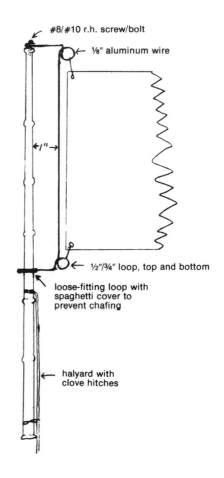

#8/#10 r.h. screw/bolt

⅛" aluminum wire

←1"→

½"/¾" loop, top and bottom

loose-fitting loop with spaghetti cover to prevent chafing

halyard with clove hitches

make a top and bottom loop at right angles to the others through which the burgee can be lashed." Mr. Erickson thoughtfully provided a drawing.

> It was not unusual for a fishing schooner on her maiden voyage and on other important occasions to fly from her masthead a huge pennant proclaiming her name. Party boats do it, but yachts never do.

Inflatable Life Rafts

Fire or sinking at sea are the ultimate emergencies for which life rafts have been designed. In the ultimate emergency, there is little time to think and no time to change one's mind or to buy any new gear.

The life raft must be easily available and must be inflated quickly. Life rafts are carried either in a fiberglass box or in a bag. If a place for it can be found on deck where it can be out of the way and firmly lashed down with quick-release hooks, one simply jerks the lanyard on the quick-release gear and throws the box overboard. The painter is kept attached to the vessel. A sharp pull on the painter fires the CO_2 cylinders in the raft, the box pops open, and the raft inflates, canopy and all.

Most life rafts consist of two inflated rubber doughnuts, one on top of the other, and a canopy supported by a gas-filled "ridge pole." The raft contains a survival kit, but it is basic at best. The survivors, warmly dressed, throw in such other food and gear as they have prepared, get aboard, cut the painter lest the sinking or burning vessel involve the raft in its own destruction, and they are on their own.

The raft is equipped with life lines and a ladder so that it may be boarded from the water, or one may just jump on top of it from a height of as much as fifteen feet. The canopy will give under impact. However, to land on a distressed shipmate from a height of fifteen feet would add considerably to his problems.

The first consideration is that the inflation gear be sure-fire. Because the two air chambers, just described as "doughnuts," must not be interconnected, lest a hole in one sink both, there is a three-way valve on the gas bottle permitting gas to flow from the gas bottle to both chambers but preventing any return flow from either. The valve is a heavy, rugged, and simple piece of hardware unlikely to fail. The firing mechanism is equally simple. A sharp pull on the painter opens a one-inch-diameter hole in the gas bottle. Because the raft may have to be inflated in frigid conditions where CO_2 will approach its liquefaction temperatures, a small amount of liquid nitrogen is added to provide an extra kick. At high temperature, of course, the pressure is much greater from both gases than it is at low temperatures, so both strength and elasticity of the fabric are important. Avon uses heavy rip-stop nylon impregnated with Hypalon, a natural rubber derivative.

Once a life raft is safely inflated with the occupants aboard, the next consideration is stability, a subject on which controversy rages among three different schools of thought. The conventional raft, of which Avon and Goodrich are examples, employs several bags of water under the periphery of the raft which fill with water almost immediately on inflation. These hold perhaps 200 pounds of water, enough to preserve the stability of the raft when a survivor boards, unless conditions are severe. Suppose, however, a violent gale of wind, a heavy sea, and a well nourished survivor or two climbing over the lee side. Some argue that as the raft rises to the steep face of a sea, the wind will get under the raft, flip it over on top of the survivors, then blow it out of reach. Supporters of this type of raft deny the likelihood of this result but cannot deny its possibility under the most extreme circumstances.

Jim Givens, seeking greater stability, designed a raft with a much bigger and heavier ballast bag holding 4,800 pounds of water. This introduced further problems. His opponents claim that the motion of his raft in passing over a cresting sea is so violent as to injure the occupants by hurling them against each other and making projectiles of the survival gear. Also, they claim that should a sea break on a Givens raft, it cannot bounce out of the way like a lighter type and the occupants may be pummeled by heavy blows from on top. Because it is less likely to roll with the punch of a breaking sea than is a conventional raft, the Givens raft is said to be more likely to disintegrate in stormy conditions. Also, there is little doubt that the Givens raft is very difficult to tow. A modification to the bag permitting the water to escape through a valve is said partially to overcome this difficulty.

Another solution lies partway between the lightly ballasted raft and the Givens raft. This raft, designed by the Switlik Parachute Company, consists of a circular ballast chamber below the lower doughnut with holes so that it will collapse under tow. The Coast Guard is said to have ordered a number of these, but not as survival gear as much as rescue gear.

The Coast Guard and the official bodies of other nations concerned with safety at sea are moving slowly in the matter of testing and granting approval. The Coast Guard refuses to approve or disapprove of any raft at present. If the raft is to be used on a yacht, no Coast Guard approval is necessary. If it is to be used on an inspected vessel, the individual raft in question must be inspected as it is packed.

The British are testing rafts in Malta, where giant machines for making waves and wind are available. The present problem is to

design instruments adequate for testing wind velocities and pressures.

Most rafts now are equipped with small weighted sea anchors designed to prevent the raft from drifting off to leeward too fast and to hold the windward edge down, thus preventing the wind from getting under it and flipping it.

All kinds of rafts have saved lives, perhaps the most famous being the Avon raft that kept one crew afloat in the Pacific for 118 days after a whale sank their yacht. Of the rafts that failed, of course, we have no record. It seems likely that no matter how rugged the conditions for which a raft is designed—wind, sea, burning oil, overloading and so on—that worse conditions can occur in which the raft will be lost. It can never be buoyant enough, strong enough, and well-enough equipped to guarantee that he who buys one will be saved.

A means of attracting the attention of rescuers is very important. The canopies of most rafts are said to be radar reflectors. This may well be so, but the shape of the canopy is such that to resist wind and water it will also shed impulses. Hence, a radar reflector is a most useful piece of equipment. The sheet aluminum ones that fold flat are the best reflectors, but they are all angles and edges and very hard to stow safely where they will injure neither the raft nor its occupants. Flares are usually provided, but despite their fierce pyrotechnic character they burn for a pitifully short time. Parachute flares may be better, but probably the most useful single piece of survival gear after the raft itself is an Emergency Position Indicating Radio Beacon. In case of disaster, it will broadcast automatically a distress call on a frequency guarded by Coast Guard and naval vessels and all commercial aircraft. A helicopter can be over you in an hour and a cutter can be alongside soon after.

It is most important that the raft be returned to the manufacturer for servicing every year. Missing or damaged articles are inspected and replaced as necessary. Flares and flashlight batteries are replaced. Food and water containers are replaced and the raft is carefully repacked. This is an expensive operation, but if it is not done, all other precautions may prove to have been futile. The inspection costs about one hundred dollars.

A new six-man raft costs about $2,000. With the change, you can buy a Narco EPIRB.

NOTE: *This article was written in March 1979. Since then the Coast Guard has approved some inflatable life rafts.*

Equipping a Life Raft
Edward H. Simmons

Our new life raft had proudly adorned our foredeck for the past season. Winter lay-up time was approaching and, following the manufacturer's instructions, we took the raft to be inspected.

We had never seen our trusted piece of equipment inflated, so we delivered it personally to the inspection station. There the seal was broken and the inflating lanyard was passed to my wife who was told to PULL . After several sharp yanks, the raft remained a limp pile of rubber. The somewhat embarrassed attendant rapidly emerged with the manual trip ring (did you know there is one?), which was also pulled. Stubbornly, the raft refused to inflate. My thoughts were ranging from the sublime, "We'll never need it anyway. Let's sell it!" to the ridiculous, "How do I inflate the raft in ten-foot seas, at night, after the yacht has sunk?" Anyway, the serviceman appeared this time with bellows and we inflated

the raft manually. The cause of the difficulty was traced to an empty CO_2 cylinder that had never been filled at the factory. The raft had no leaks. After receiving assurances that the situation would be corrected, we left the station to ponder the day's events. One thought kept recurring: if the raft was in that condition, how adequate was the survival equipment to sustain life on the open seas?

Our curiosity led to an investigation of our own gear and the supplies in other commercially available rafts. We found they contained the following:

1. Fishing gear kit	12. Graduated cup
2. Sea anchor	13. Can openers
3. Bailer	14. Seasick pills
4. First-aid kit	15. Drinking water
5. Paddles	16. Signal mirrors
6. Quoit with line	17. Hand pump (bellows)
7. Flashlights	18. Instructions for survival
8. Hand flares	
9. Knife	19. Plastic bags
10. Sponges	20. Whistle
11. Raft repair kit, including leak stoppers	21. Emergency rations
	22. Radar reflector

Some manufacturers provide small packages of tissues, insect repellent, and red signal flags. Others have opted to include for additional purchase an EPIRB, a space blanket, and double floors. Each individual item above was not necessarily available on each raft.

To the casual observer the preceding list of standard equipment may seem complete and well planned. However, a close inspection of the contents will show serious omissions and inadequacies. Based on these findings, we assembled our own kit according to the following premises: First, it is safe to assume that the kit will be used under the worst possible conditions. Second, it is better to have too much than too little. Third, the kit should be readily available for inspection and possible replacement of parts.

In the event of a shipwreck and the safe deployment of the raft, the first consideration is to be seen or heard. Therefore, no well-stocked survival kit should be without an

EPIRB. Literally hundreds of examples of dramatic rescues have demonstrated the effectiveness of these transmitters. The one selected should be waterproof and capable of being checked for transmitter output and battery condition. It's wise to carry a spare battery in your kit.

Also, no manufacturer we investigated offered a flare launcher. All rafts contained a random number of hand-held flares, which certainly are not the most current type of distress signal.

We chose to include in our kit an Olan 25-mm flare launcher with twelve red meteor and six red parachute flares. The advantages we saw over the hand-held flares were greater visibility over a wider range, and less danger to the operator and raft from sparks due to a possible flashback.

Before leaving the subject of being seen and heard aboard a raft at sea, consideration should be given to the unbreakable mirror that most rafts contain. Any size convenient to handle is satisfactory. However, the one or two we have seen had such sharp edges that we could almost guarantee a cut, or worse yet, a hole in the raft if improperly handled. Check yours.

To provide for the welfare of the crew is the second consideration in the event of a disaster. Hence, we investigated first-aid kits and found them to be woefully inadequate. If you feel sure you will suffer no more than a torn hangnail from abandoning ship—fine! However, if your injuries or those of your crew may be more severe, check your kit. We feel you will be disappointed at its contents: antiseptic and possibly burn cream, scissors, and assorted bandages—period. When we consulted our doctor, he gave us some helpful tips about first-aid kit contents: Be sure any special medication required by crew members is available—such as Synthroid for a thyroid condition or insulin for a diabetic. Carry a supply of feminine napkins and tampons. They make the best pressure bandages in the world for deep wounds and lacerations that bleed profusely.

The survival kit we assembled contained the following first-aid items:

1. Petroleum jelly
2. Sunburn–minor-burn spray
3. Smelling salts
4. Assorted bandages and tape (or cloth ties to secure)
5. Feminine napkins and tampons
6. Local anesthetic
7. Sutures with gut
8. Butterfly closures
9. Salt tablets
10. Ace bandages
11. Antibacterial cleanser
12. Painkiller tablets
13. Mild laxative
14. Seasick pills
15. Fiberglass sail battens for splints
16. Aspirin
17. Antidiarrhetic
18. Wide spectrum antibiotic

Furthermore, we carry one solar still for each two crew members. Why raft manufacturers do not include these valuable items is difficult to comprehend. To supplement this source, we carry twelve twelve-oz. tins of water. These should be varnished to prevent rust.

Our raft was equipped with the customary supply of emergency food rations. We supplemented these with the following: dried beef sticks, dried and honey-coated fruit, hard candy, and potent multivitamins.

Another excellent high-energy food source that keeps well is Appalachian Trail Bars. The recipe is as follows:

1. Mix and let stand five minutes: 1 egg; ½ C milk; ½ C oats.
2. Add and mix: ½ C peanut butter; ½ C bran or wheat germ; ½ C sesame seeds, nuts, or sunflower seeds; ½ C raisins; ½ C honey; 1 tsp. salt; 2 tbsp oil.
3. Add, ¼ C at a time, ¾ C flour.
4. Spread on greased flat pan.
5. Bake at 350 degrees 20–25 minutes until nicely brown.
6. Cut into squares and cool on rack.

These bars are stored in an airtight container such as Tupperware.

With the proper equipment, life can be sustained by food from the sea. The fishing kit that came with our raft was useless, in our estimation. To replace it, we purchased three large lures or jigs and tarred cod line, the type used in commercial tub trawlers. We added #7/0 hooks and a supply of rubber worms for bait. Also, we carry two knives in our kit. One is short with a heavy blade capable of prying open almost anything. The other is a fileting knife. We broke the points off both knives and ground the tips on an emery wheel before packing them. We also included a sharpening stone.

In addition to the preceding, the following items should be included in any well-equipped kit:

1. Space blankets
2. Can opener
3. Reusable plastic lids that fit cans in the kit
4. Mouth horn
5. Small canvas buckets
6. Two powerful hand-held searchlights with spare light bulbs and batteries—similar to Guest lights of 22,000 candlepower
7. Inflatable air mattresses—any water lower than your body temperature, 98 degrees F (37 degrees C) will cool you, in time, to the point of hypothermia.
8. Two additional five-gallon Jerry Jugs partly filled with fresh water and lashed underneath the dinghy.

All the preceding equipment would not fit into our raft canister. So we purchased a waterproof duffel to carry our survival gear. The duffel was the most practical container for our supplies because of its accessibility. Following a regular schedule, we are able to monitor the condition of our equipment, i.e., change batteries and replace food supplies when necessary.

Before placement in the duffel, all items are either sealed in plastic bags or Tupperware containers.

Two large fenders are then strapped to the sides of the duffel for buoyancy. A drogue is also attached to it with a long line. When put overboard, this sea anchor will hold the kit in a fairly stationary position. Finally, a strobe light is secured to the duffel. Then the whole rig is lashed to our sailing dinghy with floatable polypropylene line. In practice we can launch the raft and cut loose the dinghy in twenty seconds. Now we feel we have at least a fighting chance for survival.

Will the Life Raft Work?

Before sending our Winslow life raft back to the factory for its three-year check, we pulled the handle to see if it would really work. It did. It burst from its cocoon just as we expected, but it was only partly inflated. The canopy did not lift at all, and when someone boarded it, the two sides came together. Quick work with the hand pump, which comes wrapped securely in brown paper so it is hard to get at in a hurry, soon supplied enough pressure to extend the sides and lift the canopy. However, the hand pump stuck in the valve into which it must be threaded; fortunately, I had a pair of pliers in my hip pocket so was able to disengage it and use it on both valves.

If it were ever necessary to use the raft in the heat of action, it would be well to take no chances and anticipate the need by ten minutes to be sure that the raft is properly inflated and supplied.

My raft had no supplies or equipment beyond the hand pump. One should have easily accessible at least one oar, a compass, and a light. A flare gun and a radio marker beacon would be valuable if not indispensable items. If one is far at sea, of course, food, water, and warm clothes must be put aboard too. All this takes time when time is of the very essence.

Pull the cord.

43

Inflated automatically

Fully inflated

While we were experimenting, the owner of another brand of raft happened by. He had tried the same thing. At the first pull, the valve tore out. When the cylinder was tripped manually it was found to be empty.

A life raft is rather like a parachute. Until you need it, you can't tell whether or not it will work, and then it is too late. The clever fellow who sold me my raft advised me to bring it back if it didn't work!

The Maintenance-free Battery

The recently developed maintenance-free batteries now being sold for automobiles appear to have considerable advantages for marine use. The most obvious is that they will not spill unless laid down almost flat on the side.

Furthermore, they do not need periodic additions of water and they hold a charge when not in use for much longer than the usual type of battery.

The new battery is a lead-acid battery like the old one, depending for its current on the action of sulfuric acid on alternate plates of lead and lead oxide. However, there are several outstanding differences.

First, the lead in the old batteries contained antimony. The ions of this metal migrated through the acid and in time built up a coating on the lead oxide plates that made them ineffective. The new battery does not contain antimony.

An ordinary battery requires the addition of water because the water in the water-acid electrolyte breaks down into hydrogen when the battery is charged. This happens most rapidly when the battery is overcharged. In order to keep a battery up to full charge when the motor is running, the generator or alternator must keep a small amount of current running into it. The more of this overcharge current the battery requires, the faster the water breaks down, the more "gassing" there is, and the more frequently must water be added. The maintenance-free battery, using a calcium-lead alloy instead of an antimony-lead alloy in its plates, requires in a brand-new battery about one-third of the overcharge current required by the conventional type. After eighteen months of use in an automobile, the calcium-alloy battery requires less than one-twentieth of the overcharge current, thus sharply reducing water and breakdown.

In the lead batteries, bits of the lead oxide eventually flake off the positive plates and fall to the bottom of the casing. When enough of this is built up, an electrical connection would be formed between positive and negative plates, producing a short circuit inside the battery and ruining it. Therefore, the plates were supported above the bottom of the casing. In the new battery, each of the positive plates is enclosed in a plastic microporous separator sealed on sides and bottom, thus preventing the lead oxide from scaling off and still permitting the acid to come at the plates. Now the plates can be set directly on the bottom of the casing, permitting a much larger depth of acid over the tops of the plates. Thus, with decreased water loss and a much greater amount of electrolyte available before the plates are exposed, the battery will last longer without addition of water.

Even with these innnovations, however, water is still broken down by the chemical action of the battery and hydrogen and oxygen are released. If the battery is sealed, where does this gas go? The answer is that although the top of the battery is sealed to the case, the battery itself is not hermetically sealed. There is a concealed vent with a "valve" on it that releases the gas and through which the acid would slowly spill if the battery actually tipped over. It is most unlikely the battery would leak in rough seas or if the vessel were heeled to a heavy puff. If the boat heeled far enough to spill acid from a maintenance-free battery, you would have problems far more serious than spilled acid.

Thus, by using a calcium-lead alloy instead of an antimony-lead alloy for the negative plates, water loss is vastly decreased; and by enclosing the positive plates in an envelope, the reservoir of water-acid electrolyte over the battery is much increased. Therefore, water need not be added for the life of the battery. This permits the sealing of the top except for a very small orifice to permit the escape of what little gas is formed.

When asked why these batteries were not sold for marine use, a marina operator said that they were "not approved for marine use." He did not know who was supposed to approve batteries. The Coast Guard denied any responsibility for batteries. Insurance companies had no objection to the use of maintenance-free batteries. A manager of a Western Auto store said that the store would not guarantee the batteries for marine use and was guaranteeing them for use in autmobiles and trucks as a means of testing them further. One Cautious Conrad speculated that should the voltage regulator stick so that a very heavy overcharge hit the battery for a considerable period, it might heat up, gas heavily, and build up enough pressure to explode. In a boat, the results would be far more serious than in a car,

where there is a firewall between battery and passengers. However, he believed that the battery case was hermetically sealed, which it is not. It is true that a marine engine runs steadily at high speed, whereas an automobile engine frequently slows and speeds up again. Consequently, the alternator is delivering a steady trickle of overcharge with no periods of discharge; but with the overcharge rate required by a maintenance-free battery so much lower than that of a regular battery, the maintenance-free battery should be better in a boat than the conventional type.

Battery Care

Mr. Winslow Palmer of Fort Myers, Florida, says, "Regarding the reliability of maintenance-free batteries, we acquired an Oldsmobile Starfire with such a battery in May 1976. The battery expired in September 1977, for a life of only sixteen months. There was no indication of generator problems and the regulator seemed okay.

"We replaced it with a regular battery, which I keep filled with rain water. While a single experience such as ours is no evidence of the reliability of the type, I would suggest that anyone expecting to be out of touch for months on a cruise would do well to stick to the standard battery type until the maintenance-free type has had more experience on board."

Mr. Palmer continues: "The manager of a large battery-manufacturing plant pointed out that the standard automobile battery design is aimed primarily at *starting* a big V-8 engine at twenty below. The optimum plate structure and electrolyte density to meet this requirement is not necessarily the best for maximum life with a lighter load.

"He recommends that we cut the electrolyte density to around 1,200, which will extend battery life several-fold at a negligible loss in capacity. He suggested that we treat a standard battery by topping off with distilled water, give the battery a full charge with some trickle overcharge, then take out the electrolyte down to the tops of the plates and refill with distilled water.

"I've done this to the two batteries in the boat and the one in my Dodge Van with the big V-8 engine, with no noticeable effect on starting capability in either. In a couple of years or so I'll let you know how long the batteries stand up and whether I can still get the van started at twenty below, provided it ever gets that cold down here."

Insurance Anchor

The best insurance is the biggest anchor you can handle. However, the biggest anchor you can handle at forty years of age may be too big when you are sixty. Also, it may have been stowed in the bottom of the rope locker with two other anchors and their rodes on top of it. When you really need that insurance anchor, you may find yourself jammed into the forepeak trying to wrestle a seventy-five pound monster up through a hatch only just big enough for it. If night has fallen and the motion is violent, the experience may fall short of what you planned as a vacation.

Paul E. Luke, a distinguished builder of aluminum yachts and a man of ingenuity and compassion, has developed an insurance anchor that can be used efficiently and stowed compactly. He started with the well-known kedge or Herreshoff anchor. Although it has less holding power than a Danforth or CQR anchor in mud or sand, it will catch in almost any bottom and makes up for its lack of holding power per pound with greater weight. To make it possible to handle this weight, Luke made the anchor in three pieces. The first, which contains half the total weight, is the fluke. This is made in the traditional pattern and has a rectangular hole in its center, slightly tapered like the head of a pick. The shank is a separate piece, its lower end tapered to fit the hole in the fluke with the big end of the taper outside so that the greater the strain, the more tightly is the shank seated in the fluke. The stock slides in through the upper end of the shank. The ring for attaching the chain is formed by drilling out the threads in a big screw shackle and lining the holes up with the hole in the top of the shank. If the end link of the chain will admit the horn of the drilled-out shackle, there is no need of a screw shackle and a wire mousing to attach the chain to the anchor. A pin prevents the stock from sliding out, just as in the usual folding-stock Herreshoff anchor.

The anchor knocked down

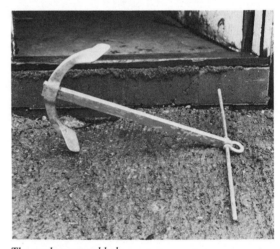

The anchor assembled

Thus, a seventy-five-pound anchor can be stowed conveniently and compactly in three separate pieces, no one of which weighs over thirty-five pounds. The pieces can be easily brought on deck and assembled at the rail, whence the anchor can be lowered over the side. These anchors are available from Paul E. Luke, East Boothbay, Maine 04544. The price, of course, varies with the weight.

46

Mayday . . . Mayday . . . Mayday . . .

"I am sure they are all right. They have a ship-to-shore radio, you know." What a comfortable thought for the home folks and also for the skipper, who knows that the air–sea forces of the United States Coast Guard will spring into action in case he has an emergency! However, the skipper better pick his emergency carefully. Any catastrophe that damages his power supply or his antenna, or which renders his transmitter inaccessible, chokes off that cry for help.

If a vessel is dismasted, she loses her antenna. If she catches fire, the radio operator may very well be unable to reach his mike. Should she ground on a ledge or bar with a sea running, soon her batteries and then her whole cabin would be underwater.

Fortunately, there has been developed for aircraft and recently licensed for marine use a compact little radio with its own antenna and power supply. It weighs only two pounds and can be carried in one hand. When switched on, it calls "Mayday" steadily for eight days (at 70°). It uses 121.5 and 243 Mhz, frequencies monitored by commercial, military, and Coast Guard aircraft, by the larger Coast Guard vessels and by some Coast Guard shore stations. If such a set can be stowed where it is accessible from the deck, chances of rescue are vastly improved, especially if one must take to a life raft. Even a man in a lifebelt in warm water would have a fairly good chance.

There are a few details to note before buying such a set. First, it is for the most desperate emergencies only, to be used after your regular set has proven ineffective. It broadcasts only a distress call, giving no name, location, or particulars of the accident. Searchers "home" on the signal, so of course the switch should be left on until help arrives.

Secondly, you must have a station license from the FCC to own one. If you already have a station license, these frequencies must be added to it. You will ordinarily be licensed only if you plan to operate over twenty miles offshore, beyond the range of a VHF set.

The cost of the instrument varies with the manufacturer from about one hundred dollars to two hundred dollars. Narco, on Commerce Drive, Fort Washington, Pennsylvania, sells one for just below two hundred dollars, and West Products, of Prescott St., Boston, Massachusetts, sells another at about the same price. There is another smaller, lighter set sold by Adler, Barbour Yacht Services in New Rochelle, New York, for a little over one hundred dollars. It is small enough to attach to a life jacket or man-overboard float. More elaborate sets are made that begin to talk as the yacht sinks from under them and float on, talking for days.

Flares: Do They Work?

There are at least three kinds of flares. The hand-held ones such as are used on the highway to warn of stalled trucks are feeble reeds to lean on in time of trouble. Some of them must be lighted with a match! If you can light a match on deck, who is in trouble? Others use a friction cap. If you plan to use this, be sure to read the directions well in advance of the emergency. No doubt when they are new they work pretty well, but one can scratch and scratch to no avail. If the flare does catch and one can hold it at a height of ten or twelve feet above the water, it will be visible for about the same distance as a lighted buoy, say six miles.

I once bought a mini-kit about the size of a fountain pen that was supposed to project a brilliant light into the night skies. I had to do a good deal of filing and fitting in daylight to make the firing pin strike the cartridge. I tested it. It projected a small ball of fire about the height of the masthead. It was all over in less than thirty seconds.

Finally, in anticipation of an ocean voyage I bought a 25-mm flare pistol. This is an expensive device, retailing for about seventy-five dollars, but cheap if you ever really need it. After informing the Coast Guard of my intention, I fired a red flare and a parachute flare on a spring afternoon. The red flare went perhaps 100 feet high, left a trail of smoke behind it, and expired very quickly. If someone were looking for you, it might be a useful aid. The parachute flare was better. It went higher, burned for perhaps thirty seconds, and left behind a trail of whitish smoke. At least one man reported the flare to the Coast Guard.

After dark, it was a great deal better. The red flare described an arc in the night sky. The parachute flare was a lot better. It lit up an area about 200 yards in radius and stayed aloft perhaps thirty seconds. It was much more conspicuous than the other flares and attracted much more attention. The Coastguardsman on duty confirmed my conclusion that the flare pistol, especially at night, is the best means of attracting attention.

It is a long night. One would do well to have a good supply of ammunition, even at ten dollars a shot.

The thoughtful skipper should remember that flare pistols come under the gun laws of some states and must be registered. Unless you want to spend a year in jail, don't bring one into Massachusetts unregistered.

No doubt other effective distress signals have been invented and are on the market. I simply report my experience with what I have seen.

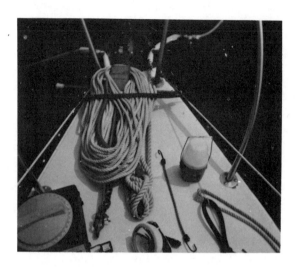

A New Marine Supply Store in Your Town
William H. Ashbaugh

Equipment is part of the fun of sailing, but it can be expensive. Even if you have more money than you know what to do with, finding creative ways to save money and improve your boat's capabilities can be satisfying. Discount auto supply stores provide a useful source of supply today. Twenty years ago such a suggestion would have elicited horror in any real sailor. "It will rust right away" would have been among the milder derisive comments. Today the extensive use of plastics in manufacturing has eliminated at least some of those problems. See for example the "anchor light" and coffee maker described, and truck equipment is often built to heavy and dependable standards.

In the upper portion of the photograph you will see a rubber truck cover tie-down being used as an anchor and coiled line tie-down.

These tie-downs are made of heavy elastic rubber with a nonrusting S hook at each end. The S hooks are here hooked into port and starboard holes of the aluminum rub rail. The tie-downs sell for less than one dollar at our local store.

When both ends of the rubber tie-downs are looped into the same S hook as shown in the lower right portion of the photograph, it can be inserted in the holes used for the jib sheet blocks in the rubbing rail further aft. Attaching a small block to the looped rubber and a line through the block up to the boom makes the tie-down an effective snubber for an inexpensive boom vang. This vang has the added advantage of elasticity so that it does not need to be reset with minor adjustments to the main sheet. Elasticity also cushions the force of the boom when the sail is slatting in a seaway. The one pictured has shown no deterioration in two years of use, but of course caution should be used so that it is not overstretched.

Cigarette lighters open up all sorts of possibilities. There are many useful accessories designed to fit these lighter sockets, and the lighter itself makes a useful tool even if you do not smoke. Hold it close to, but not touching the ends of synthetic rope and you will have a professional quality seal for the ends of nylon and dacron rope.

One popular model (Taylor) of these lighters is actually made for marine use and contains a chart lighter feature. The E and B

Marine Supply, Inc., 257 Bertrand Ave., Perth Amboy, N.J. 08861 sells this lighter. Whether this "marine model" is purchased or you get yours from an auto supply store or a junk car, these lighters should be mounted in a protected spot away from spray and rain.

The accessories designed to plug into these lighters include trouble lights. The light pictured contains a G.E. sealed-beam headlight, about ten feet of cord, sells for under ten dollars, and has been used for several years as a searchlight–trouble light.

Another useful accessory is a converter for changing twelve volts into six, seven and one-half, or nine volts in order to power your transistor radio, direction finder, etc. The one pictured is inexpensive, but make sure the one you get has enough amps for your set or it will burn out quickly.

Other accessories include:

Coffee (soup, etc.) maker—under ten dollars; plastic model gives a pint of hot coffee in ten to fifteen minutes.

Hand vacuum cleaners—under ten dollars, more expensive models available.

Portable electric air compressors—under fifty dollars for your inflatable dinghy, but don't be in a hurry.

Electric shaver converter—under twenty-five dollars.

These items are listed in the J. C. Whitney and Co. catalog (1917–19 Archer Ave., P.O. Box 8410, Chicago, Illinois 60680). However, you will usually save money by buying at your local auto supply store, as shipping and handling charges can add one-third or more to the price of catalog sales.

Obviously, all these cigarette lighter accessories are useful in your car when not aboard your boat.

Shock cords such as the one pictured in the right center of the photograph are sold for less than fifty cents at our local auto store as tie-downs for motorcycle racks. While these cords and the truck cover tie-downs are available at marine supply houses, they are usually considerably less expensive at auto stores. The cords make excellent sail furlers and are useful as tie-downs in many other situations.

Auto stores stock more than auto supplies. When the bulb in a waterproof plastic camping lantern is changed to a low-amp bulb you have an effective anchor light. The lantern pictured in the upper right side of the photo is a Ray-O-Vac #90 costing less than ten dollars with battery. This anchor light has been used over two years from Baltimore to Bar Harbor.

Even fiberglass cloth and resin can be less expensively purchased at auto supply stores as compared to a "discount" marine supply store.

As in everything else connected with the sea, caution is required in equipping your boat, from whatever source you use, but there is nothing magical about the word *Marine* attached to an item, and often a nonmarine item may be equal to its fancier cousin.

Marine hardware houses should jettison all the silly and sentimental signs they sell and make only one, which every vessel of whatever size should be required to display—ETERNAL VIGILANCE IS THE PRICE OF SAFETY AT SEA.

Claude Worth

3

Maintenance

Paid by the Hour; Judged by the Job

Have you ever wondered why boats fitted out in a boatyard often look so much better than the do-it-yourself backyard jobs? What can boatyard labor do that the owner cannot do himself? One answer is that the boatyard worker puts in more time. Just look at the bill! The yard worker is on the job five or six days a week, knowing that what he does not finish today will be waiting for him tomorrow morning. The pressure on him is to do a good job, for the quality of the yard is judged by the appearance of your boat. If he doesn't know that, his boss does.

On the other hand, the owner usually works only two days a week. His eyes are fixed on getting afloat by Memorial Day. He makes a schedule in his mind, paints between showers, and skimps on the sanding. He knows that what he does not finish this Sunday night must be done next Saturday and the delays are cumulative. If he paints on Saturday, he cannot afford to leave the boat alone for a week but must lean a ladder against the rail on Sunday where the paint is dry to the touch but still soft and green, scuff it up, and promise himself to touch it up later.

The yard man has the proper tools and he uses them from February to the Fourth of July fitting out boat after boat. He has "the feel of the shillelagh" and uses the tools with finesse born of practice.

Many yachtsmen are as careful and skillful as yard workers, but we never notice their boats as anything but well maintained. It is the hasty weekend worker's boat whose topsides show last year's nicks under this year's paint, whose varnish is darkened under the shine, whose skiff's bow fender smirks awry.

Tips on Painting

Whoever writes the directions on the paint can is a perfectionist. "The surface must be completely clean, dry, free from dust and grease and sanded smooth." The man who starts at 7:00 A.M. and works all day at it can accomplish this, but where does his time go?

He knows that you have to take off as much paint as you put on. He tears into the job with a power sander, frequently replacing the paper and being very careful to hold it flat against the boat and to keep it moving to avoid making flat places. Then laboriously he sands the edges of chips, nicks, and bumps by hand and either spot-primes them or wipes them with trowel cement and sands again. Any imperfection in the old paint will show right through a new coat of gloss. It is slow, fussy work.

Then everything must be wiped clean and the dust allowed to settle again. Then he lays on a coat of flat paint, well brushed out, and works on someone else's boat for several days. Then on a warm sunny morning—he can afford to wait for it—he and a helper will lightly sand the undercoat, wipe it clean again, and paint a finish coat, working around the boat in opposite directions. They will then depart and leave the job for several days without messing up the green paint by laying a ladder against the rail.

Boot top and waterline will be painted from the scratch on the hull, not with masking tape. Paint creeps under masking tape; and if the tape is applied over paint not quite hard, the paint will come off with the tape.

When your boat is not ready on time and you tell indignant stories about boatyard excuses: "Forty days of rain in May this year . . ." remember that the yard is in no hurry to go sailing and is judged by the shine on your topsides.

The black finish on many cast aluminum fittings eventually wears off. An indelible Magic Marker makes a neat touch-up job easier and less messy than paint. If your rub rail is also aluminum, those embarrassing docking scratches can be hidden immediately.

Learned the Hard Way

Before you open the paint can, wash your hands—but don't rinse them. Rub the soap right in until it dries and disappears. Then when you come to clean up afterward, the paint will slide right off.

When you finish painting for the day, take time to wipe dry the groove in the top of the paint can and scrape off any paint caked on the surface next to it. Clean the edges of the lid also. This assures an airtight seal when you put the lid back on and prevents the formation of a skin on the paint. Some people blow into the can before clamping down the lid, claiming that this mystical act drives out oxygen from the can. Store the can upside down to be certain no air leaks in.

Suspend brushes in a full can of thinner

and they will pretty nearly clean themselves overnight.

Paint the deck last, after you have launched, finished the engine work, stepped spars, and set out the mooring. Otherwise you are certain to get it mucked up and the scars will haunt you all summer. Paint the deck on Sunday and go away at once. Deck paint, particularly, dries quickly to the touch, but the film remains flexible for a long time. If you step on it, you raise wrinkles in it that catch dirt and look terrible.

Mix nonskid compound with deck paint in about one-third the recommended proportion. This will make a surface rough enough to prevent slipping in boat shoes and smooth enough to keep reasonably clean with a mop. Stir frequently, for the stuff settles out and you will have slick patches and sandy patches.

In planning decor for the deck, stick to one color as much as possible. Cutting lines takes time and provides many chances for unsightly slips. The traditional color for decks is a sandy buff, originally produced from oil and ochre. Whatever color you choose, pick one easy on the eyes. Gray and green in light shades are good. A dark color makes a hot cabin. Avoid large areas of dazzling white in the cockpit or afterside of the house.

Neglected varnishwork where the wood has darkened under the film can be restored by removing the varnish and treating the wood with oxalic acid. The crystals can be bought in a drugstore. Mix them into a paste with water and plaster onto affected places. Wear rubber gloves.

The man who writes the directions on the varnish can is a dreamer. He says to flow the varnish on with a full brush and in the next sentence orders us to avoid sags and runs. Don't put it on too thick or too thin! Gummy sags are tedious to repair. They must be carefully skinned off with a sharp chisel, allowed to dry hard, and then sanded smooth. Brushing varnish too thin makes little specks and bubbles in the surface, but they can be dusted off with a light sanding. If you have a big area like a hatch cover to varnish, lay the varnish on across the grain of the wood and then smooth it down with the grain. Move the brush slowly and you won't get too many bubbles.

A good quality brush is essential for fine work. It is expensive, so, like any good tool, it is worth taking care of. Never let paint dry in it. With the best of brush cleaners you will never get it really clean again. Little specks will be always working out of it. Keep separate brushes for paint and varnish. Most common oil paints can be cleaned in paint thinner, but this does not seem to work so well with varnish. Gasoline does very well but is a dangerous expedient.

Notes on Rigging

The best reason for taking your mast out in the fall is that you can inspect it in the spring. Here are some of the things to look for.

Inspect every terminal fitting on the standing rigging for hairline cracks. Use a magnifying glass and wipe the fitting with a dirty greasy rag to emphasize any fault. Examine turnbuckles, toggles, mast tangs, and lifeline fittings.

Inspect fastenings through or into the mast for corrosion. A sandy, salty encrustation is a danger sign.

Replace any worn servings. Use the stout black marline with real tar in it if you can find

Protective copper sheathing at the masthead should be inspected for rot.

it. A touch of grease on the mallet will help to run the serving on smoothly, but too much makes it loose and sloppy. Many people paint servings white so any rust becomes evident. With stainless rigging, though, either black paint or varnish and lampblack does very well.

Look closely at the masthead sheaves. Repairing or replacing these is difficult once the mast is stepped. Look for undue wear or signs that sail or halyard has chafed against the fittings.

Winches call for special attention. Read the manufacturer's directions carefully and disassemble a winch only with the greatest care. They are complicated machines and must go together just so. Also there are little pawl springs that are easily lost.

In a wooden spar, look for cracks in glued joints. Work glue into any open cracks and clamp down hard.

Rot seldom attacks a spar where it is well ventilated, but poke suspiciously with your knife just above spreaders or bands or where strips of fiberglass or brass may have been installed to take the chafe of boom or gaff.

Look carefully at the ends of the spreaders where rot may have started under the fitting that takes the wire. If tape or chaf-

A bronze cleat bolted to an aluminum mast has caused serious corrosion.

A taped spreader-end is an invitation to rot.

ing gear has been put on to protect sails, be sure that it has not generated a rotten spot in the wood, which could cost you your mast when the wire comes away. Especially if the spar has been left in the boat for some time, check the place where the mast coat comes and also the heel of the mast where it stands in the step.

Grease every shackle pin and mouse it with marline. It is a pleasant job and will give you confidence in the strength of your gear.

Oil metal or plastic blocks with a pressure oil can and carefully wipe off any excess. Some fibers are damaged by oil and all fibers are damaged by blocks that run hard.

Wooden blocks should be cleaned and greased. Remove the covers over the pin and tap out the pin with a nail set. Notice that the pin comes out the way it went in. One end will have a pair of little vanes crimped in it to prevent its turning in the shell of the block. Hit the other end. Clean off caked grease on the pin and in the bearings of the sheave, grease with soft grease (not the hard water-pump grease), and reassemble. Do this, of course, before you paint or varnish.

Don't oil snap shackles, especially on the head or clew of a sail, unless they are very stiff and corroded. A well-oiled snap shackle can slat itself open with devilish ease and then someone may have to go aloft.

You will probably step the mast as soon as the boat goes overboard. Be sure everything is rove off properly, especially at the masthead. If you have to reach the top of the mast without benefit of a halyard to go aloft on, try this: get alongside a vessel with a mast taller than yours. Run the highest halyard you have in working order to the chain plates on the far side of the other vessel and heave down hard. Run one of his halyards to the chain plate on the far side of your boat. This heels the two masts toward each other. Now go aloft on his mast and reach the top of your own.

Working aloft can be very pleasant and can give you a new point of view on your boat. Indeed, the whole world looks different from forty feet in the air. The harbor looks bigger and the yard smaller. However, it is a scary business if not done properly.

Have a bosun's chair with the sling running under the seat and built at least twice as strong as it ever needs to be. Wear a safety harness and snap on when you get to where you are going to work. It inspires confidence. Have one man tend your line and keep an eye on it constantly lest someone with his mind on another problem should release the winch brake. Don't let him stand under you, though. Even with a bucket for your tools, you could drop one.

Slides and mast hoops must be lashed to

53

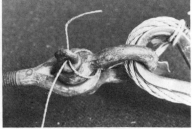

Left: By September this shackle will be dangerously weak.

Right: To mouse a shackle pin, take a turn of marline through the eye.

Left: Take several more turns and pass the ends under the turns in opposite ways.

Right: Take two turns across the original turns and fasten with a square knot.

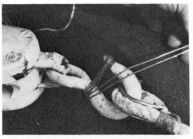

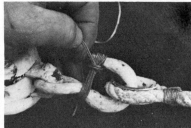

Left: To mouse a hook start with a lark's head. Pass the doubled marline around the lip of the hook.

Right: Take a hitch around the original turns at the lip end of the mousing and tie off with a clove hitch.

Left: A wooden block disassembled for cleaning.

sails so they lie at right angles to the plane of the sail. This requires a square lash.

Renew zincs. They disintegrate rapidly and thus afford some clue to the rapidity with which more important elements would disintegrate were there no zincs to absorb the galvanic action. The picture at right shows the deterioration of a zinc bolted to a stainless steel plate on an iron keel next to a bronze propeller and rudder post.

Safety

People who get hurt are usually in a hurry. Take time to set the ladder firmly alongside the boat and to lash the top to the rail. Not only will the ladder stand firm, but you are less likely to return and find it leaning against another boat.

In a boatyard, wear shoes with thick soles. There are nails everywhere, and just one nail through the sole of your sneaker will put you out of business for half a day.

Never touch an ungrounded power tool. Nowadays all tools have a ground connection and most outlets are of the type to take the three-prong plug. If you must use a converter, be sure the tail is grounded to the connection box. If your hands and feet are wet, you could get a lethal shock, especially from a 220-volt line.

Leave the beer until the work is done. No one works efficiently with a bottle in one hand. Also, the least uncertainty in footing or balance can lead to a bad fall.

Burning paint is a common cause of fires in boatyards. The burned residue falls on the ground in heaps and sometimes smolders along until after quitting time and then blazes up. You don't often hear of people being blown up from smoking around the highly volatile solvents in paints and cleaning agents, but the carelessly dropped match or butt may smolder unnoticed until you are out of sight. Most yards have fire extinguishers readily available. Locate one.

Don't spring your back! Get help with the heavy stuff; bend your knees and lift with the legs. An awkward load is as dangerous as a heavy one, especially if you are a little out of shape. Turning over a dinghy or picking up a coil of line from behind you will do it. Falling overboard with your boat on the cradle can be more dangerous than when she is afloat.

The Dinghy

Because you will be using her as a work boat, leave the dinghy until last; but then do a thorough job on her, for she is your representative on the float. First scrub her out thoroughly with a bucket of hot water and a stiff brush. Get out all last year's sand, shells, and dried bait. Rinse with a hose, and wax or paint her. If she is to be kept afloat, she will need a coat of copper paint on her bottom. Renew the lanyards on the oarlocks and the lashings that hold the fender strips on the sides; they will wear out soon anyway. Renew the painter and check the ring bolt to which it is attached. Be sure that there is another at the stern. She will tow much better in a following sea with a line astern. Finally, paint the name of your yacht on her stern, pretty up the varnish trim, buy her a new cushion or two, and paint your name and address on the bow seat so she can find her way home if she goes adrift.

The Old Man says that the reason so many people use outboards on their dinghies nowadays instead of rowing is that modern yachts are so damned ugly that they can't stand looking at them as they row away.

Before You Launch

Seacocks are best inspected before your boat goes overboard. As soon as the weather is warm enough to work barehanded, it would be well to take each one apart, inspect it, lubricate it, and reassemble.

First, remove the locknut. Be sure you have a wrench that will fit it. The whole seacock is made of bronze, a much softer metal than the steel wrench. If the wrench does not fit tightly on the nut, it will slip and round off the corners. Then nothing but a vise-grip or stillson wrench will do the job, and the nut is ruined. If the nut moves reluctantly, give it a squirt of WD-40 and wait a minute.

Then remove the next nut in the same way. Perhaps now you can wiggle the handle back and forth enough to loosen the core of the seacock and pull it out. If not, give it a squirt of WD-40 down in the place where the hose is attached, take a light hammer and a punch or big nail, and tap the center of the threaded end. Do this gently, and *never* tap the threaded end directly with a hammer. Once those threads are damaged, you must pay for a machine job of rethreading or buy a new seacock. Neither is inexpensive, and both take time.

When the core comes out, clean it carefully with a rag and solvent. Gasoline will do if you do it outdoors and wear rubber gloves. Do not succumb to the temptation to put the wire brush to it. The core is accurately machined to fit into the housing and make a water-tight seal. Rough it up and it will leak.

Clean the inside of the housing in the same way. Wipe the core with vaseline or soft grease, not the stiff water-pump grease, and reassemble. Set the first nut tight enough so the sea cock turns a little stiffly against the grease. Then with a thin wrench, hold the first nut, turn the second down on top of it, and pull the two snugly together. Usually if you simply hold the lower nut still and set the other down on it, the whole assembly tightens up so you can't move the sea cock. Therefore, while you turn the top nut clockwise, turn the lower one a little counterclockwise to meet it.

If you have not taken the bilge pump apart, cleaned it, and replaced worn diaphragms and seals, now is the time to go at that chore, for you may need it in good operating condition on launching day.

If your battery has been sitting idle all winter, April is a good time to check its charge. One of the best treatments you can give it is to put it in your car. It can stay in its plastic case and should be firmly tied down so it cannot possibly bounce around. Connect the positive pole of the boat battery to the positive pole of the car battery with a jumper cable. Connect the negative pole to the corresponding negative pole. If your car has a negative ground, as many cars do, you can simply ground the negative to the engine block or the frame of the car. It is most important, however, to connect like poles to each other or your batteries will explode in a torrent of hot sulfuric acid.

Be sure the jumper cables do not chafe against anything, and check the level of the electrolyte occasionally.

This treatment will keep your battery active and charged up for a month and is much better for it than slapping a fast charge on it the night before you want to start the engine.

If your boat carries a bowsprit or boomkin, there is no better time to look closely at the chain plates, shackles, and the stay itself. These parts wear and waste away unobtrusively, and when they let go, the results can be devastating. With the vessel ashore, it is easy to replace a worn shackle and mouse the new one with serving wire. Turnbuckles caked with paint can be started, greased, set up, and locknuts tightened down or cotter pins properly installed and taped. Worn servings can be removed, renewed, and repainted.

This is a good time, too, to check the propeller, the shaft, and the key, locknut, and cotter pin that hold the propeller in place. After considerable use, the corners of even a hard key will become rounded off and may slip or jam. Remember that the propeller, shaft, and nut may be made of soft bronze and one crack with a steel hammer can spoil a carefully machined fit.

While you are poking around the stern, look at the fitting which supports the heel of the rudder and the pintles and gudgeons that hold it in place. These take great strain and in an older vessel may show serious wear. Look, too, at the place where the rudder post enters the hull. It may show wear and corrosion.

Now get a light and creep aft inside the boat. Look at the point where the rudder post comes up through the stuffing box. If it is rough, scaly, or corroded, be suspicious. If these things let go, they usually do so without much warning, so it is well to look at it. While you are in there, take off the stuffing-box nut, shove a finger full of water-pump grease up into it, and set it down again as much as you can without making the rudder action at all stiff.

If you want to make yourself feel better about the danger of losing your steering, drill a hole in the after upper edge of the rudder. If something vital breaks, at least you have a chance of getting a line through it and regaining some control.

It is just as well, too, to look for loose

caulking at this time. Don't worry about a piece of putty that seems a little loose but is still firmly in place. When the planks swell, she will take hold of it. Pieces that are loose enough to drop out should be replaced with fresh putty.

Check out the depth finder, Kenyon, and any other underwater gear. The surface of the transducer should be clean, smooth, and bright. It is usually not covered with copper paint. However, through a long season, it may grow whiskers and need a shave. Be gentle.

Screens over water intakes for head and engine cooling water should be cleaned and reinstalled with sharp new screws if the old ones are worn. Often the screw and the screen are of different enough metals to waste away the screw. The same situation may affect the lag bolts holding the stern bearing for the propeller shaft. Also, if the keel is of sour oak, it may eat away a bronze lag. However, if the stern bearing has not been leaking and seems firm, it is better not to disturb a lag bolt.

If after all this you have found no trouble, which is probably the case, you will sail with greater confidence. If you do find trouble, you will have found it when it is most easily and inexpensively repaired. And this may be the year in which you are tested.

Fitting Out Notes

• Before you start, assemble a small box of indispensable tools. It will save you overhauling your main toolbox a dozen times a day. You will want to have quickly available at least the following: a sharp knife, a Phillips screwdriver and an ordinary screwdiver, a putty knife, a nine-inch adjustable crescent wrench, a pair of narrow-nosed pliers, and a pair of vise-grips.

• Time spent keeping the scene clean and in order is time well spent. People get hurt tripping on things and waste untold hours stepping around and over them and looking for other things underneath them.

• A ball of marline, a roll of plastic electrical tape, a roll of the tape that plumbers use to seal joints, a can of WD-40 for loosening frozen threads, and a can of hard grease are supplies it is well to have within reach.

• Don't let paintbrushes stand in a can of thinner with their bristles resting on the bottom of the can. Drill holes in the handles and suspend them on a wire or nail across the top of the can. They will clean themselves in twenty-four hours.

• Bring your fire extinguishers aboard with the first load of gear.

• If your gasoline engine proves reluctant to start or runs haltingly, go through its electrical system carefully. Disconnect every wire, one at a time, and with a little emery paper or fine sandpaper shine up every terminal and the screw that sits in it. If there is no terminal, install one by cleaning the end of the wire and squeezing on a terminal with vise-grips. Install new spark plugs. With an ignition file, clean the surfaces of the points where they come together and be sure that they are the right distance apart. If your instruction book does not give the proper clearance, try .020 inches. Be sure the battery terminals are clean and tight. If she ran last year and if she is getting clean gasoline, she ought to run.

• A diesel engine runs at such high temperatures and pressures and must be machined to such close tolerances that the amateur without a bench, a micrometer, and precision power tools can do little more than change filters without causing expensive damage. Know when to quit and call in the expert.

• Keep a first-aid kit handy and use it. Hands made soft by a winter ashore are easily infected by minor injuries, especially blisters and rope burns.

• Renew zincs, even if there still seems to be a good deal of metal left. You can see the zinc corrode, but you cannot see what corrodes if a big chunk of zinc is not there.

• Wire or mouse with marline every shackle. Shackles have a way of unscrewing themselves at awkward times. Fishermen do not use shackles on moorings for this reason. They forge a big ring into the end link of the chain, then pass the other end through the staple in the rock, through the ring, and pull tight. Drill and wire all nuts and turnbuckles, too.

• Don't work alone unless you love to do

it and there is absolutely no alternative. You will be tempted to lift something too heavy or grab for something just out of reach or continue long after quitting time. Two people accomplish more than twice as much as one and have more fun.

• If yours is a wooden boat, do not sail her for at least a week after she goes overboard. Much of a boat's strength lies in the compression built up as her planks close down on the caulking and on each other. To sail her too soon puts an unreasonable strain on her fastenings and may make her leak for the rest of her life.

• However enthusiastic or impatient your crew, do not leave float or mooring on your first sail of the season without being certain that your anchor line is coiled and clear to run, that the bitter end is made fast, and that the anchor shackle is wired properly.

• Remember that doing and undoing makes work for damned fools.

• NEVER pick up a power tool from the water without pulling the plug first. A lady in an English boatyard dropped her power drill overboard, reached down to pick it up, and electrocuted herself despite immediate efforts to revive her.

Fitting Out Help

As weekends warm up and you get into the fitting-out jobs, you can use a good deal of help from those who look forward to sailing with you in the summer. They have perhaps made a rash promise at Christmastime and it is time to call them on it. However, there are some preparations to be made and procedures to be followed that will vastly increase their efficiency and their pleasure in whatever tasks you set them to.

First, be sure you have enough equipment. Sandpaper you will need in large quantities, with blocks to wrap it around. You will need as many putty knives as people, for most men will use one and shove it in a hip pocket for future use.

Clean up your paintbrushes and have them soft and dry. If you need new ones, get them before Saturday. Have at least a gallon

of paint thinner and a number of coffee cans for mixing and cleaning. If your household cannot supply rags, buy paper towels galore.

Be sure you have masks for those sanding copper paint. The stuff is very irritating, and some brands are as poisonous to people as to barnacles.

Check out the toolbox for common weapons like screwdrivers, pliers, and adjustable wrenches. It is well to have an extra jackknife or two in the toolbox, for someone is sure to forget his. If you plan to use a power tool, have a *long* three-wire extension cord with a ground plug and a converter if that should be necessary.

If the yard cannot promise you a ladder, bring a safe and solid one with you.

You better supply lunch for the crowd, too. It will be appreciated; and after all, you are getting free labor.

When your volunteer workers show up, you must give each one a clear idea of what you want him to do and put the tools in his hand. Of course, the expert rigger need only be asked to check out the standing rigging or to overhaul spinnaker gear. However, the enthusiastic but inexperienced helper will soon lose his zeal if told simply to sand off the side of the house. Get down beside him and start the job. Show him about how much you want taken off and give him a definite and fairly small amount to do at a time.

When you get all your help at work, start one of the grubbier jobs yourself, but let it be one you can drop, for the rigger will want you to look at what *may* be a hairline crack in a turnbuckle, or the engine man may find that he cannot start a vital nut. Also, you must stop occasionally to inspect the work of the sander and to encourage him on his way.

It is a great help to have a "gopher boy," a boy who, when you want something, will "go fer" it. Introduce him to the manager of the yard store, for the boy may be up there quite often. Between jobs give him something quick and interesting to do, for young minds have often a short attention span. Maybe he would enjoy being the official photographer.

Remember that most of your workers may be more accustomed to shuffling papers than to pushing sandpaper. They knock the skin off their knuckles and are likely to tire easily. Take fairly frequent breaks. An hour and a half at a clip is probably enough, and a six-hour day is a long day at the yard.

When the whistle blows for lunch, knock off. It will probably be pretty early, but that's all right. Send the gopher to the car for the lunch, and let it be a good one. Beer goes well for those who like it, but especially on a warm April day it promotes spring fever, often in a severe form.

In the afternoon you may find yourself busy taking care of your workers. Everyone loves to paint. You, however, must see that the paint is properly stirred, boxed from can to can, and thinned to the proper consistency. The painter must be provided with a small can of paint, a suitable brush, a rag, and a bit of thinner. You may have to run ahead of him with masking tape and follow up behind him with a rag to pick up drips.

If any of your crew uses a power tool, be sure that he knows how to use it, for an accident is your fault. If the rigger must go aloft in a bosun's chair, stand the gopher boy next to the pin on which the halyard is belayed and order him under pain of keel-hauling to let no one touch it. The boy better not stand right under the rigger, though, lest he drop a wrench.

No smoking. Fitting out is an inflammable business, and a boatyard on fire is tragic.

An afternoon coffee break will be welcome. After it, start no new job, but put your crew to finishing up what is in progress. Allow ample time to pick up tools, sweep up the mess you have made, close paint cans properly, suspend brushes in thinner if they are to be used again next week, and leave all in good order.

A beer or a wee nip at quitting time leaves everyone enthusiastic about coming back next Saturday. The discouragement of inadequate equipment, not enough tools, insufficient or unclear direction, and the poison of waiting around with nothing to do will have been avoided. As owner you have to Tom Sawyer your help a little; make them feel that it is a privilege to whitewash a fence.

Laying Up

Laying Up Afloat

A wooden boat in tight and sound condition is best kept afloat through the winter. Her seams remain tight and her weight is supported by the surrounding pressure of the water rather than by her keel. One owner who kept his boat afloat for twenty years, hauling her only to clean and paint her bottom, averred that he could scratch a match on the top of her keel in the spring. For fiberglass and aluminum boats, lying afloat is a desirable alternative to hauling. Any boat is damaged more by sun and drying wind than by cold salt water. The weight of the boat resting on the keel exerts a tension on deck beams designed for compression strains and reverses strains on every part of the fabric. It is especially important with aluminum and fiberglass boats to check carefully the possibilities of galvanic action before laying up afloat. Renew zincs on fiberglass boats and be sure aluminum boats are thoroughly painted.

If your boat is to lie afloat, the danger from ice in northern latitudes can usually be avoided by selecting a protected anchorage where the tide keeps the water stirred up so that ice does not form. A thin sheet of ice sometimes skims over a salt water cove on a still, cold night. This ice is soft and mushy from the top but cuts edgeways like a saw. Some owners nail rough boards around the waterline to protect against this, and some float a boom of logs around the boat. However, most boats seem to survive skim ice pretty well if a responsible person watches them. There is practically no defense against the heavy ice that may form after a week or two in a very hard winter. With an offshore wind it moves off in heavy pans with an irresistible force, taking wharves, floats, moorings, boats, and everything else with it. However, in a well protected cove, this is most unlikely to happen.

A recently developed defense against ice is "bubbling." During cold spells, air is pumped through perforated pipes on the bottom of the harbor under the boat. The rising bubbles raise warmer water to the surface and

thus prevent ice from forming around the boat.

Freezing is another principal danger and one many insurance policies exclude from their responsibility. Because the water outside the boat does not get below the freezing point of seawater, water in the bilge is unlikely to freeze hard. However, any seawater standing so as to be largely surrounded by very cold air may very well freeze. Scupper pipes, such as those that drain self-bailing cockpits, rudder and center-board trunks, and seacocks are good examples. Scupper pipes may be protected by plugging them tightly from the outside, sucking out the remaining water inside with a rubber tube, filling the pipe with antifreeze, and corking lightly to prevent evaporation. Hoses attached to seacocks should be disconnected, drained, and the top of the seacock filled with antifreeze and capped. Rudder trunks and centerboard trunks ought not to freeze and usually are safe, although I know of one boat that burst her rudder trunk and sank at her winter mooring during a record cold snap. It is one of the chances you take.

A boat laid up afloat is likely to "sweat" on the inside from condensation. Air below the waterline is comparatively warm and damp compared to the colder air above. As the warmer air rises, moisture condenses on cold surfaces. Conversely, on warm, damp days, the warmer air from outside condenses on surfaces still cold or at the temperature of the seawater outside. The best defense against the dampness caused by sweating is thorough ventilation. Blowholes in the cover at the bow and stern are essential. One can lay the supports for the cover over the rail, providing an opening under the "eaves" all the way around the boat and still protect the decks from rain and snow. However, the structure must be well tied down or the whole roof may blow away.

Winter moorings should be extra heavy and should be chain from anchor to deck. The weight of the chain acts as a spring so that the boat can give to winter gales and to any surge that may penetrate from outside. The chain must be heavily wrapped with chafing gear wherever it touches the boat, for even gentle motion will chew down a wooden rail very quickly. If the boat is moored out in the cove, she should be moored bow and stern in the direction of the prevailing winds. If she is moored alongside a wharf, at least two moorings should be laid off in the harbor so the weight of the chains will hold her away from the wharf. Fender boards should protect her from the wharf or float.

No matter how extensive your precautions—and you should leave nothing undone—some responsible person nearby should watch over the vessel, going aboard once a week to see that no water has accumulated in the bilge, to check moorings and chafing gear, and to see that all is well.

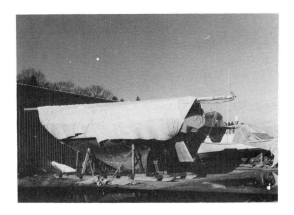

Hauling Out in a Boatyard

If your boat is hauled by a yard, you may usually have her stored either inside a shed or outside. If she is outside, she should be covered with a frame and tarpaulin and well ventilated, and the cover should be well carried down on her southern and western sides to protect her as much as possible from sun and drying winds. It is well to have her hauled as late as possible in the fall and launched as soon as the weather permits painting, so she will dry out no more than necessary.

The bilge should be drained as dry as possible and handfuls of salt thrown into it to ensure that any water left in it will not freeze. All seacocks should be left open and all tanks and water lines drained, for she will freeze hard all through her. One advantage, however, is that any worms that may have crept into inaccessible places will be frozen too.

Great care must be taken to see that the boat is properly supported on her cradle. A boat with a long, strong keel can rest squarely on it with wedges fore and aft. Supports under the bilges should be braced firmly both athwartships and fore and aft, and should bear on wide wooden pads, not directly on the planking. Boats with short keels and long overhangs must be firmly supported and wedged up under the overhangs to prevent a tendency to sag at bow and stern.

If the boat is to be stored inside—a somewhat more expensive and desirable solution—the same support is necessary but of course no cover is needed and ventilation need be no problem, for all hatches and ports can be left open.

Before committing your boat to a yard, it is well to have the yard's responsibility and yours clearly stated in writing. For instance, is the yard responsible for acts of vandalism, for gear stolen, for gear mislaid? Do you expect to pay extra for storage of spars, dinghy, and battery? Is it intended that the yard clean the bottom when the boat is hauled? What work is the prerogative of the yard and what may the owner do himself? Must the owner purchase all material used on the boat at the yard store, or may he bring it in from outside? When must the bill be paid? When all this and more is clear, your insurance company should be informed so that everything is properly covered.

Laying Up at Home

For small boats easily floated onto a trailer and towed behind a car, whether of wood or fiberglass, this is an excellent solution with considerable saving in yard bills and maintenance expense. If the boat is so big that it must be lifted by a crane or Travel-lift, loaded on a hired flat-bed trailer, and then skidded off in your yard, the local costs of such a service must be weighed against the yard bill and the owner's time. This is such a complex problem that generalizations are not of much help. For instance, one must consider the ground rules of the local yard. Some insist that the owner must leave his boat and walk away, leaving all rigging, engine, paint, and repair work to yard personnel at yard rates. Others permit owners various amounts of work and even, occasionally, use of tools. At home, of course, you are your own boss, but this may raise a problem of time and expertise.

Unloading a five-ton boat from a trailer

can be a long and difficult task involving a powerful winch or tackle, generous supplies of blocks and skids, a pail of grease, and some knowledge of the rigger's trade. A serious failure could mean expense far beyond a yard bill and possibly serious injury. Cleaning and painting, which look so easy when the job is six months away, require tedious hours in April. The help of friends so glibly promised on New Year's Eve may fail to materialize productively in the spring. Your image of yourself, umbilically connected to the house by an electric cord, snugly building cabinets or a chart table aboard your yacht on a January Saturday, may dissolve under the pressures of skiing, business, or family needs. Maybe you should consider whether you would be better off to work at your own profession and pay a professional mechanic to overhaul your engine.

Provision for support and ventilation at home is of course the same as it would be if she were in a yard. However, if you plan to work aboard, consider a heavy clear plastic cover instead of an opaque canvas one. The plastic lets in a surprising amount of light and heat on a sunny winter day.

Finally, consider every laying-up chore not as something done at the end of a sailing season, but as the start of a new one. It makes the winter shorter.

Cutting Your Yard Bill

With hourly labor charges at boatyards running high, anything that the owner can do for himself will serve to reduce significantly the coat of maintaining his boat. How much one can do depends partly on the yard. Twenty years ago, boatyards lived by building wooden boats in the winter and summer and putting their capable and experienced crews to hauling, storing, and maintenance jobs in spring and fall. With wooden yachts now economically prohibitive, the yards are driven to providing enough maintenance work to keep capable men busy the year around. Therefore, many yards now insist on doing all work on stored boats at hourly rates. Others insist on doing varying amounts. If you can find one that will allow you to work on your own boat, here are a few jobs that can save some money.

Sails

Surely you can unbend your own sails, spread them out on a wharf, and wash them down on both sides with a fresh-water hose. When they are thoroughly dry, inspect them carefully. Look for chafed seams where the sail rubs against the after shroud when running before the wind or where a slack lee backstay may rub against it. Look carefully at tack and clew grommets, the rings in the corners of the sail. The usual method of installing these is to sew around an iron or brass ring and then punch a brass eye inside the ring to protect the stitching. If the stitching is worn, pry out the eye, restitch, and punch in a new ring. After half a dozen of these repairs, you will have saved the cost of palm, needle, twine, wax, and a grommet-setting tool.

Look carefully at the headboard on your mainsail or mizen. It may well be bent, twisted, or badly chafed. Maybe you can fix it right then on the wharf, but you may have to mark it for the sailmaker's attention. Look at every slide on luff and foot. This may be tedious, but you are in a sense being paid what the yard would charge for the work. Worn seizings can be easily replaced. Study the reinforcing stitching around batten pockets and reef cringles, especially at the clew. Look carefully at the tabling or "hem" along the leech of all sails, especially jibs that must cross mast or forestay in tacking. The cloth may be rotten here and need extensive patching, but in some cases a careful stitch or two will save it. In any case, the thorough inspection will save time in the sail loft.

Fold and bag the sails, label each bag, and store in a dry place. Many skippers make a point of hanging sail bags from rafters in such a way that rats and mice cannot get at them. The rodents like to build their nests in cotton sails, but Dacron is less attractive. Even so, it is well to hang the bags up and perhaps to put a wad of newspaper in the bag. Newspaper makes better nests than dacron or cotton. Sails needing repair should go to the sailmaker at once in order to insure early attention. Some sailmakers give lower rates for fall work.

Rigging

At least, before the boat goes into the yard, you can remove covers or tape from the turnbuckles at the lower ends of shrouds and stays. Remove cotter pins, be sure the turnbuckles turn easily, grease the threads lightly with hard water-pump grease, and replace the cotter pins without spreading them, leaving the rigging a bit slack so all the rigger need do is pull the pin in the toggle or in the jaw of the turnbuckle. A rigger can spend an expensive hour trying to free a frozen turnbuckle with WD-40 and a torch and end by ruining it at your expense.

Take booms and gaffs off the boat yourself, wash them off in fresh water, especially if they are aluminum, run an oiled rag over tracks and reefing gear, and store at home on the rafters of your attic or garage.

If the yard will permit it, arrange to have the mast lifted out on the day you bring the boat in. Then you can detach all rigging from the hull yourself, bring her under the derrick and knock out the wedges. You would do well to let the yard rigger attach the sling and supervise actually lifting the spar. He is well acquainted with his own gear. Have him lay the mast on horses on the wharf. Here you can inspect all the upper ends of the rigging. Either take the rigging off and store at home or lash the rigging to the mast with twine and have the yard store the spar on a rack in their spar shed.

Engine

Beyond cleaning it thoroughly, there may not be much you can do about the engine before you take the boat to the yard, for you will have to have it running in order to deliver the boat. However, if the yard will permit it, after the boat is made fast to slip or mooring, drain the water jacket, coat the threads of the drain plugs with hard grease, and replace them. Start up the machine, disconnect the water intake from the sea cock or heat exchanger, and plunge the intake hose into a large bucket of antifreeze containing a rust inhibitor. Run the engine until antifreeze comes out the exhaust. Stop the engine and plug the water intake. This fills the jacket with antifreeze. As the machine runs its last, squirt some oil into the carburetor air cleaner to spread it through the valve chambers. Remove the spark plugs, pour a tablespoon or two of oil into each cylinder, and turn the engine over twice to spread the oil over the cylinder walls. Replace the plugs. Wrap a rag around a pine plug and tap it into the exhaust pipe to discourage air circulation and condensation.

Consult the yard about fuel tanks. In general, they should be full and capped or empty and open in order to prevent condensation.

After the boat is hauled, drain the fresh-water cooling system if the yard will permit you to work under the boat.

Take the batteries home, check the water level, and put them on a trickle charger. The cost of the charge will come back in savings on battery storage the first year, and prolonged battery life in years to come.

Cabin

Obviously, before the boat goes to the yard, take everything out of the cabin that will move. This includes not only such obvious items as bunk cushions but also the stove, lamps, charts, instruments, anything on the shelves or in the lockers, tools, spare parts, the cabin table—everything that will be better off ashore and that will obstruct the free movement of air through the boat. Remember that under a winter cover she will be subject to considerable change in temperature and humidity, even with ventilation at bow and stern, and condensation will be a real problem. Scatter Ajax or Comet or some kind of scouring powder on shelves. It will discourage mildew, and in the spring it can be wiped up with a damp rag, leaving the shelf clean.

Drain the water tanks, lines, and pumps. Be very sure there are no pockets of water left to freeze and burst pipes. Attractive and persuasive arguments have been adduced for putting gin or vodka in the water tank to prevent freezing. This sounds great, especially with a view to spring, but the physics professor calculates that the amount of vodka necessary to lower the freezing point to an antifreeze level would fit out the skipper's liquor locker for the winter.

Pump some kerosene through the head to keep pump leathers and valves soft. Close sea cocks and disconnect hoses. Drain out all water, and leave seat and cover open.

Clean the icebox thoroughly. It is of great importance to leave the door open. Because it is second nature born of ingrained habit to close icebox doors, tape a block on the inside of the latch or even remove the door. If it stays closed all winter, it will be musty all summer, and condensation in the insulation or behind it will encourage rot.

On Deck

Of course you will remove your compass, but also take all other instruments not permanently attached. They are unnecessary temptations to thieves and vandals and are better kept at home. Take also any blocks that can be easily unshackled. Anchors and roding can be left, except that anchors are now so expensive that they are well worth stealing. Certainly no coil of nylon anchor line should be left on deck, for sunlight will attack it even if moth and rust do not. Mop, boathook, fenders, and dock lines should be clearly labeled with waterproof magic marker and left to protect the boat. You may lose the lines and you may find the fenders protecting someone else's boat in spring, but it is just as well to leave them aboard.

Clean up. This is tedious work, and surely the boat will get dirty again, but sand, mud, grease, and dirt sets up into something like cement in the course of the winter, and some boatyard man will spend a long time and many of your dollars getting deck and topsides ready to paint. The less of that kind of work he has to do, the better off you will be.

If the boat is to winter in the water, consider the cockpit scuppers. If they are fitted with seacocks, you can close them, disconnect the hoses, and let the cockpit drain into the bilge. If you do, throw handfuls of salt into the bilge if your boat is wooden. If there are no seacocks, you may be able to ram rubber stoppers into the scuppers from outside. Suck out what water you can get, and dump a cup of antifreeze into the pipe from above. All this is to prevent the water in the scupper pipe from freezing, bursting the pipe, and sinking the yacht. It is not a problem except in a hard winter in high latitudes, but it has happened. The pipe, although at or below the level of the water outside the boat, is surrounded by air. If that air gets below 27 degrees F, the water in the pipe could freeze.

The Dinghy

If you can, take it home and save the storage charge. You may take better care of it than the yard will. In any case, clean it thoroughly. If it has an outboard motor, run it in fresh water for fifteen minutes and fog it out by squirting oil into the air intake. Empty the gasoline tanks and leave them upside down and uncapped to prevent condensation.

Lash oars, oarlocks, rudder, and spars inside the boat and store the dinghy sail as you do your other sails.

All this takes time, but it will seem worth it when things go together easily in the spring and you are sailing in May with the yard bill paid.

Thoughts on Choosing a Yard for Winter Storage

Location and price per square foot are probably the last considerations in choosing a yard. You could probably be persuaded to travel quite a way by land or water or to pay a considerably higher price by other significant factors.

How much work do you want to do yourself? Some yachtsmen would rather spend their time working at their own professions and spend their money employing professionals to work on their boats. There is a certain logic in the idea, to be sure. In this case, find a yard to which you can deliver the boat on October 15 and which will have her ready to sail away on June 1. This will be expensive, and some yards insist on providing this kind of service and no other. If you choose this type of yard, however, it is worth spending an hour or two looking at how other boats in the yard are being cared for. Are they properly supported on their cradles? Are the cradles on level ground? Is there a fire hydrant nearby? Is there a fence around the yard? Are spars properly supported on level racks? Is the machine shop an orderly place? Are mooring pennants, dock lines, lifts, and railways sound and well maintained?

If you want to work on your own boat in the yard, ask how much work the yard will permit. Some yards insist on doing all the work below the rail. Others permit you to do whatever you wish yourself but forbid your bringing in an outside carpenter or mechanic to work on your boat.

Should you elect to do some of the work yourself and have the yard do some, consider not only the hourly rate the yard charges but also who will do the work. Some small yards maintain a carpenter and a mechanic and then employ high school boys or transient labor to do the rush painting in the spring. Sometimes these people do a very good job, but not always.

Who will put on the winter cover? If the yard is to do it, take a careful look at the covers on other boats. The first thing to look for is ventilation. There should be a peek hole at bow and stern. If the supports for the cover rest on the rail, be sure that they are padded and tied down. See that the supports are close enough together so that the cover will not sag into pockets that can collect rain and snow. After your own cover is on, be sure that no stovepipe, corner of the cabin house, or rail stanchion makes a hump in it. The toughest canvas will soon chafe through under the action of the winter wind. Try to arrange a site on the north side of a building where the sun

cannot strike. A big power cruiser will do as well as a building.

Investigate the availability of electric outlets and sill cocks for hoses. Will the yard allow an electric heater aboard so you can work in the cabin on winter Saturdays? Will they let you burn off paint with a torch? Do they rent tools? Will they let you use their bandsaw, planer, or drill press briefly? Is there a charge for these services?

We now come to the most significant point of all, a consideration far beyond price. What kind of people run the yard and work in it? I know yard owners and employers who consciously put on an act for customers, flattering them and their boats, making promises that they cannot or do not keep, and treating them with contempt behind their backs. Others will get up if it blows in the night to check mooring pennants or dock lines and drop by on Sunday afternoons in September and October to see that the weekend sailors have left their boats and tenders safely. Some carpenters are of the "Oh, . . . it, nail it where it is" type, while others will fit a knee or a new plank like a cabinetmaker.

The latter person expects something of the owner and deserves to get it. He expects the owner to care about his boat, that he show skill in handling her under sail or power, that he bring her in clean and tidy with her gear shipshape. He expects your appreciation of his work too. If he goes to extra trouble and does a good job on a tricky piece of repair work, he will appreciate your noticing it. He will also respect you for pointing out a shoddy paint job and asking him to do something about it, for even the best of painters, rushed by the season, occasionally paints too soon before a shower or too late in the day.

Often these kinds of people are found in small yards in the less popular harbors. Their yards are picked up, their landings in good shape, their shops tidy. But they do not work for nothing, nor should you expect them to.

It is, of course, perfectly proper to question any item on a bill that looks unreasonable. If you arc charged thirty dollars for unstepping a spar that two men did in fifteen minutes, you are entitled to an explanation. It may appear

that use of the "hister" involves a flat fee. It may be an office mistake.

Ask about the terms of payment. Many yards require a payment of half the storage charge when the boat comes in, or before December 31. Some will refuse to let you take the boat out of the yard in the spring until bills are paid. In any case, pay promptly. It is a great help to the yard to have the money in hand and it certainly sweetens your relationship to have the reputation of paying on the line year after year.

Ask about taxes. Some towns tax boats as personal property if they are within town limits on April 1. If there is a tax, are the assessors predatory, or merely unreasonable in their estimate of your yacht's value?

Ask about insurance. Usually your own insurance, less deductible, covers damage to your boat and the yard assumes liability for injury to its own employees. Check it out. What happens if you fall off a yard ladder while working on your own boat?

Ask about timing. When must you bring the boat in? Can you sail it on weekends from the yard's mooring? Will they pump the boat occasionally if necessary? When will they unstep spars? When will you be hauled? When, given decent weather to paint, can you be launched in the spring?

Plan your winter work. Inspect everything as you take it ashore, and go through the boat, inside and out with the yard manager as soon as the boat is hauled. A dozy butt, a worn rudder post or shaft, a dent in the keel where you bounced over a ledge should be noted and repairs planned early. If the boat is to be moved

into a heated shop for extensive repairs, plan that her stay there be brief, for she will dry out badly if she is a wooden boat.

Many yards will have a contract covering matters like these. Go over it with the manager carefully, less as a legal document than as a statement of mutual intentions. If there is no formal contract or if it is sketchy, write a letter explaining your understanding of what is to be done so that you can return to it later in case of disagreement. It is unlikely in the right kind of yard that anyone will be sued, but it is well to have the agreement clearly understood.

Finally, stop in once a month in the winter to look the boat over, to discuss repairs with the carpenter or mechanic, and to pass the time of day. You are entrusting to them a valuable piece of property about which you care deeply.

Grounding Out

How is it possible to keep the bottom of your boat clean throughout a long season without an expensive mid-season haul-out? Sending a diver overboard to scrub the bottom with a brush is a losing game. In the first place, he can't scrub hard enough underwater to do an efficient job. Second, even if he could, he would do more harm than good, for the poisonous material in antifouling paint is easily removed from the surface and then its value is nil.

If your boat can stand on her keel, you can adopt the fisherman's expedient of grounding out. This is simply bringing your boat alongside a wharf at high water and allowing the tide to leave her leaning against the wharf high and dry. It is sort of a controlled shipwreck.

There are a few important precautions to be observed. First you should secure the permisssion of the owner of the wharf and inspect the site carefully at low water. Remove any rocks. If there are bed timbers there for grounding, be sure that they are sound and spaced properly to support your boat. Check the supports of the pilings the boat will lean against and, if you are in any doubt, shore them up.

Select a day when the high water comes about six or seven in the morning so the boat will be drying and you will be painting in the heat of the day. It is well to pick a day when the night tide is higher than the morning tide, but as she won't take bottom at the very peak of the morning tide, you will probably be able to get her off all right in the evening.

Bring the yacht alongside and position her with bow, stern, and spring lines next to the piles against which she is to lean. Obviously, these should be as far up the beach as possible. Put out all available fenders and remember that as the tide goes, she is going to drop some. A fender board is a very useful protection.

Seat your crew along the side of the boat next to the wharf to keep the boat about eight inches to a foot away from the pilings and to encourage with their weight a list toward the wharf. As the tide begins to ebb, you will notice a wet band around the pilings above the water, and as this grows wider, you will become aware that your boat has grounded. She will touch on the after end of the keel first and if necessary can be pivoted around that point for the next fifteen minutes. Soon she will be hard aground with her stern cocked up and her bow dropping as she comes down on the length of her keel.

Now unsnap the main halyard from the sail and snap it into a strap around one of the timbers of the wharf. Don't use a plank. Get around a piling or a sill. Heave down on the halyard to give the boat a very positive list against the wharf. Don't do it until the yacht is hard aground on the length of her keel or her bow will pull in toward the wharf and she will not bear where you planned. Don't pull too hard, especially if she is resting on bed timbers, for the great leverage of mast and winch could skid her keel away from the wharf. All you need is a definite list.

As the tide goes, assemble your weapons. You will need an old broom or stiff brush. A new broom is too floppy and a wire brush is too stiff. You will need a bucket, a gallon or two of the strongest chlorine bleach available, copper paint, brushes, thinner, stirring sticks, extra cans or paper paint pots, old clothes, and boots. Don't go barefoot or use sneakers. People throw very sharp things off wharves, and you can't always watch where you step.

As soon as you can get at the bottom of the boat, wade in and slosh on the bleach. This seems to release all the algae and grass by its mere presence, so very little scrubbing is necessary. Pull your hat down hard, for the bleach is very strong stuff and very painful in the eyes. If your skin is allergic to it, wear rubber gloves.

Have your mate follow with a bucket and rinse off the boat. If you can, rig a fresh-water hose. The force of the jet will help to remove the slime, and fresh water dries more quickly than salt.

When she is clean, let her dry until the tide starts to come. Mix your paint thoroughly, "boxing" it from pail to pail. This is more important with copper paint than with other kinds because much of the antifouling material is in suspension and settles out quickly. When the tide gets almost to the keel, start painting. One man on each side can paint a forty-foot yacht ahead of the tide. It is not necessary that the paint dry hard before the water covers it. It is better if it stays soft. Copper paint will stick to quite a damp surface as long as there is no standing water on it.

The man with the steadiest hand should cut the waterline. Don't fuss with masking tape; copper paint creeps under it anyway. For a mid-season job, run your line a hair below the existing line and a little unevenness will never show. Once when I was carefully cutting in a waterline, a passing fisherman advised, "Just take a confidence drink and then walk right around her."

When the painting is done, go home and clean up. However, plan to be back at least an hour before she is due to come off. Before she floats, the halyard must be cast off, and she usually comes off before you expect her to float anyway. As her bow comes up, cast off bow and spring lines, put a little steady strain on the stern line, and she will slide off, clean and painted for the rest of a long season at the cost of a day's work, a pail of paint, and a bucket of bleach.

Antifouling

Magellan and Drake used a mixture of tar and tallow put on hot. Every few months they careened their vessels on a beach, burned off the accumulated weed, and repainted.

In Nelson's day they sheathed ships with copper plates. This was much more successful, but the copper ate up iron fastenings with galvanic action. Because the planking was fastened with wooden treenails and very little iron was used, they did not fall apart quickly.

Nineteenth-century whalers hove down alongside a New Bedford wharf, caulked the hull, covered it to the waterline with felt soaked in tar, covered that with pine sheathing, and nailed sheets of copper over that. Thus the copper was insulated from the hull, the vessel was protected from teredos, and she stayed quite clean for a long time. At the end of a three-year voyage, the copper would be very thin or worn away altogether in places. The vessel would be hove down, stripped, and the process repeated.

The copper in the presence of salt water slowly oxidizes and breaks down into other salts. These wash away, presenting always a clean surface. Copper ions in the water seem to discourage marine animals and poison those that attach themselves to the copper surface.

Not only are they poisoned, but they wash off as the surface erodes.

Sheathing modern yachts with copper is clearly impractical because of the weight, expense, and the insulation problems. Therefore, the modern practice is to use copper paint, whose principal active ingredient is copper oxide. The liquid in the paint is there to make the copper oxide stick to the boat and to release the oxide little by little, allowing it to escape into the water just as the copper oxide did on the whalers. Furthermore, the surface of the paint is soft, so that if a barnacle does sit down on it, he is poisoned first and then washed away as the surface wears down.

Any problem of galvanic action on fastenings and underwater metal can be solved with zincs, which are more active than copper, iron, or any other metal likely to be exposed. Aluminum boats present a special problem. Obviously, a copper paint on bare aluminum would very quickly corrode the aluminum. A special paint containing tributyltin fluoride instead of copper is used and it goes on over two coats of special primer.

Because of the nature of copper paint, it is important to launch the boat before the last coat of bottom paint is hard dry.

Racing boats that require a hard underwater surface use copper paint with a different vehicle, but the purpose is the same. Hard as it is, it slowly deteriorates, releasing the cop-

per oxide and keeping the surface clean. Thus it is obvious that scrubbing the bottom of a copper-painted boat is counterproductive and wasteful. Either race her dry and paint with a hard paint or leave her in the water and repaint as the old paint is used up.

In buying copper paint, look for the amount of copper oxide in the can. Copper oxide is what you are buying. The Sailor went through a marine supply store recently with a spring balance weighing copper paint cans and came out with the figures in the accompanying table. The items are listed in order of the cost per gallon.

Note that the most expensive paint, Copper-lux, has by far the most copper oxide in it and per pound is the least expensive. Three coats of Red Hand would cost about the same as one coat of Copper-lux and would not give as much protection. However, there are other considerations. The temperature of the water, the amount of animal and vegetable life in it, and the way the boat is used are important considerations.

If your boat lies to a mooring most of the summer in warm waters and you want her clean and ready for you on departure day, you must use the point that gives the best protection, the paint that has a high percentage of copper oxide, and a vehicle that allows it to leach out rapidly.

If you keep the boat in colder waters and

Brand	Cost/gal.	Wt./gal.	% CuO	Wt. CuO	Cost/lb.
Copper-lux (qt. x 4)	$100.00 (sale)	23 lb.	67.5	15.53	$ 6.44
Woolsey Vinelast (qt. x 4)	77.95	17	48	8.16	9.55
Bottom-Kote	66.90	16.75	45	7.54	8.87
Vinylux	66.50	14.25	45	6.41	10.37
Interclub bronze (qt. x 4)	51.80	12.00	31.5	3.8	13.63
Supertrop	41.00	13.5	24.8	3.35	12.40
Intercop	36.95	13.25	29.1	3.86	9.58
Red Hand	33.85	12.5	22	2.75	12.31

CAUTION: This table represents principally the products of the International Paint Co. and the pricing in one retail store. The weights were taken with a spring balance and hence are approximate only. The purpose of the table is not to recommend one kind or price of paint over another but to demonstrate the range of prices and active ingredients. Graphites and special racing finishes are not included except for one copper-bronze.

use her constantly, one or two coats of a less expensive paint may go the season. One authority, speaking of New England waters, said categorically, "Buy the cheapest paint which weighs thirteen pounds per gallon!"

If the range of tide exceeds the draft of your boat and if time is not of the very essence, you can put on one coat of a less expensive paint at fitting out time and ground out in the middle of the season before any growth appears on the bottom. Wash down thoroughly with Clorox, rinse off, and repaint. It will cost but the price of the paint and Clorox and a grubby day's work.

On the other hand, if you have to pay three dollars a foot plus labor to go on a railway and then pay the yard to clean and paint, the most effective paint you can put on in the spring is worth $100 per gallon if it will carry you through the season.

World's Best Antifreeze
William H. Ashbaugh

Fall and winter days often provide the best sailing weather. Unfortunately, many boat owners feel they must give up sailing the moment there is danger that their auxiliary engine might freeze. If it was possible to prevent engine freeze-ups easily, many could enjoy a much longer sailing year, and it is possible to do just that with the world's best and cheapest antifreeze —air.

Engines that use raw seawater for cooling are difficult to protect with the usual antifreeze. By disconnecting the cooling water inlet hose and putting it in a bucket of antifreeze, it is possible to distribute antifreeze throughout the cooling system as the engine is cranked—but this is a cumbersome procedure and more appropriate as a lay-up drill than as an end-of-sail routine. Far easier is draining the engine—thus distributing nonfreezable air throughout the system. Most engines have at least one drain, but you will need at least two others. If you have a water-lift silencer muffler in which the cooling water is discharged with the exhaust gases, you will need one drain for the low point on this silencer. The second drain must be placed just inside the inlet

seacock so that the water pump and inlet hose can be drained. Check with your engine dealer on placement of these drains. Check also to make certain that the interior of your cooling system is made of a noncorroding material, as frequent draining could hasten rusting of interior surfaces.

A number of types of drains are available, from the simple sheet-metal screw screwed into the underside of your water-lift silencer (muffler) to seacocks. A useful petcock drain for attachment to your seacock inlet is that used by plumbers when they need to tap into an existing pipe (for a humidifier, etc.). These fittings are available at plumbing supply houses. They have the advantage that no threading is required because they have their own pressure clamps, which attach them to the existing pipe (or seacock) after a small hole has been drilled in the fitting to which they are to be attached. Once the drains are installed, all you need to do at the end of a day's run is to close the seacock, open the drains in the muffler, engine block, and intake line, and crank the engine until the system is dry. Pulling out the center coil lead will prevent the engine from starting, although a brief run without water will probably not hurt it.

Now you can leave your boat knowing that her engine has the ultimate antifreeze— air.

How to Ruin a Boat with a Caulking Iron

When a boat leaks, the inexperienced owner's first reaction is to ram some cotton in the seam with a hammer and a caulking iron. There are several ways this can damage your yacht irreparably.

Caulk her too hard when she is dry.

A seam in a wooden boat is built with one beveled edge to make a "half vee" for the caulking. Not only is the cotton or oakum intended to prevent water from leaking in between the planks, it is also intended to force the planks against each other and thus make a succession of separate boards into one single shell, giving strength and stiffness to the

70

whole structure. If the seam is caulked too loosely, it may not leak, but the vessel will "work" in a seaway. If she is caulked too tightly, especially if the wood is very dry, when the plank swells it will push so hard against its neighbors that it will either pull the fastenings or buckle in the middle and split. In either case, a haulout and major repairs are necessary.

Make a hollow seam.

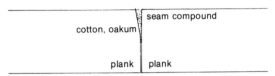

It is possible for the overenthusiastic amateur to hit the iron so hard that he drives the cotton clear through the seam into the inside of the boat. This, of course, cannot be easily mended. No amount of putty will fill the hollow seam to give it the stiffness it needs, and the cotton inside the boat will act like a wick to draw water in. The only solution short of a new plank is to roll two thicknesses of cotton together and tunk them in gently so they do not go through. Do not tack a batten on the inside to caulk against. Your first tap with the iron will spring it away from the inside of the plank.

Caulk a seam
which has no caulking in it.

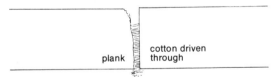

The planking of a lapstrake or clinker-built boat like a dory is ordinarily not caulked. The planks are set in paint and fastened every few inches with clinch nails.

If you find a place where the planks do not fit closely, especially if the boat has been out of water for some time, and you ram a piece of cotton in with a caulking iron, you will merely spread the seam farther apart and extend it fore and aft. The cure is to launch the boat, swamp her, and let her swell. If the seam still

How to ruin a boat with a caulking iron: hit the iron hard with a hammer.

fails to close, hold a maul against the inside of the nearest clinch nail, dig out the putty over the head, hold a nail set against it and give it a good rap or two with a hammer. This should pull the seam down. Then go along the seam for a foot or so each way, giving each nail the same treatment.

Frequently, seams where deck houses or hatch coamings come to the deck are not caulked and may leak. Do not try to caulk them, or you will simply extend your problem. If the seam is not caulked, the coaming was probably set in bedding compound and tightened down with a bolt. First clean out the crack. Then work a *little* bedding compound or one of the patented rubberlike mixtures into the crack and tighten down on the nut. It will probably be hidden under a plug in the timber under the deck, but it has to be there.

Caulking is an expert's job. A good caulker uses a mallet, never a hammer. He can

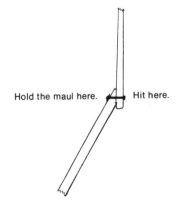

Hold the maul here.   Hit here.

tell by the feel of the iron and the bounce and ring of the mallet whether the caulking is going in too hard or too loosely or whether he is about to make a hollow seam. Call on the expert for expert work.

Microbial Contamination of Diesel Fuel

Dorothy J. MacFarlane

A sailor out of Miami is enjoying the warm breezes, lazily circling in the ocean. As the breezes lull, he starts his auxiliary engine for the trip back to port. A few yards away, the engine stops. A quick check of the situation reveals a slimy black mass on the fuel filters.

The boat owner probably has in the fuel tank a relative to the "mold" that grows in jelly jars, a fungus that actually lives in fuel oil and "eats" fuel.

Fungus probably got into the fuel tank the same way it got into the jelly jar. Perhaps a microscopic spore, the "seed" form of the fungus, dropped in out of the air when the cap was off, or contaminated fuel was put into the tank.

Fuel is very clean when it leaves the refinery, as the temperatures used to make fuel are high enough to sterilize it. Anywhere from then on through the delivery system, it can get contaminated.

There are at least three conditions necessary for the contamination to grow into a problem—water, temperature, and time.

Diesel fuel has a small amount of water dissolved in it. As fuel warms during the day, water can be absorbed, only to condense out of solution as it cools at night. This is one way water bottoms are formed below the fuel in storage tanks. Fungus grows best at the point where the fuel meets the water surface—both food and water are here within easy reach. As the fungus grows, it can form large mats. When the oil is sloshed, by filling or wave action, the mats are distributed around the tank, where they cling to surfaces. The mats carry trapped water with them and actually produce additional water from fuel breakdown. Then this water enhances further fungal growth.

At proper growth temperature microbial life flourishes. Cold does not kill it, but does slow it down. Fuels are warmed by the sun, or, in some marine diesels, by being cycled through the hot engine. This warmth then promotes growth.

Fungus grows slowly. Constantly moving fuel doesn't build heavy water bottoms and tends to sweep away spores and small mats of growth. In tanks such as those used for auxiliary engines, home heating fuel, idle boats, or aircraft, growth is promoted by fuel stagnation.

However, fuel movement is no guarantee againsty fungal contamination. Once a fungal strand attaches, it is probably there until it dies or is removed.

Effects of these growths are many and harmful. Most evident is the clogging of fuel filters. Slimy black, green, or brown masses collect on the filter material and catch dirt, rust, and water. Filters can plug completely, or even burst.

Fungal debris can bypass the filter, to clog or damage fuel lines, injectors, and cylinders. Growth that attaches to tank surfaces holds water and products of fuel decomposition against the surface, causing corrosion and pitting. Some types of growth can actually eat their way through tank linings. Where walls are damaged, flecks of lining fall into the fuel, eventually reaching the filters or injectors. This can lead to coking of injector nozzles.

Do you have contaminated fuel? Fuel should be clear and light colored, with a clean odor. Contaminated fuel is dark and smells like rotten eggs. The characteristic slime will appear as a dark, slick blob on filters, surfaces, fill lines, fill caps, and in fuel lines. Injectors may coke rapidly. The Boron Oil Co., 1876 Guildhall Building, Cleveland, Ohio 44115 supplies a Microbe Monitor Test Kit for about seven dollars. With it you can determine in forty-eight hours or less whether you have a microbe fungus infection.

If you have the problem, there are certain steps to follow. The first and perhaps most important is good housekeeping. This means keeping water bottoms at a minimum, storing fuel in clean tanks, watching filters for beginning problems, and perhaps prefiltering fuel through special filters to remove water. Avoid purchasing fuel you think may be suspect.

Avoid additives that contain detergents: these suspend even more water in the fuel, and may enhance microbial growth.

If these measures are insufficient to control microbial contamination, you may have to treat with a fungicide, such as BIOBOR JF ® fuel fungicide. Should the tank become badly fouled, drain the fuel and dispose of it—according to local disposal codes, of course. Clean the tank if possible, and inspect all parts of the fuel system for damage. With tanks that are an integral part of the ship's hull and cannot be cleaned, watch fuel filters for pieces of attached fungal mat that die and break free. A fuel fungicide will kill fungus, but that doesn't necessarily mean that the mats will dissolve or disappear immediately.

Contamination of any magnitude seldom occurs in gasoline-type fuels, but diesel, kerosene, and turbine fuels are very susceptible. Careful maintenance and proper treatment can save time, aggravation, and many dollars in damages and repairs.   —D.J.M.

A Biological Approach to Oil Spills

While Dorothy MacFarlane and the oil merchants are busy trying to eliminate organisms that feed on fuel oil and plug up our filters, Dr. Ananda M. Chakrabarty at General Electric Research and Development Center is working to develop a strain of bacteria that will flourish on a diet of fuel oil. Dr. Chakrabarty seeks an organism that will eat oil spills.

Because oil is such a complex mixture of compounds, as yet nothing will eat all of the components of oil, and most of the bacteria are poisoned by the toxic products of the others. Dr. Charkrabarty has developed a way of changing the germ cells to develop an entirely new organism that can consume the principal components of oil and will die out when its food is consumed. Considerable success has been achieved by combining cells with different strands of DNA and irradiating the ''super-microbe'' with ultraviolet light to ensure stable reproduction.

The new organism consumes most of the components of oil but must now be thoroughly tested for its impact on the environment after it has finished with the oil.

A more detailed account by Kim Cottrell of this project is published in *Sea Frontiers*, vol. 23, #1 and is obtainable from The International Oceanographic Foundation, 3979 Rickenbacker Causeway, Virginia Key, Miami, Florida, 33149.

The Ailing Engine— for Beginners Only

If a gasoline engine, apparently in excellent health, suddenly dies without noisy, traumatic symptoms, there probably isn't very much wrong with it. There are essentially four systems that combine to make the engine run. A bit of dirt, corrosion, or water in any one of them may stop the whole machine.

Electrical Systems

Electric current to make a spark goes from the battery to the spark coil to the distributor to the spark plugs. Start with the plugs. Take one out without burning yourself, for it will be hot. If the prongs are brown and more or less clean, respectfully replace it. If the prongs are sooty or a piece of black stuff lies between them, clean it off. Wipe the porcelain part clean if it is at all dirty, replace the plug, and try to start her up. If she does not respond, ground a screwdriver with a wooden or plastic handle firmly against the engine head and bring the shaft within a sixteenth of an inch of the top of the plug. With the switch on, press the starter. If you see a bright little spark, all is well with the electrical system. Move on to the fuel system.

If you do not see a spark, follow the heavy wire from the spark plug back to the distributor, a plastic spider with wire legs reaching out to each plug. Into the middle of it comes another wire from the spark coil. Press each wire in the distributor firmly down into its socket and do the same with both ends of the connection to the coil. Try her again.

Now take the end of the wire out of the

middle of the distributor, holding it with a dry rag. Bring it close to bare metal on the engine block. If you get a bright spark, the problem lies in the distributor. Loosen the spring clamps that hold the cap on, carefully lift it off, and wipe out the inside thoroughly with a dry rag, paying careful attention to the metal nubs under each wire. If these are dirty, *gently* scratch them clean with a knife or fine sandpaper. Lift off the rotor in the middle of the distributor. On top of it is a piece of spring steel with a brass button in it. Clean this carefully and bend the spring up a little so it will make a firm contact with the button in the middle of the cap. Replace rotor and cap and try again.

Take off the cap and rotor again. Under the rotor lie the "points." These are two bits of metal on a spring, which open and close as the rotor turns. With your screwdriver, ground the points to the frame of the distributor. If you see sparks, shut off the switch, turn the engine over until the points separate, and with an ignition file or a bit of sandpaper gently clean the faces of the two contacts. If they are rough, burned, or badly pitted, you have doubtless found your trouble. Put it all back and try again. If still no spark at the plugs, study the points carefully and see how to move them very slightly together; a quarter turn at the most should be enough. Try again.

If there was no spark at the points, try grounding first the terminal on the coil where a thin wire runs to the distributor and then the other terminal. If you have sparks on the first, then you have a complex problem in the distributor. If none and there is a spark on the other terminal, the coil is shot. If no spark on either terminal, the trouble lies in the switch—ground each terminal to check it—or further back in generator or voltage regulator. There isn't much the untutored yachtsman can do about these machines, but check to be sure all connections are tight and clean. A good squirt with silicon spray on wires, distributor, plugs, coil connections, and elsewhere can do no harm and may make the difference.

Fuel

If you have a spark on the plugs and she still won't run, check the fuel line. Of course there is gas in the tank, but you better check it anyway and be sure the valves are open. Turn her over with the choke full on and smell for gas. If you do not smell gas, gently loosen the connection where the fuel line goes into the carburetor. Hold a cup under it and have someone press the starter. If gas gushes out, catch it all, tighten the connection, mop up, and with a hammer or wrench gently tap the side of the carburetor. There is a float valve in it like the float in a toilet tank. If that is stuck, it will shut off the gas.

If no gas gushes out of the pipe, shut off the gas at the tank, take the strainer apart, and clean it thoroughly. Before you replace it, wipe clean the pipe from the tank and blow through it while someone opens the valve. You should hear bubbles in the tank. Reassemble the strainer, turn the gas on, watch for leaks, and try her again.

If there is gasoline running into the carburetor, spark on the plugs, and no action, she may be flooded by a faulty automatic choke. Take the air cleaner off, hold the choke open, and try her vigorously.

If there is still no response, it is time for an heroic measure. While the starter turns the engine over, squirt a small dose of Sure Start into the air intake. This is largely composed of ether, a violent explosive, so be very gentle with it. If she does not catch now, she needs the attention of an expert.

Cooling Systems

If your engine suddenly smells hot and the heat guage goes over the top, shut her off at once. Disconnect the water intake hose from the engine. If water only oozes through, blow back through it, poke it out with a wire, or go overboard and clean the intake. If it is clear, the thermostat may be stuck. It is usually to be found where the cooling water comes out of the engine, to be recirculated or dumped into the exhaust. Tunk it gently with a hammer. You can take the thermostat right out and run the engine without it. It will run cool, but it will run.

Lubrication

There is very little you can do for this system. If the oil pressure drops badly, shut off the engine and sail home. If you run the engine without proper lubrication and cooling, it will "freeze" and, after cries of pain, will stop forever.

To perform the operations described, you should have with you:

- two screwdrivers with plastic handles
- a set of ignition wrenches and a file for points
- a set of flat wrenches
- a small crescent adjustable wrench
- a pair of vise-grips
- a piece of fine sandpaper
- a small hammer
- a can of silicone spray
- a can of Sure Start

Yachting tells of a yacht reported missing after a race in the Caribbean. She turned up far from the finish. Her disabled motor could not charge her battery, so her LORAN was useless, and her skipper could not find the finish.

Winter Survival for Your Mooring

If you live in an area untroubled by ice, you need simply haul your mooring chain to the surface, bend on a piece of ½ inch nylon line long enough to reach bottom at the highest tides, and buoy the other end with something big enough so it will not be run down and cut off by passing motorboats. This scheme permits the chain to lie in the mud where it will rust less than it would suspended in salt water, for the mud tends to keep the oxygen from it.

However, ice raises a serious problem. Salt water ice is quite soft and mushy if you try to walk on it, but edgeways it is much stronger. Even a thin layer will saw and cut a stout line. Furthermore, if your mooring is in a cove that might freeze over heavily, it is possible that an offshore wind might move several acres of ice at once, its enormous momentum cutting off or dragging with it whatever is frozen in. This is even more likely to happen if a fresh-water brook runs into the cove.

There are several possible defenses against ice. The first is to employ someone with a "hister" to pull your mooring up and set it ashore. You can't beat that for security and for an opportunity to inspect the chain. However, if you have a very heavy granite block, for instance, this can be expensive.

Another alternative is to work your mooring into shallow water. At low water, haul the chain as nearly up-and-down as you can with winch, halyard, or come-along. Rig a bridle around your boat and let the tide lift the mooring. In case the mooring is "caught down," it is well to have a hatchet handy to cut the bridle before the yacht is pulled under, but this is a most unlikely possibility. At high water, run in shore as far as you can drag the rock and cast off. Repeat the process if necessary on successive tides until the rock is in water shallow enough to be visible at low water. Drop the chain on top of it. In the spring, simply hook up the chain with a boat hook, bend on your pennant, lift the rock off again with the tide, and drop it wherever you want it. This is, to be sure, a time-consuming method and in some harbors may entail the risk of having your mooring stolen. If you can hook it up, so can anyone else.

Another alternative is to bend on a long, light chain in place of your pennant and run the chain ashore. At dead low water, shackle it around a rock, a wharf piling, or a stake driven into the bottom. In the spring, under-run the chain and bend on your pennant again. This alternative has many advantages: your chain lies in the mud where it won't rust, your mooring remains in its permanent position so you can occupy the same berth year after year, the mooring itself is invisible, and the little chain is inconspicuous. The drawbacks are the cost of the light chain if your mooring lies well offshore, and the remote possiblility that some scoundrel will discover the chain and make off with the whole rig. He would have a big project on his hands and would find it a difficult task to accomplish inconspicuously.

A third alternative is to buoy the chain with a line that will allow the buoy to float about a fathom below the surface at low water. You, who know just where to look because you have taken bearings and ranges on the spot, can find the buoy in the spring and hook it up. It must be a good buoy, though, to stand being submerged for a whole winter without becoming waterlogged. A steel or aluminum net float might make it, or a buoy of hard, closed-cell plastic, but a buoy of ordinary plastic or wood might not. This is a risky alternative and may involve the nuisance of dragging for your mooring with a grappling or the expense of hiring a driver.

A fourth alternative is to attach a "winter stick" to the chain with a line long enough to let the stick float just out of water. Ice cannot saw off a 6×6 timber; and if the ice freezes around it and and starts to move out, the stick should be pulled down through the ice by the weight of the chain and the mooring so the ice will float over the top of it. The principal disadvantage of this plan is that the end of the chain is held up off the bottom by the buoyancy of the stick. Thus it is subject to rust and is chafed and worn by the motion of the stick in the tide and sea. Either saw off the worn links in the spring or shackle a fathom of heavy chain to the end of the mooring chain in the fall so the short piece will take the wear during the winter.

You must adapt your strategy to your particular needs, of course.

4

Bosun's Work

An Effective Mast Coat

One of the most difficult places to seal is the place where the mast goes through the deck. Years of failure have evolved the following effective if rather complex procedure. You must think of it before the mast is stepped.

1. Cut a doughnut of ¾-inch plywood whose inside diameter is about ¼ inch larger than the mast hole and whose width is about an inch. Set it in bedding compound and screw it down solidly to the deck.

2. Cut a circle from heavy paper whose circumference is considerably greater than that of the ring. Cut a slit along a radius. By overlapping the edges of the slit, make a cone whose angle is that of the finished mast coat and fasten the edges with paper clips.

3. Cut away the bottom of the cone until it will sit on the ring with about ½-inch overlap, enough for a seam.

4. Cut off the point of the cone until it will just slide easily over the butt of the mast.

5. Mark the point of the overlap, open out the cone, cut off the surplus overlap (allowing for a seam), and use the paper for a pattern to cut a piece of canvas.

6. Sew a band of canvas about 1½-inch wide to the top of the truncated cone so that when it is in place the strip will come on top of the cone to shed water over the seam. Remember that the skirt will go down inside the cone when the mast coat is in place.

7. Sew another skirt about an inch wide to the bottom of the cone so that it will fit down over the ring.

8. Now double-sew all seams, including the edges of the overlap, and work the mast coat over the butt of the mast to a point above the deck level.

9. With the mast in place and the wedges driven home, pull the skirt down to the top of the wedges so the lower skirt will cover the ring, and lash the upper skirt tightly to the mast with half a dozen turns of marline pulled as tight as you can pull them.

10. Turn the cone down over the wedges. The lower skirt should now fit down over the ring. Butter the outside of the ring with bedding compound.

11. Get several hose clamps of as great a

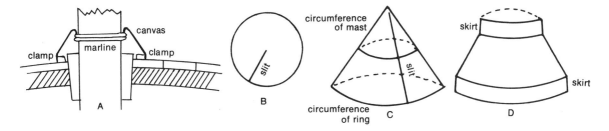

length as you can find, put them together end to end, and work them down over the skirt. Set them up until the bedding compound squeezes out.

12. Paint the whole works with several coats of deck paint.

Note that by this method it is unnecessary to drive tacks into either mast or deck and that it will work as well with a metal mast as with a wooden one. Also, this mast coat can be easily removed and replaced without damaging it. Keep the pattern, however, for canvas will wear out.

Jib Downhaul—The Easy Way

Oldtimers rigged downhauls on jibs because going out on a plunging bowsprit to wrestle down headsails in rough weather was uncomfortable and dangerous. Even with a modern knockabout rig, a downhaul can be a great help and comfort to a short-handed crew.

When the wind gets over Force 4 and the wet and windy foredeck is too bleak for sunbathing, the skipper calls for a smaller jib. On an ocean racer manned by a large crew of athletes, this is a stimulating challenge, but to the office worker or his wife on vacation, it can be an ordeal. It is just about possible for an active man to take a sail stop in his teeth, to cast off the halyard and run it over his shoulder, scramble out to the pulpit, brace himself, haul down the sail while he controls the halyard so it won't foul and go up the mast in a bunch, tie the stop around the luff so the sail won't climb the stay the instant he leaves it, work his way

The mate douses the jib.

aft again, and subdue the thrashing sail. With a downhaul, it is a cinch.

Seize two or three half-inch bull's-eyes—doughnut-shaped pieces of wood or brass like a thimble, only round—to the luff of each jib on the starboard side. Seize a small single block to the starboard side of the foot of the forestay. When you hank on the jib, run a light line from a cleat under the starboard rail forward of the shrouds through the block and the bull's-eyes and snap it into the snap shackle at the head of the sail. Hoist the sail and pull the downhaul snug so it doesn't slat about and get fouled up.

When the sail must come in under difficult conditions, the mate carefully drops the coil right side up in front of him on the foredeck and casts off the halyard from the winch, leading the fall over his left shoulder. He seizes the downhaul in both hands and from the comparative security of the foredeck hauls the sail down. If the halyard fouls, it will catch under

Quick and positive action

strains are greater, the stretch is vastly greater, and the problems involved in casting off can be nearly insuperable if the common knots are used.

To attach a heavy line to a light one, you cannot use a simple square knot. Either the small line will pull through the bight of the large one or it will jam into a twist impossible to release. The answer is the sheet bend illustrated. If the knot is to be under intermittent strain, it is well to half-hitch the light line around its own standing part and seize the end of the heavy line to itself. Although this knot sometimes sets up very hard under strain, it can be worked loose by prying the standing part of the small line up through the bight of the large.

Two heavy lines can be joined with a carrick bend. The ends of this knot can also be seized down to help prevent a jam.

his left arm. The sail comes down quickly, all the way, and is held down tightly so it cannot climb the stay. Downhaul and halyard are belayed and the clew twisted up.

Of course, if the humane skipper will bear off and blanket the jib with the mainsail, the operation can be carried out more comfortably. The declaration often seen in books that the big jib, blanketed, will simply drop at your feet does not seem to be borne out by experience. There are occasions, too, when one cannot bear off, such as when shooting a mooring or coming alongside a float. Then the speed and positive action of the downhaul is much appreciated, and at such times it is very helpful to have the crew conveniently located on the foredeck rather than balanced in the pulpit.

Handling Heavy Lines

Dock lines, anchor lines, and tow lines represent problems a little different from those we daily encounter with sheets and halyards. The

Sheet Bend

Sheet Bend with half-hitch and seizing

Carrick Bend

Carrick Bend completed

To make the end of a heavy line fast around a mast or piling, use a bowline. It is not only a quick and easy knot to tie but can be released by "breaking its back," that is, by bending the top of the knot forward and back to work the standing part back through the top loop. If a bowline is to take heavy strain and is to be used where it can be watched, shove a stick through the knot as illustrated. The stick can be knocked out and the knot easily loosened.

The towboat hitch is the best way to make a hawser fast to a bitt. It never jams, can be easily tied with the stiffest lines, and can be cast off a turn at a time so the line can be eased slowly over the bitt.

Beware of the clove hitch. It will surely hold, but, especially if wet, it will jam up very tightly when a heavy strain stretches the line and then is released. The square knot can pull up so hard that a sharp knife is the only an-

swer. Half hitches are also likely to jam hard, but less likely to do so if a round turn is taken first.

An anchor line should always be spliced around a thimble and shackled to anchor or chain to minimize chafe, but if you must use a knot, take a round turn through the anchor ring first to minimize chafe. The lark's head is also a knot unlikely to chafe.

Any line running unprotected by a stationary object will chafe, sometimes to a surprising extent. The picture on the next page shows a one-half-inch dock line after a week's use. One strand is gone and the rail is deeply gouged. A length of plastic or rubber hose will help to protect the line. If the end will not go through the hose, cut the hose spirally and snap it over the line. It is well to seize it to the line to prevent its working up or down.

Bowline—back view

*a. Turn around
bitt with bight
under.*

*b. Drop bight over
bitt and pull snug.*

*c. Circle bitt
again, bight under.*

*d. Drop bight over
bitt, pull snug.*

Only on big vessels using very heavy hawsers is a light heaving line necessary. A small yacht can usually get close enough to float or wharf to get a dock line ashore. The trick is to tie a bowline big enough to go over a piling easily. Make fast the bitter end of the line. Coil down the rest of the line on deck with the bowline end uppermost. Seize the loop about a quarter of the way around its circumference and in the same hand hold the standing part. This makes a fairly heavy handful. Hold in your left hand several big coils. Stand clear of the line coiled on deck, swing your right arm several times to build up momentum, and with your arm quite straight throw the line underhand, getting power from legs, waist, and shoulders. Finish the swing with your right

arm pointing at the target. Let the coils run freely off your left hand. When the man ashore has the line over a piling, take in slack, catch at least one turn around a bitt, and ease the line as the strain comes on. Keep your hands well clear of the pinch.

A vessel can be held close alongside under very difficult conditions with a single spring line and the engine. With the line over a piling abreast the vessel's stern, hold the spring on a bitt well forward. Run the propeller "slow ahead." As the bow comes in, turn the rudder gently away from the wharf to hold the stern in. When you are ready to leave, turn the rudder toward the wharf to skid the stern out. Reverse the propeller, then back until the line is slack and can be cast off and until the stern is well clear. Then go ahead, swinging the stern gently toward the wharf and the bow away. Take it slowly, use plenty of power, and you will look like a real steamboatman. (See Fig. 1, page 82.)

To make a vessel fast alongside in a berth where she is to lie for some time, use spring lines fore and aft (Fig. 2). In a small boat up to about forty-five feet, one pair of springs will suffice. Run one from the forward bitt aft to a piling astern and another from main sheet cleat or quarter bitt forward to a piling just ahead. A bowline leading from the bow to a piling just ahead of it and a stern line leading to one just astern will prevent the vessel's swinging her bow or stern off while the springs pre-

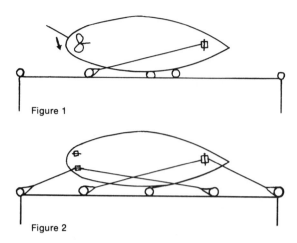

Figure 1

Figure 2

vent her from ranging ahead or astern. If there is considerable rise and fall of tide, make each line as long as possible so the rise of tide will make proportionately less difference in the length of the line required. At Saint John, N. B., and Grand Manan, where the tide rises twenty to twenty-five feet, fishermen are tied alongside with no need to tend lines with every tide.

When you must use a piling on which another vessel also has a line, do not just dump yours on top of his. Pass the eye in your line up through the eye in his and then put it over the pile. In this way either may cast off without disturbing the other's line.

Keep your dock lines and anchor rode clean and dry. Dock lines in particular get greasy and dirty. Soap, water, and elbow grease will get off the grease and remove abrasive particles of dirt. Dry the line well before stowing it. The manufacturers claim that synthetic rope like nylon is not subject to rot. However, to stow wet line in the confined space of a rope locker will make a musty, mildewy cave out of what should be sweet and clean. Natural fiber ropes, of course, will rot badly if stowed wet. All lines should be protected from heat and acid.

Probably your heavy lines will last as long as you do. However, you can tell when they begin to lose strength—they will look very round. The lay will be much less prominent than it is in a new line. Open up the lay and scratch the corner where the protected fibers turn over the edge of the strand to face the

weather. If the fibers break and fuzz up, the rope should be replaced at once.

Old line can be used as a bumper around the dinghy or the float or it can be stranded and pulled apart for rope yarns. Various kinds of ornamental work are easily done in pliable old rope and dress up a yacht or summer cottage. Anyway, don't throw it out. It will surely come good.

Splicing Nylon Line

The proper way to secure the end of a line to a shackle, an eyebolt, or a ring is to eyesplice it tightly around a split thimble. This protects the rope against chafe and eases the sharp bend the rope would have to take were there no thimble.

However, with nylon, polypropylene, or soft-laid dacron, a heavy strain accompanied by sudden sidewise jerks can so stretch and twist the line that the thimble pops out of the splice and turns over, releasing the line to chafe on whatever the splice is around. The Sailor spliced a thimble in the painter of his dory. After towing her through a violent head sea, he beheld what is shown in the picture.

To prevent this from happening, splice in the thimble loosely and put a heavy strain on the line with a tackle or a come-along. Then while the line is still tightly stretched, serve up the splice, squeezing the two parts of the line tightly together right up to the point of the

The splice jumped the thimble and chafed on the bronze eye.

The loose splice under tension

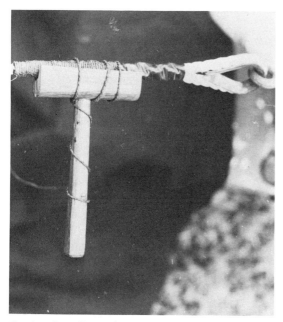

Serving the splice under tension

The finished splice with the tension relaxed

thimble. Use a serving mallet if there is room to swing it. If not, take an old leather mitten, cut off fingers and thumb, and sew a piece of stout leather to the back where the marline would otherwise cut your hand. Pull the marline as tight as you can without parting it. When the serving is finished off and the strain is released, the elasticity of the line will cause it to shrink very tightly around the thimble. The serving will take some of the strain too, preventing the splice from stretching.

Setting Up Rigging

The standing rigging of a modern Bermuda-rigged sailing yacht is a complicated and sensitive system that generates enormous strains. Consider first the athwartship pattern of a comparatively simple system. The purpose of the system is to keep the mast straight when the weight of wind in the sail comes on it. If the rigging is too slack on both lower and upper shrouds, the mast will bend just above the deck, taking some of the draft or belly out of the lower part of the mainsail. If the lower shrouds are tight and the upper ones slack, the mast will bend to leeward at the spreaders, taking the draft out of the upper part of the sail. If the upper shrouds are too tight and the lower ones slack, the mast will bend out to leeward in the middle, increasing unnaturally the belly in the luff of the sail and tightening abnormally the leach or after edge of the sail. If both shrouds are too tight on one side, the mast will stay more or less straight but the boat may go better on one tack than the other. Finally, if all shrouds are too tight, a tremendous compression strain is exerted on both mast and spreaders. If a spreader collapses under strain, the mast will probably go too. There ought to be just a little slack in the lee rigging.

Now consider the fore and aft support. Few modern yachts under forty feet carry running backstays or jumper struts. The mast is supported by a forestay and a permanent backstay, both running to the masthead. A measure of support is afforded by double lower shrouds, one forward of the mast and one aft. Again, we would like to have the mast stand straight, but also we would like the forestay to be bar taut, not to let the luff of the jib sag to leeward at all. At first glance, this can be accomplished by setting up the backstay and headstay in such a way that the mast is straight and both are humming taut. Should this develop a bow in the mast as a result of the heavy compression strain, the lower shrouds can take it out. To be sure, this increases the strain but it does remove the bend. On more careful consideration we see that under the strain of a big genoa sheeted aft with all the power of a winch operated by an athletic arm, the forestay and backstay must stretch a little. Even the substitution of rod for wire does not totally eliminate this. Also, the mast will respond to the increased compression strain exerted by both shrouds and fore-and-aft stays by compressing and bending a little. It is also possible, especially in an older boat, that the shape of the hull itself may respond by raising the sheer at the chain plates, buckling up the deck, and developing a "banana effect" by raising bow and stern. The result of all this is a slight sag in the forestay. Further efforts to eliminate this by further increasing the strain on shrouds and stays can lead only to decreasing, never to eliminating, the sag in the forestay. Something will part.

Notice that some insurance companies assess a penalty on boats with hydraulic tighteners.

Racing men, of course, must balance these strains against weight, developing the lightest possible rig that will stand the strain. However, the cruising man is not going to windward under the same physical and emotional strains and can afford to beat down the bay at a slightly more relaxed pace than the racing man going for the weather mark. To assure a happy cruise for his crew and a long life for his boat, he should carry a little slack in his lee rigging, a little sag in his forestay, and maybe even a slight bend in the top of his mast to ease the strain on mast, rigging, chain plates, and hull. A boat used successfully for cruising for several years when tuned up and sailed hard in an ocean race sheared off the bolts holding the stem head fitting to which the forestay was shackled.

Part of the fun of racing is its desperate nature. We "walk the duck to her," climb the weather rail, and let her roll her lee deck under. Port tack crowds starboard, just nips under his bow. Caution is drowned. We're in a boat race!

Spars are lost, sails blown out, boats capsized, and occasionally people are hurt; but seldom is any damage done that money won't fix, and triumph is worth it.

However, when the recklessness extends to design, construction, and fitting out, give pause. Masts are built so lightly that if it blows hard, they may collapse; if it doesn't, we may win. Boats are "skinned out." Useful navigational aids are forbidden. Sails are limited in number—who will take a storm jib? When ratings are lowered for going to sea short-handed, the game begins to look like Russian roulette.

5

Seamanship

Seamanship vs. Showmanship

To land at a float, whether with a steam yacht or a launch, the seamanlike way is to come in slowly with just enough way on to steer the boat. As you range alongside, the mate steps quietly ashore and passes a stern line around a stout cleat. With an easy squeak of the line, the yacht will swing her stern and her whole midship section gently against the float. Pass a bow line and you have her. No one even has to give an order.

The showman comes in at six knots and roars into reverse with a swirl of white water. The mate leaps six feet to the float and passes a line. It screeches around the cleat and the stern swings out. The skipper shouts profane orders through a bullhorn. Someone rushes aft with a stern line. Hastily coiled and flung, it falls short. And so goes the hurrah's nest. It may be good entertainment, but it is bad seamanship.

The *Sailor* would not even mention such an obvious point if he did not see yachtsmen who appear to think that such a splash and hurry is evidence of their command of the situation. Someone is likely to get hurt.

Maneuvering in Strong, Gusty Winds

We had stolen the weekend and were determined to go sailing on a blustery September

Saturday. Perhaps it would be the last sail of the season. We promptly got ourselves into one of the most awkward positions we have seen in almost half a century of yachting.

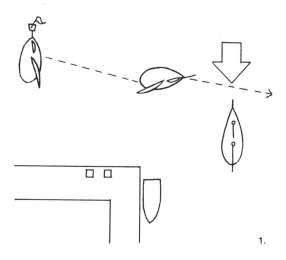

1.

Lying on the mooring, head to wind, we reefed the mainsail, cleared the staysail to hoist—being sure the downhaul would run clear—and put extra stops on the jib. We belayed both sheets at what would be about right for sailing with the wind abeam, for steering and trimming sheets would take more hands than we had. It seemed simple to drop the mooring, have the mate set the staysail, run aft to the wheel, and sail away, as shown in Drawing 1, above.

85

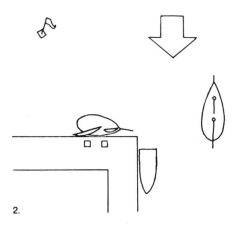

2.

Drawing 2 shows what happened. No sooner was the mooring gone and the staysail half set than the sloop quickly swung broadside to the wind and the mainsail filled. She heeled far down to starboard and, before she began to sail ahead, swept sideways down on the float. The two gas pumps on the float prevented slacking the main sheet, for the boom would have wiped them off. The wind and harbor chop had us plastered against the float. With the mainsail full, it would have been very difficult to lower. The skipper, standing at a wheel to which the vessel could not answer, contemplating a sail he could not lower, felt checkmated.

However, the vessel herself solved the problem. As she slammed and bounced against the float, she moved enough to gain a little headway, and scraped along the float. As her bow came clear, still without much steerage way, the staysail pushed it to leeward. As her side slid clear of the corner, she was already headed to leeward of the little schooner anchored off. Once clear, she leaped ahead, picked up steerageway, dragged the end of her main boom across the dodger on the stern of the cruiser moored on the front of the float, passed astern of the schooner, luffed, saluted the open-mouthed onlookers with a wave of her staysail boom, and turned herself over to the skipper again.

The incident tells us that when the wind gets up over twenty knots, we have to rethink the procedures for maneuvering in close quarters. In the situation just described, the thoughtful skipper would have known that before she began to sail ahead the sloop would take a knockdown. She was standing still, indeed floating astern, and swinging to take abeam a breeze that another skipper told us later was gusting to forty-three knots. With her rail underwater and her keel no longer vertical, with all the windage of spars and rigging above the reefed mainsail and of her upturned weather side, and with the mast inclined at a steep angle so the forward drive of the sails was not fully developed, she must slide bodily to leeward at no small pace. Once plastered against the float with no way to take the pressure off her by lowering the sail, there seemed to be nothing we could do for her.

How should the maneuver have been made?

One can only speculate, but perhaps had the mainsail been trimmed a little closer—not hard on the wind but generously full and by— and the staysail been quite slack, the mainsail would have filled earlier, the staysail would not have driven her off so hard, she might have picked up way more quickly and worked by the end of the float and ahead of the schooner. Maybe this is one of those circumstances for which we have an engine.

The problem of making a landing at a float or picking up a mooring must also be reconsidered in a strong breeze. Where under ordinary circumstances the skipper would come up to leeward of a float and range gently alongside, he finds that even though with a heavy breeze the boat moves much faster, she will not range against wind and chop nearly as far as she would in moderate conditions. Therefore, she must be sailed right up to the float.

This looks like a perilous situation. A boat weighing five to eleven tons moving at six to seven knots is to be stopped next to a float only as long as the boat. The boat must be close enough to pass two lines to the float and catch turns quickly before she drifts astern and puts a heavy strain on them. If she comes in too fast, she will tear the float up by the roots and perhaps hurt someone. If she comes too slowly, she will be in irons to leeward of the float, may fall off the wrong way, and drive ashore. There is a way to save this situation under sail and it is just as safe and easy as using the engine.

If your boat will sail under mainsail alone, take in everything else. A reefed mainsail with its center of effort farther forward may actually be handier than a full mainsail. Get into a position well away from the float—say about two hundred yards—and a little to leeward. Sailing full and by, you should be able to fetch the lee corner of the float comfortably. Head for it. As the vessel picks up speed, slack the main sheet a little and luff some. It helps a great deal to have a good man on the sheet, because trimming it is probably a two-hands job. Bring the boat in slowly, balanced between leeway and forward drive. Be sure to keep her moving ahead enough to steer her, and let her luff enough so she does not come charging in. When you get close enough, put the tiller hard to leeward, take a pull on the main sheet, and lay her alongside.

At this exciting moment with the sail snapping and cracking overhead, the chop splashing up between boat and float, and everything at a standstill for an instant, your mainsheet man must get out a spring line before the boat starts astern, and your foredeck hand must get out a bow line before the bow swings away from the float. If it is done properly, it is a neat and controlled maneuver with little likelihood of failure. If you are nervous about it, make a few practice runs well offshore.

Approaching a mooring, you can use the same method. You will find it easier than making a float, because if you miss, you can come around and try again. It is most important in

making a mooring to come in slowly enough so that the foredeck hand has time to get a turn on the bitt before a strain comes on the pennant. Once he has it, the sail should be snatched down at once, lest while she is taking up slack in the mooring line she pay off, fill the mainsail, and charge about the harbor.

If your yacht will not sail under mainsail alone, you will have to use your smallest headsail with the mainsail on the approach. Sheet it quite flat to hold her head to leeward so you can bear off when you want to. Filling the main will help you to bring her up. At the last moment, have the foredeck man take in the jib just before you lay her alongside.

Power boats have similar problems when the wind gets up, for many of them have high bows and deck structures and little grip on the water forward. Also, their rudders are small and require a vigorous stream of water in order to produce any significant turning effect. Remember, too, that the rudder does not turn the bow; it turns the stern *away* from the direction in which you turn the wheel. Also, with any considerable breeze, power must be kept on right up to the last moment.

Technique will vary with the particular boat. However, if you can approach from dead to leeward with enough forward motion to give good control, you will find that stopping will be no problem. A touch of reverse will do it. Lying alongside with the propeller turning slowly ahead against a forward spring line may be the easiest way to lie.

If you cannot approach from dead to leeward, come in on an angle, balancing leeway against the forward thrust of the propeller and the push of the rudder to leeward against the stern.

Suppose you find yourself in the position of the yacht in Diagram 4. In calm or moderate weather, you would round up under the stern of A, range slowly to windward, reverse on top of the mooring, giving the foredeck hand plenty of time to gaff it aboard, and then ring off the engine. When it is blowing, the solution is more complex.

As you pass the stern of A, moving slowly, turn the wheel to port. The rudder moves to port and starts the stern moving to

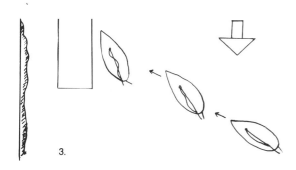

3.

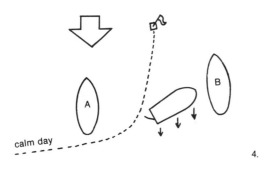

calm day

4.

starboard. However, the weight of the wind on the bow forces the bow to starboard, too, and the windage of hull and superstructure accelerates the drift. Consequently, the yacht moves bodily to starboard and a collision with B is imminent. If the skipper waits one second too long, it is inevitable. He cannot turn to starboard and go astern of B, for it is too late. If he hits the throttle hard in order to send a stream of water against the rudder and push the stern to starboard, he will either swing in broadside, or, as the yacht gains headway, either hit hard on the side of the bow or cuff the stern as the stern swings rapidly to starboard. To reverse with full power may save B, but it will put your yacht quite out of control, with the bow blowing down to leeward and no stream passing the rudder to control the stern. The secret of success is to go ahead strongly on the engine just as you start the turn. This will skid the stern to starboard more quickly than the bow can blow off and will get the stern to leeward of the bow. Then cut the power and ease up to the mooring going ''slow ahead.'' The man with the boat hook must show good form, for the boat cannot be held over the mooring for long. Once she loses way, the bow will blow off to one side or the other. To maintain control, should the mooring be missed, power must be vigorously applied and the stern swung quickly to leeward of the bow.

To get into a champion mess and to provide entertainment for the Sunday sports fishing off the wharf, approach the mooring too slowly, so the foredeck man can just reach it as the yacht loses way. Before he can get it aboard, the yacht will drop back and put a strain on it. In an effort to help, the helmsman

goes ahead on the engine, but the bow has swung off so the boat does not move directly toward the mooring but away at an angle. The foredeck man, one hand on the boat hook and one on the life rail, is pretty well stretched out. Either he drops the boat hook or he lets go the hand rail and goes overboard or the buoy line parts and the mooring goes to the bottom. In reversing to avoid B, the helmsman winds the dinghy painter in the propeller—and from there on the picture is too frightful to contemplate.

Hints on Light Weather Sailing

Plenty of books deal in frightening detail with the procedures for weathering hurricanes, but few have considered as carefully the solutions to problems of light weather sailing. The basic principle is to get the boat moving and then to maintain its momentum. This is especially true with a heavy cruising yacht.

First consider the rigging and set of your sails. The mainsail should be set full, with as much draft as you can get into it. This is achieved by easing the clew outhaul a little so the foot is straight but not bar taut and doing the same with the luff. Also ease the leach line. There probably won't be wind enough to flutter the leach and it certainly should not be allowed to curl up at all. Do not use the vang unless the sea is rough. With a gaff-headed sail, ease the peak enough to slack the leach, but not enough to make a hard ridge from throat to clew.

The jib should be set loosely too. The luff should be tight enough to eliminate as much sag as possible, but not so tight as to make wrinkles. A light set of sheets might be substituted for the usual half-inch dacron and the sheets can be tied directly into the clew of the sail, thus eliminating the weight (and expense) of a snap shackle. The snatch block for the sheet should be moved aft a little from its usual location to tighten the foot of the sail slightly and to ease the leach.

Of course you will use the biggest jib you have and will be ready with mizzen staysail, topsail, jib topsail, and any rag you can hang up. A jib hung under the main boom when sailing off the wind will catch air otherwise deflected under the boom. Attach the tack of the jib to the end of the boom and stretch the luff along the spar.

The next consideration is helmsmanship. Be alert. Most of your instruments, if you have them, will be useless. The feel of the wind on your face is the most useful instrument you will have. In going to windward, start by easing the main sheet a foot or two more than you would ordinarily do, and ease the jib as far as you can without luffing it. You may be sailing only six points (sixty-seven degrees) from the wind instead of the usual four points (forty-five degrees), but at least your boat will be moving through the water. As she gathers way, she will make a little more wind by her own forward progress and will pull it ahead a little. Maybe you can gently trim sheets a grind, but move cautiously and sacrifice distance to windward to forward progress.

Distribute people so that the boat is heeled slightly to leeward, thus, the weight of the boom will hold the sail out. Don't overdo it, for most boats are built to sail more or less upright. Urge people to sit still. Rushing about the boat will upset whatever balance you have achieved and destroy what momentum you have built up.

Avoid tacking, jibing, or sudden turns. Momentum once lost is very slowly regained. Sailing in company with another yacht in a ten-knot breeze, we had once occasion to luff. The other yacht at once gained on us, and long after we had borne away and were sailing full-and-by again, she continued to gain. If you tack, you will practically kill your forward progress and will have to build momentum all over again.

Seek the drafts coming down off the lee sides of islands and along shores against which the wind blows at an acute angle. Avoid the dead spots that build up to windward of points and headlands that the wind meets at right angles. Seek smooth water and fair tidal currents.

Watch other boats carefully. You can tell a great deal about where to hunt the breeze from their course, angle of heel (if any), and trim of their sails.

Try to avoid a situation in which you will have to run directly downwind, unless you have a spinnaker and a crew to set it. Not only is progress slow, but whatever progress you make decreases rather than increases the apparent wind, the force of the air which actually hits your sail. Also, whatever sea there is rolls you about, slats the wind out of your sails, collapses the jib, and renders you and your crew hot and uncomfortable. A broad reach with headsails full and a discernible motion of air is much more comfortable.

If the sea is sloppy and the weight of the boom is slatting the wind out of the sail, have someone lean against the boom to steady it. This is really better than a vang and easier than rigging a boom tackle forward, because it provides a steady and flexible forward pressure against the sheet without flattening the sail.

Above all, it should be reemphasized that the helmsman must stay alert to the feel of the wind, the set of his sails, and the progress of the boat through the water. However enthralling the conversation, he must not forget his job.

If the wind falls lighter and the sea is choppy, give up and start the engine. Your crew will applaud the decision, however disappointed you may feel; and you can take courage in remembering that "the wind bloweth where it listeth" and another day will be better.

Sailing Out of a Tight Spot

You are lying to a mooring in the sloop *Bowl* pretty well surrounded by other moored yachts and not far from a lee shore. Your engine, let us suppose, is out of action and you don't like your mooring, the proximity of the shore to leeward, or the way the wind and chop are building up. You decide to move to a more sheltered harbor.

It has begun to breeze up—eighteen knots already—and the situation looks awkward. If you swing off to starboard, on the port tack, you will foul *Cup* and both of you will land on the beach. If you swing to port, you cannot count on moving fast enough and going close enough astern of *Dipper* to tack between her and the dinghies tied to the float, now leaping in the building chop and slamming their gunwales together. Try the following plan:

Take a piece of strong light line (three-eighths-inch dacron, for instance), and whip the end so that no knot can prevent its running freely. Tie a bowline around the bitt under the mooring splice and pass the whipped line up through the splice, pulling through the whole length of line.

Set your mainsail and take the stops off the jib. Be sure everything is coiled down and is clear to run, with the jib halyard ready to hoist.

Now take the mooring pennant off the bitt and grab the light line coming up through the spliced loop. Slowly slack off this line until you are almost at the end of it, the vessel lying to the doubled line leading off her port bow, with the mooring buoy well out ahead. Make the end of the light line fast with a turn around the bitt and a bight tucked under the turn so it can be released by a quick pull on the end.

Set the jib with the sheet slack. There will now be tremendous slatting about, but ignore the noise. Make the jib sheet fast at about where it would be on a close reach (1). With wheel and main sheet in hand, ask your mate to push out the jib to port. The bow at once swings to starboard (2). Trim the main sheet; as soon as it fills, let the jib come over to starboard. At once the yacht starts to sail ahead but soon fetches up on the mooring as it pulls her bow to port.

Turn the wheel to port (tiller to starboard), have the mate hold the jib out to starboard, and tack. As she comes around, the mate will release the jib. Ease the main sheet a grind and sail with the wind abeam. She will quickly gather way (3), and this time as she comes up against the mooring (4), she will pull pretty hard. Again the mate holds the jib, this time to port, and you tack. This will leave you headed off on the port tack, still just to leeward of the mooring. The mate must release the jib and pull the end of the light line, freeing it from the bitt (5). Drop it and grab the bowline. Pull in as fast as possible, letting the light line reeve through the loop in the pennant.

You will now be abeam of the mooring, sailing fast and under good control. As the whipped end of the line zips through the splice in the pennant, you are free, and easily to windward of *Cup*. You can now pass between *Cup* and *Spoon* and go on your way.

It is well to be sure that your foredeck hand has a sharp knife, for should the whipped end foul the pennant, you are going to be ashore in short order with *Cup* and the dragged mooring around your neck. If it jams, he cuts; but he cuts your line, not the mooring.

This is a neat trick. It takes courage to do it under pressure the first time, so maybe a practice run is in order on a moderate day with no other boats around.

Practical Anchoring

Most sailing books recommend scope anywhere from three to seven times the depth of water and we have read of round-the-world sailors who rode out gales of wind with ten times as much scope as the depth of water. But in crowded New England harbors in the summer you can't go by the books.

If you anchor a thirty-foot boat in three fathoms with thirty fathoms of scope your stern will swing through a circle over four hundred feet in diameter. At seven times the depth you will swing about 310 feet, and at three times the scope you will occupy a circle over half as wide as a football field. How, then, does one anchor with any degree of safety in a crowded harbor?

There are several factors working in your favor. The water is comparatively shallow, the bottom is mud or clay, the harbor is well protected so that it is unlikely any big sea will get up. Also, you will be either aboard or nearby to keep an eye on the weather.

Add two other factors in your favor. Use as heavy an anchor as you can conveniently handle. Thirty-five pounds isn't too much to haul without a winch. Any anchor less than twenty pounds is largely decorative, even on a small boat. Second, use about three fathoms of five-sixteenths or three-eighths chain between the anchor and the rode.

90

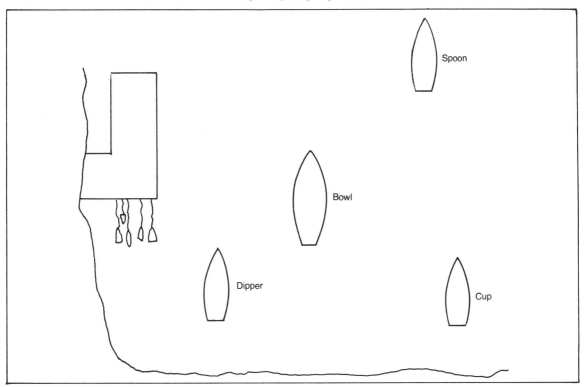

Figure 1

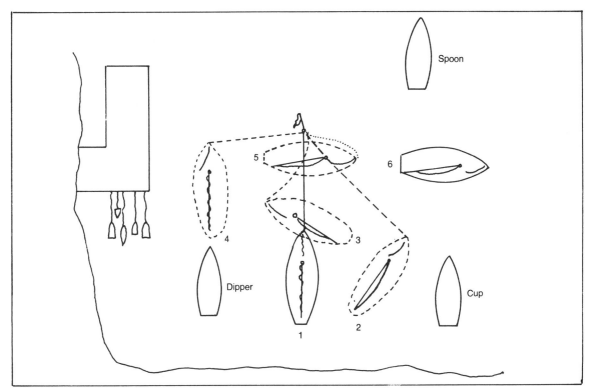

Figure 2

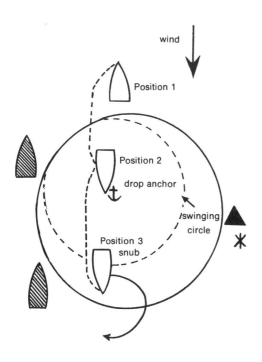

wind

Position 1

Position 2

drop anchor

swinging circle

Position 3

snub

Finally, you can anchor so that the hook really takes hold and does not just rest on its elbow on the mud. Do it this way. First, as you sail in, take your time and look around. Pick out the biggest hole you can find among the anchored yachts. Then sail gently up to windward of the hole, luff, and drop mainsail and jigger (Position 1). Be sure the anchor is on deck or hanging over the side and that all the gear is clear to run.

When the mainsail comes down, turn the yacht sharply on her heel, slack the jib sheet, and sail gently down the wind into the "hole" where you plan to lie. With about one fourth of the hole astern, drop the jib and let go the anchor, paying out scope freely (Position 2). As you begin to come close to the first boat to leeward, snub her up hard on the bit (Position 3). She will put her nose down in shocked surprise and spin her stern around. The line will squeak on the bitt and you will notice the taut line twist a little as it stretches. The anchor will dig in halfway to China and take solid hold.

Before you go ashore, take in enough scope to float you about in the middle of the space available. The anchor rode will take

quite a steep angle, but as long as the wind does not come on to blow hard, you will be all right.

If It Blows in the Night

If you find yourself anchored on short scope in a crowded harbor with your anchor well set by your having sailed it in, you probably are safe enough on a quiet night.

However, if you are awakened by the "whooo" of wind in the rigging, the squeak of anchor rode on the bitts, and a swash of a chop breaking alongside, you cannot trust an anchor on short scope. With your pajamas snapping around your ankles, slack off as much as you can without hitting anyone. Remember that boats with high bows are likely to sail around their anchors as the wind gets up, so make allowance for this, especially if your own boat has this bad habit.

If the anchor rode now leads out from the bow and meets the water at an acute angle, you are probably all right. Line up a couple of lights ashore or watch your position relative to some fixed object, not another boat, for a while.

If you are not satisfied that the anchor is holding firmly, there are two things you can do. First, slide a piece of ballast down the anchor line on a big shackle. This turns the strain on the anchor in a more nearly horizontal direction and also acts like a spring to take some of the jerk and snap out of the strain.

If the wind continues to increase and the future looks to be in question, it is time to turn out the crew for anchor exercise. Get your big anchor on deck and have your crew lower it gently into the stern of the dinghy. It is better to row the dinghy than to use the outboard for this maneuver because you can hold her under the bow more easily with oars. Also, with you, a big anchor, and the motor in the stern of a dinghy, and with the drag of the anchor rode astern, you may find that she will not look up into the wind.

Row to windward, making an angle with the original anchor rode of forty-five to sixty degrees. Take out all the line, which your crew has been passing out as you rowed, and dump the anchor overboard.

Back aboard, take a good strain on the new anchor to get a solid bite, divide the strain between the two, turn in, and sleep soundly.

Trip Lines and Foul Anchors

If you want your new anchor to live a long and useful life, use a trip line on hard bottom. As the diagrams and pictures show, this is merely a way of tripping the anchor intentionally. It shifts the strain from the shank to the commercial end of the anchor. For anchoring in mud, sand, or clay, a trip line is unnecessary, but on rocky bottom or where the bottom may be foul with old moorings, it is almost a necessity.

Bend a light line a little longer than the depth of the water to the crown or fluke of the anchor and attach a buoy to the other end of the line. Coil the trip line down carefully on the foredeck. As the rode goes out and the trip line comes taut, drop the buoy. It will float out ahead of the yacht as she drops back.

When you are ready to go, haul the anchor in the usual way. If it is caught in the bottom, gaff up the buoy, which will now be floating under the bow, slack the rode, and put a strain on the trip line. The anchor should now come up easily.

If you are anchored with a trip line and the anchor breaks out without your having to use it, the trip line with the buoy on the end will stream out astern as you gather way. Get it in quickly before you put your engine in gear or it will almost certainly foul the propeller.

Fishermen use a variation on the trip line when anchoring on rocky bottom to fish. The rode is attached to the crown of the anchor and then seized to the ring with two or three turns of marline. The line is *not* passed through the ring, thus the marline takes the

full strain of the boat. If the anchor is "caught down," the rode is pulled taut. Every time the boat goes down on a sea, a little more line is gathered in. When she tries to rise to a sea, a heavy strain is put on the rode. This parts the marline, the strain comes on the crown of the anchor, and it breaks out easily. Obviously, this is not an arrangement one should use if he were anchoring for the night or were to leave the yacht, for a marline seizing is nothing to bet your boat on.

If your anchor fouls and you have no trip line rigged, there are several things you can try before cutting the rode and abandoning the anchor.

1. If you are under sail, try sailing it out. Veer scope about equal to the depth of water, in addition to what is out when the rode is up and down. Set mainsail and jib. Back the jib. As the mainsail fills, sheet the jib to leeward. The yacht starts to sail ahead and brings up short on the rode. This forces her to tack. As she comes about, sheet the jib on the new lee side and sail across the anchor. Again she will bring up hard and be forced about. This time as you cross the anchor, gather in scope and catch a couple of quick turns on the bitt. She will hit the rode hard when it is almost up and down. Something ought to give.

2. The next alternative is to let out all the scope you can and run a circle around the anchor with the engine, keeping a heavy strain on it all the way. If nothing happens, turn and circle the other way. That ought to twist her out!

3. You might get it, particularly on a

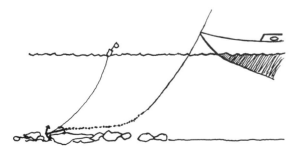

stockless anchor like a Danforth or a CQR, by tying a running bowline around the rode and weighting the loop with a sounding lead or a piece of ballast. With the rode up and down, drop the loop to the bottom in the hope that it will go down over the shank of the anchor and pull from the lower end like a trip line. Go off in the skiff to tighten the loop so you can pull on it at as much of an angle as possible. Then slack the rode and pull straight up on the trip line.

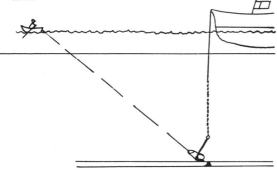

4. There is one more "last chance" alternative. At low water, heave the rode as taut as you can, make it fast around the mast with a stout rope stopper, and wait for the tide. This will put an increasing strain on the rode until something lets go. Of course it is possible that nothing will let go and your yacht will stand on her head. When this situation develops, be sure the rode is slack and that everyone is standing clear. Then cut the stopper.

5. A diver with scuba gear is your final recourse, but he may cost more than a new anchor.

Foul Hawse

A boat lying to two anchors as she swings to shifting winds and tides is almost certain to twist the anchor lines around each other. With one line out on each side of the headstay, one must clear them either by turning the boat around several times or by getting out in a skiff under the bow and passing the coil of one line around the other—a tedious job at best.

By accident I discovered an easier alternative. Lying in an anchorage beset by swirling tides, I needed a second anchor to prevent swinging into other boats and to prevent fouling my first anchor. The water was not deep,

so I bent my little fishing anchor to the bitter end of the first anchor line and led it from the *same* side of the headstay as the first anchor. Having rowed out all the line available and taken a strain, I had only a fathom or so of line left aboard in a bight to make fast to the bitt, both ends being in the water.

Of course, she wound up the lines under her bow as she swung to wind and tide over a period of several days. However, when it was time to go, I had but to clear the bight of the line from the bitt and the chock and untwist it from the deck.

Even if you have to use two separate anchor lines, if they lie on the same side of the headstay, the untwisting can be done from the foredeck, where a heavy coil of line is much easier to handle than it is in a tiddly skiff under the bow. Extra care must be taken, of course, to parcel the lines against chafe, for one of them is certain to be pulling across the stem at first; and after they twist up, they will chafe heavily on each other if there is any sea running.

A Second Anchor

In addition to the vessel's ordinary working anchor, she usually carries a bigger one and a smaller one, neither of which is much used.

The heavier one is, of course, an insurance anchor. The threatening hurricane, the heavy squall, even the smokey sou'wester in an exposed anchorage will be reason to wrestle the big one on deck. Its weight depends less on the size of the boat than the strength of the skipper. Few of us can handle much over seventy-five pounds in the awkward shape of an anchor. If the boat needs one bigger than this, it should be carried lashed down on deck where two men can get at it simultaneously, but with weights like this a windlass is practically necessary. One helpful solution is the Luke anchor.

Opinion differs widely on the most useful shape for a heavy anchor. Many favor the Danforth. There can be little doubt that it is a powerful device, once dug in. There are those of us, though, who have hauled a Danforth a considerable distance across a hard bottom, even with long scope. The Herreshoff anchor, a slight variation on the traditional stock-and-fluke type, is not very efficient for its weight but is easier to dig in, and once well planted is unlikely to drag. The possibility of the rode's fouling the projecting fluke as the vessel swings is not important when it is used as a second anchor, for the vessel will not swing around it. It is good in almost any kind of bottom, even eel grass, which will choke a Danforth or a plow. The latter, besides being choked by grass, is sometimes slow to take hold but has enormous holding power once dug in.

Whatever kind and weight of anchor you favor will be of little use unless it is laid out properly. Sad experience teaches that a length of chain next to the anchor is important. This is partly to resist chafe on rocks at the bottom, partly to keep the rode next to the anchor lying flat so it does not foul the anchor or break it out every time the vessel swings slightly, and partly to put sag in the line and keep the strain on the anchor as nearly horizontal as possible.

One may reasonably interrupt here to ask why one does not use chain exclusively. Many people do, and Hal Roth, an experienced world-wide voyager, insists upon it. But for the coastwise vacation cruising man, who anchors every night, there are objections. The first is the weight of a chain rode. One hundred and fifty feet of five-sixteenth-inch chain weighs about 175 pounds. That is quite a weight to carry in the bow of a small yacht when added to the weight of a storm anchor. Furthermore, if you use chain, you need a windlass, and that is heavy too. Also, someone has to pull that anchor. In five fathoms of water, the chain alone will weigh about thirty-five pounds. And chain is hard on the hands.

Although it is true that the weight of the chain makes a fine sag to keep the strain on the anchor horizontal and serves as a spring to ease the jerks produced by heavy seas, when the chain becomes nearly taut under heavy strain both of these advantages are lost. Chain has no elasticity whatever, and under storm conditions will jerk the anchor violently from no very advantageous angle.

Finally, chain is quite expensive. Five-sixteenths galvanized chain is listed at about two dollars per foot.

If we use a combination of chain and nylon rope, we have advantages of both. Three or four fathoms of chain will prevent chafe, keep the rode next to the anchor flat on the bottom in moderate conditions, and provide some spring. In heavier weather, the nylon will provide stretch to cushion shocks. It is lighter to stow, easier on the hands, lighter and easier to haul, and much less expensive. The chain should be shackled to the ring of the anchor with the heaviest shackle whose pin will go through an end link of the chain. The pin should be greased, set up tightly, and well moused with stainless-steel seizing wire so under no circumstances can it turn. The nylon rode should be loosely spliced around a split thimble too large for it. Then it should be pulled as hard as possible with a windlass, come-along, or a tackle. The splice will pull away from the thimble under strain. While still under strain, the splice should be tightly served with marline to pull the two parts tightly together against the point of the thimble. Thus it is unlikely that the eye will stretch and allow the thimble to capsize and chafe the unprotected line against the shackle connecting nylon and chain. This shackle, too, should be greased and moused.

The bitter end of the nylon should be whipped and the very end sealed with a match. Do not touch the melted nylon. It is very hot, clings to the fingers, and gives a painful burn. The end should then be tied around the mast or bitt below decks so it cannot escape.

The most important consideration in laying out a second anchor is to do it soon enough. If you wait until the wind is singing in the rigging and the sea is rough enough to plunge the bow deeply into each wave, you will be working on a wet and unstable platform under tense conditions.

The practice of taking a second anchor out in a dinghy is a relic of the days of sail. It is a difficult and dangerous procedure and usually involves dumping anchor and chain overboard in a heap—a two-man job under the best of circumstances. It is a great deal better to lay out anchor, chain, and line on the foredeck and then to motor ahead and out to one side, dragging the slack line of the first anchor from the bow, and then to lower the second anchor to the bottom. As the boat drops back, pay out chain and line so the chain lies on the bottom well away from the anchor. Before the first line comes taut, take a strain on the second anchor line to set it firmly into the bottom and then even up the strains on the two.

The final touch to the rig is the generous application of chafing gear in the chocks. Layers of canvas or burlap firmly lashed to the rode so it cannot slide up or down will do very well. Even better is a length of hose cut in a spiral and snapped over the line.

Should the weather deteriorate further and get really dangerous, ease off on both lines to provide maximum scope, readjust chafing gear, and slide weights down the rodes a little more than halfway. "When you have reached the end of your rope, tie a knot and hang on."

Should conditions moderate, turn in. A second anchor induces sound sleep.

A Light Anchor

Any cruising boat should carry a light anchor, by which I mean just enough anchor to hold the yacht in good conditions with someone around to keep an eye on her. Something between ten and twenty pounds is about right. It is big enough to hold you while fishing and is a great deal easier to haul up out of 100 feet of water than your usual cruising anchor. What if it does drag a little?

If you are caught in a foul tide and light air, you can lie to the light anchor until the tide turns or the wind comes in enough to move you.

If you must anchor for the night in a tidal river or any harbor where you lie to the tide, you can use the light anchor to prevent you from swinging all over the neighborhood. Bend the light anchor to the bitter end of the rode you are lying to and carry it out on the same side of the headstay or bow pulpit as you carry the anchor to which you are lying. Take

it out far enough to use up most of the rode. This will help to disentangle the anchor lines after they have become twisted together as the boat swings. Instead of hauling the small anchor first and passing the heavy coil of wet roding around, over, and under the other line, simply slack off on both lines until you find yourself holding the bight of the line and untwist it.

There are some harbors where a stern anchor will keep you lying bow or stern to the swell when otherwise you would lie across it and roll interminably. Monhegan, Georges Harbor, Little Harbor at Portsmouth and Tarpaulin Cove are examples on the New England coast.

Another use for the little anchor is to pull the vessel's stern around so she will lie with the stovepipe on the lee side, thus stimulating the draft. Often the stove will not draw at all with the pipe on the weather side but will blow back, to fill the galley with smoke, and drive the cook on deck with streaming eyes. A bucket over the smoke head helps, but getting the stovepipe to leeward removes the cause.

In rigging the little anchor, it is well to use a short piece of chain to prevent chafe against sharp rocks or the cans, broken bottles, and other detritus with which many harbors are carpeted. Shackle the chain around the crown of the anchor, be it kedge, plow, or Danforth, and take two turns of stout marline through a link and the ring. If the anchor gets "caught down," a heavy strain on the rode from directly above the anchor will part the turns of marline, capsize the anchor, and permit you to bring it easily on deck without the nuisance of a trip line. Of course, it would be folly to go ashore and leave the yacht lying to such a rig, but the premise is that the light anchor is used in conjunction with the regular anchor or that someone remains aboard.

For such purposes as we suggest, a separate rode need not be carried. Most wise skippers carry enough spare line to rig a new main halyard or main sheet. This should be long enough and strong enough to serve as a rode for the light anchor, and as it is used but seldom, it will not hurt the spare line.

The little anchor is easily stowed in

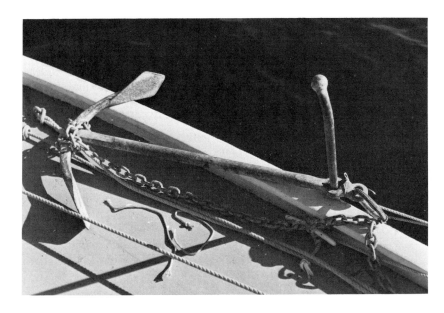

chocks on deck where it is quickly available, and the coil of rode is light enough so that it can be hung on a hook in the forepeak, whence it can be quickly pulled on deck through the fore hatch. The wise skipper will stop the coil with marline or sail twine in three or four places.

Thus, the well found cruising yacht should have at least three anchors: a storm anchor as big as the owner can conveniently handle, a working anchor sufficient to hold the yacht in ordinary conditions in a protected harbor, and a light anchor for the uses described above. The storm anchor and working anchor should each have its own rode, the length dependent on the depth of water to be expected. About 200 feet is enough for most coastwise cruising. With a piece of stout chain next to the anchor and nylon rode spliced around a thimble, stretched, and served with marline, and with a convenient means of running a weight down each of the heavy lines, you should be able to sleep soundly under anything but the most desperate circumstances.

The Rode Rider

You may come on deck some morning in the small hours to find the rain blowing out straight and a mean chop building up. The yacht throws her bow up to the rising sea and yanks upward sharply on the anchor rode. The wind and sea drive her back hard and the rode stretches. Between puffs the weight of the chain and the elasticity of the nylon pull her ahead. She swings away from the next puff, sails ahead at an angle to the wind, fetches up hard on the rode, tacks, and sails across the wind to bring up again, yanking and twisting the anchor. Getting another anchor on deck and setting it from the dinghy is at best a risky procedure. It is time for the Rode Rider.

This is simply a heavy bronze tube hinged to open lengthwise and fit over the rode. A shackle holds the parts together and supports a heavy weight such as a thirty-pound chunk of ballast. Snap the Rode Rider around the rode, shackle on a weight, bend a light line to the eye provided, and slide the Rider down the line about two-thirds the distance to the anchor. The situation improves at once. When the yacht rears back on a sea, she cannot pull the rode tight and yank the anchor, for she must lift the weight first. The higher the weight is lifted, the nearer the rode is to becoming straight, the harder it is to lift it further. To straighten out the line entirely would take infinite strain.

As the sea passes under the yacht, the strain eases and the weight sinks, but at no time can the rode go slack, so there is always a strain on the rode, holding the vessel's head to

The Rode Rider

ham, Massachusetts 02026 for less than twenty dollars.

Of course, you can merely hang a weight from a shackle fitted over the rode, but a shackle is more likely to chafe the line than is the Rode Rider. You could have a blacksmith make an iron shackle with the central part wider and curved up so that no sharp edges touch the line, but this is likely to be as expensive as the Rode Rider and to take a long time in the making. You may seldom need the fitting, but it is a handy thing to have in the locker.

the wind. Therefore, she is much less likely to yaw with the strain on her bow holding her to windward.

If the wind shifts slowly, she will walk around the anchor, changing the direction of her pull on it gradually, and never letting the rode get slack enough to foul a fluke. Should the anchor bread out as the result of a sudden wind shift, the Rode Rider, lying on the bottom and causing the anchor to pull parallel to it, will make it easy for the anchor to get a new bite quickly.

The Rode Rider is available from James Bliss and Company, Route 128, Exit 61, Ded-

Notes From the Sailmaker: Sea Anchors

Nathaniel S. Wilson

Under some conditions storm sails are not enough to heave a vessel to. Sometimes it is

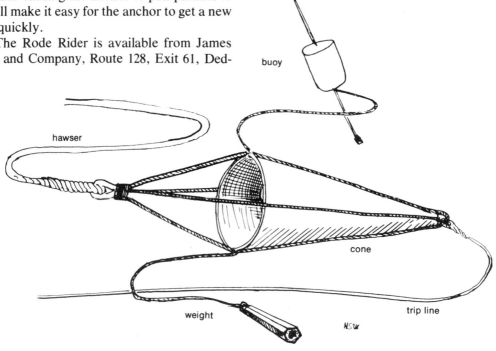

98

possible to drag a long line from the bow that will make enough drag to make the bow lie within several points of the wind. In small vessels under fifty feet a proper sea anchor may be the best solution. There can be many variations to the design, but it is important to keep it simple and effective. In theory the anchor is not to go to the bottom and hold but must lie about a fathom below the surface and yield somewhat to the pressure of wind and sea. A weight may be needed to sink the sea anchor, and a marker is attached to show its position when it is set. When the time comes to haul in the anchor, one may find the drag sufficient to make the hearty weary. With a trip line attached to the small end of the anchor, it can be easily collapsed and hauled aboard.

The cone-type anchor is an old and proven design. It can be adapted to almost any size of vessel and is easily stowed. What size anchor is required for your boat? The diameter of the opening in the cone should equal in inches the waterline length of your boat in feet. The cone sea anchor is constructed of heavy canvas. Heavy dacron can also be used, about twelve- or fourteen-ounce. The cone is constructed of four triangular cloths heavily roped. The opening is maintained by an iron ring.

To use the anchor, a heavy nylon hawser, led through the hawse pipe or chocks at the bow, is attached to the bridle at the open end of the cone. The trip line is attached to the tapered end. Both trip line and hawser are coiled clear to run free. The helmsman rounds the vessel up, way is reduced, and she is hove to. As she pays off to leeward, the cone is lowered into the sea, and both trip line and hawser slacked away. It may require 250 to 300 feet of line to get the advantage of the hawser's elasticity and drag. The hawser is made fast to the bitts or around the mast. Chafing gear at the chock is very important.

With the sea anchor holding properly, the boat will ride easily and fairly dry. The bow should be two or three points off the wind. You may find that no sail is required once the anchor is out. You may have to try different combinations of sail and rudder angle to get proper trim.

Should you lose your sea anchor, one can be improvised. A dinghy can be swamped and used as a sea anchor. Also, spars can be lashed together and a bridle attached to their ends. To get more drag, the luff of a small sail may be lashed along the spar and an anchor attached to the clew to create an effective drag.

If you are thinking of taking a long cruise offshore, consider adding a sea anchor to your equipment. You may never need it, but it is good insurance, and if you need it, you will need it badly.

While the cook gets breakfast, have all hands roll up their pantlegs and wash down decks with mop and bucket. Done daily, this keeps the corners and scuppers clear of the accumulation of soot, sand, cigarette ashes, and crumbs. It keeps the deck tight and is good for the crew, too.

Running Aground

Don't Run Your Boat Ashore

"If you have never run ashore, you have never been anywhere," said the old salt. Running ashore is as sure as sin, but *don't* let it happen on *this* cruise.

Some shipwrecked skippers are violently surprised by the sudden jolt of keel on rock. "I had no idea there was a rock there! It is 'uncharted'!" It happens to many of the most experienced. I have seen a fishing vessel high and dry on a ledge because the helmsman had a transistor radio next to the compass. An experienced party boat skipper and former naval officer put his vessel on a rock one calm evening in his own home waters and had to call the Coast Guard to take off his passengers. Five destroyers proceeding down the West Coast at night in thick weather with perfect confidence in their confident leader piled up side by side in a multi-million-dollar shipwreck.

Protection against this sort of disaster is psychological. The skipper must cultivate a suspicious disposition *as a habit*. The local chart should always be spread out where he can quickly refer to it, parallel rules and dividers nearby. A quick cross-bearing—one need not make a big show of it—will assure him that he is where he intends to be. A glance at the sounding machine will confirm it. When two islands come in line, he can lay his rule on the chart and be sure that all is well. When he passes a buoy he notes the set of the tide and is suspicious of a clump of lobster traps or of another vessel changing course ahead of him. He is ever alert for the galvanized bucket left next to the compass by the enthusiastic fisherman and is ready tactfully to relieve the helmsman who is eating a sandwich with one hand, holding a beer can in the other, telling a story with both hands, and steering occasionally. The skipper's wary state of mind must become habitual. He must put it on when he leaves the mooring—like a mental seat belt.

Sometimes the skipper can see disaster coming and can do nothing but helplessly watch it happen. I have seen a disabled powerboat drifting toward a lee shore, the skipper pulling violently and helplessly on the starting cord, the mate waving the ensign upside down and shouting for help. Ashore, the cottagers waved back in friendly fashion. Often a sailing yacht getting underway will sag into her neighbors before she gathers steerageway or without way enough to tack or room enough to swing off before the wind and jibe, will slip sideways ashore, the skipper standing helplessly with helm a-lee.

Some people have engines always ready to respond instantly to the starter button. However, before a boat can turn sharply under power, she must be moving ahead. A burst of power from the propeller may just jam her hard aground before she finishes her turn. And the iron mule may balk when most needed.

There are two time-tested items that will give the skipper another chance in such situations. The first is a light anchor with a long length of light roding kept under the fore hatch, ready to drop instantly. I saw an old gentleman in a small sloop miss stays off a rocky shore. With no undue haste he stepped forward and dropped his anchor off the weather bow. He came aft, sheeted his jib, and sailed directly for the shore, still without enough way to tack. At the last minute he cast off jib sheet, went forward again, and hauled on his anchor line. The sloop stopped short, turned in her own length, and sailed back over the anchor as he took in slack. He lifted the anchor aboard, stepped back to the tiller, trimmed sheets, and continued unperturbed.

The disabled powerboat can often be held off a lee shore with a light anchor, even in deep water with a considerable sea running. The anchor should be light enough to be handled quickly and easily. Length of roding is far more important than strength. Modern synthetic lines are so strong that a three-eighths-inch line will be big enough for the purpose and will stow compactly enough so the forepeak can accommodate up to two hundred feet of it.

The other defense against approaching disaster is a long oar, with rowlocks on the stern and on each gunwale. With a little practice in smooth water, one can learn to scull over the stern. With a ten-foot oar held in both hands, a practiced man can move a surprisingly heavy vessel against the wind. The motion is a figure-eight from side to side. Once the vessel is moving, she can be kept moving

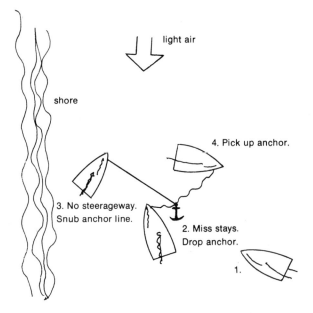

shore

light air

4. Pick up anchor.

3. No steerageway. Snub anchor line.

2. Miss stays. Drop anchor.

1.

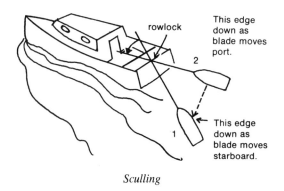

rowlock

This edge down as blade moves port.

This edge down as blade moves starboard.

2

1

Sculling

quite easily at a rate of perhaps one knot—anyway, enough to move her *away* from the rocks. In rough water, sculling is much more difficult and less efficient, but it can be done. Bahamians often scull their sloops for long distances in calm weather.

The rowlocks on the gunwales are particularly useful on sailing vessels. A few vigorous strokes with an oar on the lee side can give you a little steerageway and help the vessel to come about. In quiet weather, fishermen without power used to stand to the tiller with an oar in a rowlock to leeward and with one hand gently, steadily, push her ahead and to windward, providing a little forward motion to increase the effect of a gentle breeze and prevent undue sag to leeward.

Granted a ten-foot oar is an awkward affair to carry, but it is not nearly as awkward as being aground.

Getting Off the Bottom

If you just "tunk" her a little on a ledge or slide onto the mud on a coming tide, you will have no trouble getting off. Let fly all sheets and swing the bow toward deep water, either by pushing with a long oar or by running out an anchor and pulling the bow around. Then get all hands forward, sheet everything down hard, and run the engine ahead two bells and a jingle. With the forward drive of both sails and engine, the strain on the line, and the reduced draft caused by the weight forward and the heeling effect of the sails, she ought to slide off. If she won't come, try rocking her a little

to give her a start and to break suction. If she still won't come, shut off the engine, take in sail, and keep a steady pull on the anchor line. Don't pull too hard or the anchor will just come home through the mud or sand. The coming tide will soon lift you off.

If some good samaritan comes rushing up in a powerboat offering to pull you off, you may do well to refuse his assistance. The tide is coming, you will soon be off anyway, and you may do your boat more harm than good by hauling her over the bottom.

However, if the tide is well up and is ebbing when you run ashore, you will have to move fast to get her off, for her buoyancy decreases rapidly as the water leaves her. A drop of two inches in tide will cause a twenty-five-foot cruising-type boat to bear down on the bottom with a force of about fifteen hundred pounds. With a tidal range of six feet, the tide drops about a foot an hour. In a little over five minutes, your boat will weigh a ton, and this is a weight you will not move by getting out and pushing. If she has struck hard enough to slide up on the ledge or bar, you won't move her anyway.

Let us assume, however, that she is not very hard aground. Slack sheets at once, move everyone forward, and try the engine in reverse. It probably won't do any good, though, for marine engines have very little power in reverse. Try rocking her a little. While this is going on, have someone get the anchor into the dinghy and run it out astern. Lead the rode through the stern chock, and with everyone still forward, put a strain on it. If she won't slide off the way she went on, carry the rode forward and try to turn the bow toward deep water. Trim sheets, crack on the power, rock her, and see if she will come. If not, you will probably have to lay over the tide.

About this time, your friend in the motorboat may appear to tow you off. If the tide has not gone too far, it may be worth a try. However, if your boat has a detached rudder or a very short, deep keel, you may do more damage by pulling her off than by letting her lie over the tide. Should you decide to give it a try, remember that it is your boat, and the

101

responsibility for handling forces greater than those you usually encounter is yours. Take command yourself.

Get the crew onto the tow boat if you can do it quickly. It will get them out of harm's way and will relieve your boat of that much weight. Make the tow line fast to a bitt or to the mast. No cleat, even one that is through-bolted, will stand the strain of an enthusiastic helping hand on the throttle of someone else's boat.

The Sailor cannot too frequently or too forcefully remind his readers of the danger of a snap-back from a parting line. A tow line could kill a man. A one-fourth-inch pot warp could inflict a painful wound.

Urge the tow boat to take up the strain gently. The line will come taut, squeeze the water out of itself, and begin to stretch. You will be hard aground and the tow boat will be moving slowly ahead, stretching the line, and feeling sure that he is moving you. Before he stops moving, before the line reaches its elastic limit and parts, signal him to ease off.

Unless your crew is in danger, there is not much use in calling the Coast Guard. They will probably refuse to pull you off anyway, because ungrateful owners whose boats have been damaged have sued them. You will have to lay over until the tide comes again.

You are now in for an anxious, wet, dirty ordeal. For the first hour or so, you will have to work fast. Decide first whether to let your boat lie over on her side or to hold her upright.

The short-keeled boat with a detached rudder probably won't stand on her keel without excessive strain. She is likely to fall forward on her face or to pivot on her keel and fall over sideways. A yacht with a long keel may rest comfortably on it. Thus, she will avoid the danger of starting a plank or breaking a frame by resting much of her weight on a small area of her planking as she lies over on the bottom.

Suppose you decide to hold her up. You are going to balance her on her keel, leaning a little *away* from the side that affords the strongest support. At once, before the tide goes any further, heel her that way. Assume a convenient tree or boulder ashore. If there is none, your biggest anchor on the longest scope is the best you can do. Attach the rode to your strongest halyard and run it to the masthead. A sheet bend is the best knot for this work. Seize the two parts of the rode together and take a half hitch around the standing part of the halyard as in the accompanying illustration. Run out your next heaviest anchor on the other side and rig it the same way. Then take up on your first line and pull the yacht nearly upright. Take a modest strain on the other halyard to prevent anything from tipping her the wrong way and throwing a heavy strain on the weaker side. A spare anchor or a pig of ballast hung on the weaker line will help to steady her.

Be sure any loose rocks are out from under the keel as she settles. Tend the lines as the water leaves her until she is solidly on the

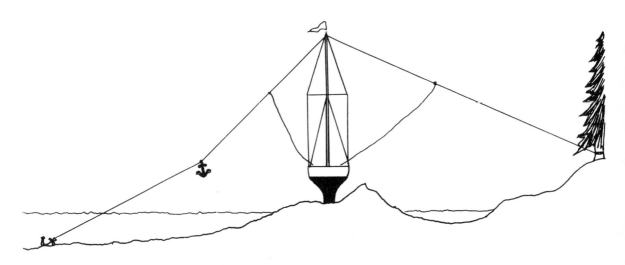

bottom. Then leave her. The less jiggling, the better. You can shove some shores under her bilge, but be certain that the top of the shore has a wide bearing on the plank.

When she is high and dry, you can make any necessary emergency repairs, but do no heavy hammering. When the tide comes, collect your gear, get an anchor into deep water, and slide her off as she floats. If it is rough, it may be well to arrange for a tow boat so she will pound no longer than necessary.

Should you decide to let her lie over on her side, you will have a great deal of hard work to do in a hurry. First, heel her to the side you want her to lie on. Other things being equal, it is better for her to lie "uphill," but it is most important that she lie on the smoothest bottom possible. Move loose rocks to provide as wide and smooth a bed as you can. You will probably be working in water waist deep, with the boat heeled toward you, so it won't be easy. As the tide goes, shove under her any kind of padding you can find to spread her weight onto as wide a bearing surface as possible. If you are lucky you might find some two by six planks near high-water mark. A number of round logs of about the same size with the cabin floor boards on top of them would be good. Push your life preservers in on top of the boards as the bilge comes down.

While this is going on, your crew should be busy aboard the boat. Large water tanks can be emptied to relieve some of the weight, especially if their fastenings are at all in question. Shut off all valves in fuel and gas lines. The hull will be under great strain and may twist in unforeseen ways, possibly starting pipe and tubing connections. Batteries should be taken ashore if possible so they can be kept level. If they must stay aboard, chock them up so they will not spill, and strengthen supports so they cannot shift. Remove from the elevated side any heavy things that might fall across the cabin. Close and latch doors and drawers. Remove or drain kerosene lamps whose gimbals may not allow swing enough to keep them up upright. Extinguish every spark of fire and allow no smoking, for enough gasoline could spill from a carburetor or feed line to blow up your boat.

Once the boat is resting firmly on her bilge, she will go no farther, and what has not come adrift already will probably stay. Do not try to lift her with a pry. You may punch a hold in her.

When the tide comes, will she rise? If she has a narrow, water-tight cockpit, she probably will. A wide cockpit or a raised deck hull with big "windows" could mean trouble. She might fill over the rail before enough water has come under her bilge to float her. Empty oil barrels lashed under the bilge are said to help a lot, but the difficulty of finding the barrels and lashing them securely may be insuperable. You may be able to use the dinghy or empty water jugs or any buoyant object. A line from the masthead to something solid might help, but if anything slips and she falls back, she could be badly damaged. As soon as she lifts her rail out of water, she will be all right, of course. Then get an anchor into deep water, restow gear, and be ready to take her off as she floats.

If the grounding has done serious damage to the hull so that she leaks badly, it may be better to leave her aground and summon expert help. Minor damage near the water line can be repaired with duct tape, available at builders' supply stores. Fiberglass boats should carry cloth and resin for emergency repairs. A wooden boat can be patched temporarily with canvas, paint, and battens. There is an epoxy putty that will not only adhere to wet surfaces but will actually set up under water if you can hold it in place long enough. The Pettit Paint Co. markets it under the name of Polypoxy, and a similar product, Epoxybond, is available from Manhattan Marine, 116 Chambers St., N.Y. 10007. Damage to unprotected shafts, propellers, struts, and rudders is usually beyond the skill and the toolbox of an amateur. A tow boat, a boatyard, and the insurance company should be notified.

If you ground in a heavy sea where the vessel will pound dangerously, of course the safety of your crew is your first concern. Get all hands into life preservers, radio the Coast Guard, inflate the life raft, burn flares, and consider the fate of the boat last. This is not a grounding but a shipwreck.

Man Overboard

Don't Jibe–Think

A skipper with a member of his crew overboard finds himself instantly on the fine line
between adventure and disaster. Only by
coolly making the right decisions and by following them up with clear and positive action
will he save his friend's life. Let's think out
the situation and explore our alternatives.

To make it easy, suppose a good day with
a fifteen-knot reaching breeze and a smooth
sea. Our sloop has four men aboard, including
the skipper. Sam falls overboard.

FIRST: GET THE LIFE BUOY OVER THE SIDE. To
give Sam a fighting chance, it must be done
quickly, for at six knots a boat is traveling
about ten feet per second. If it takes only five
seconds from when Sam hits the water to
when the buoy goes overboard, he has a fifty-
foot swim to begin with. It will be more than
twice that if the buoy is not on deck and clear
to throw. The buoy must have a light on it and
a pole weighted so that it will float upright.
Otherwise Sam will never find the buoy at all.

SECOND: TELL SOMEONE TO WATCH SAM IN THE
WATER, never to take his eyes off Sam for any
reason, no matter what happens aboard the
sloop. Once lost, it is very difficult to find a
little thing like a human head among the wave
tops.

THIRD: THINK. Figure out what must be
done to get back to Sam as quickly as possible. Clearly, there are two alternatives: to jibe
or to tack. A jibe is quicker than a tack, so the
skipper bears off, has Bill cast off the boom
vang, and then tend genoa sheets. The skipper
runs down to leeward of Sam, who by now has
reached the buoy and flag, jibes over, luffs up,
and Jack and Bill help Sam aboard. In three
minutes more, the sloop is on her course again
and all is well.

Now let us imagine what would happen if
the skipper acts on the basis of a book he has
read and after the first two steps, without an
instant's hesitation for reasonable thought,
puts the helm up and jibes. The mainsail, still
held by the boom vang, is flat aback, unless
the vang parts, the pad eye is pulled out of the
deck, or the boom breaks. The genoa is also
flat aback. The boat stops short and without
headway cannot be steered. The genoa drives
her down-wind backward and poor Sam is going to have a long, cold wait of it at best while
the mess is straightened out.

Suppose instead of a pleasant fifteen-knot
breeze it is blowing twenty-five knots with a
cresting chop running. Now the jibe is a dangerous maneuver indeed, even with vang cast
off and one man on the genoa sheets. Furthermore, Sam, who may have been wearing oil
clothes, has farther to swim in rougher water
and with less chance of finding the buoy. Perhaps the best chance now lies in bearing off,

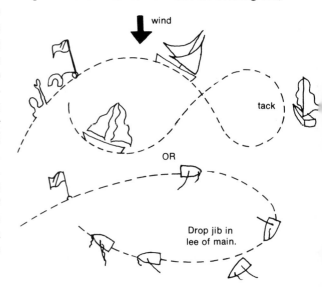

wind

tack

OR

Drop jib in
lee of main.

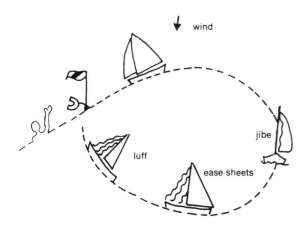

wind

jibe

luff

ease sheets

dropping the genoa, jibing with the main sheet trimmed flat, and edging up to Sam under mainsail alone. If the boat cannot be handled under mainsail alone in a strong breeze and a chop, the skipper should have known it before this.

Suppose now a yawl running off under spinnaker, spinnaker staysail, and mizzen staysail. With the buoy in the water and Jack watching Sam, the skipper, right off the top of his new yachting cap, jibes. Chaos! The spinnaker thrashes about, winding its clinging one-half-ounce nylon around every stay, shroud, and halyard. The main boom slams into the mizzen staysail, either parts the luff wire, tears the top off the mizzenmast, or breaks the boom. The spinnaker staysail is aback; there is no way on the boat, and poor Sam has a dim future.

Maybe the best solution in this case lies in the skipper's sailing a steady course, the crew's getting the light sails in, and then reversing the course under engine in the hope that Sam will be found hanging to the buoy confident and unperturbed.

Suppose it is dark or foggy—or both? Suppose a child falls in? Should someone else go overboard to help? Suppose poor Sam is knocked silly by the foreboom before he goes overboard or is cracked on the back of the head by the bow of the skiff just as he gets his head out of the water? Suppose the sloop is under power with that lethal propeller whirling under her stern, sucking in everything ahead of it?

The point is that after throwing the buoy and flag and after telling someone to watch the man in the water, the skipper must decide what to do on the basis of his knowledge of the conditions, his boat, and his surviving crew. He must have thought out the problems ahead of time and must have practiced picking up cushions, charts, hats, anything that falls overboard, so that when Sam's day comes, the skipper will be able to decide quickly the best course of action.

Recovering a Man in the Water

Suppose a man falls overboard on a pleasant day into warm water? The skipper is at the wheel, the proper procedure has been practiced, and the yacht promptly returns to the victim and is laid alongside him. Although he will probably get home alive, his problems are far from over. Getting him over the rail may be a bigger challenge than at first appears.

In a quiet harbor a man dove from the deck of my sloop, which has a freeboard of about eighteen inches, to photograph his children taking a morning dip. The children were reluctant, and the father got quite cold before he gave up. He returned to the boat, passed his camera to his wife, and seized the swimming ladder with justifiable enthusiasm. The man was heavy and the old ladder broke. His efforts to climb the rail failed because the instant he reached over his head to grab the rail, his feet slid under the boat. Our efforts to haul him aboard failed because he was a big man and there was nothing to get hold of. Finally I grabbed a thrashing ankle and hauled that over the rail; and among the three of us, he got aboard. It almost ceased to be a joke.

Imagine the situation in a boat of higher freeboard. The man in the water cannot reach the rail. The people on the boat, by lying down on deck, can just reach the water. They grab the victim's hands. Now what?

If the crew is strong enough, even pulling from a very awkward position, they can yank the man on deck like a halibut; or a loop of the jib sheet for a foothold may do the job if it doesn't slide under the boat. However, if the man is too tired and cold to help himself, a line should at once be passed around his body, under his shoulders, and pulled tight so he cannot slip out of it.

Several years ago a writer made some experiments on getting a man out of the water after a line had been made fast to him. One scheme was to attach the line to the main halyard and winch him aboard. It was a painful procedure and required one man on the winch and another to tend the line and assist the sufferer, but it worked. Another method was to attach the line to the lower main-sheet block, hoist the man to the end of the boom, and swing him aboard. The most ingenious method was to detach the lower sail slides from the mast, lower a bight of the sail over the side, conduct the victim into the hammock thus provided, and by hauling on the halyard, roll him aboard. Efforts to climb into the stern of a dinghy or to swamp a dinghy, get the man into it, and thence aboard the yacht present real difficulties when you actually try them, for a dinghy is a skittish little shell. It rolls, flips, or bounces away, even if the man in the water is quite active and alert. However, he may quickly tire himself out, lose hope and courage, and become almost helpless. You might even lose him.

Some years ago a fishing party boat capsized in Block Island Sound early in the season. Life-jacketed survivors floated about in the cold water for an hour or more before a yacht happened by. The crew of the yacht, able-bodied people, got the helpless survivors aboard only by sending a man down a boarding ladder to get a line on them and muscling them up over the side. It was a slow and exhausting process.

On the other hand, I knew a small woman, crippled in one leg, who fell off a Cal-40. Almost before she got wet, she reached up, grabbed the rail, and hauled herself aboard. Neither she nor anyone present knew how she was able to do it, and of course she was never able to repeat the feat—nor did she care to.

In a powerboat the problem may be even more difficult, unless her cockpit, like that of many fishermen, extends nearly to the rail. It is much easier to lift with your feet low. A boarding stage over the stern would be a great help if the engines were shut off—not just put

in neutral but shut off. Indeed, this advice goes for any vessel, even an outboard. Anchor if you have to, but keep those lethal propeller blades still once the man is near the boat.

Difficult as getting a man aboard may be in ordinary conditions, it is incalculably more difficult if it is rough and blowing, the water is cold, and all hands are tired. No sound and generally applicable rules can be laid down, and practicing the operation with a live target is difficult and fraught with peril too. One might summarize thus:

1. Stop the engine.
2. Get a line under the man's shoulders.
3. Keep him out from under the bow or stern where he might be struck by the overhang.
4. Carry a stout boarding ladder that can be rigidly attached to the rail in any weather.
5. Never fall overboard.

Child Overboard
Robert C. Duncan

If a child does go overboard in spite of all precautions, instant and agonizing decisions face the skipper. In August my four-year-old son was on the foredeck one second, and I saw the soles of his shoes going over the rail the next. A firm push on the tiller to leeward and a quick grasp for his life jacket as he floated within reach of the cockpit had him back aboard just as quickly. The elements of the situation demanded instant decisions and actions. They came as naturally as heading into the wind below a mooring. Experience and preparation produced positive results.

The most impressive aspect of the entire affair was my reaction after the fact. During the immediate moments of drying off a surprised and wet child, the clarity of "what would have happened if" became disturbingly relevant. Such thoughts brought on a real feeling of shock. I felt slightly cold and a bit shaky with a clammy skin. Once the shock had worn itself out, I considered two fundamental questions: 1) Did I make a mistake in judgment that resulted in the accident? and 2) Once events had developed, what brought about a favor-

The boat

able conclusion? The answers are enigmatic.

It was a quiet day. We were less than twenty yards from the mooring. Roger had his life jacket securely fastened. He was on a dry deck on his hands and knees. He had been "helping" under direct adult supervision. Children need such experience and activity if they are to grow into and respect good seamanship.

On the other hand, we were alone. He was only four years old. He could not swim. He had never been alone on the foredeck before. He was thinking about the approaching mooring and not about his footing.

Being a harsh judge of my own performance on the water, I concluded that an error in judgment had been made. Roger was not yet ready to pick up a mooring buoy alone on the foredeck.

Yet my wife saw the entire scene from a wharf less than fifty yards away. She concluded that there had been no error in judgment. "If there had been, I would have let you know. He had a life jacket on and the light wind conditions were exceedingly favorable. Roger was being given a chance to try something new under direct experienced supervision." I am still not entirely convinced, but such support provides perspective.

The answers to the second question are easier to find: preparation and experience. Roger's life jacket is indispensable. Any skipper who allows a nonswimmer in a small boat without one is irresponsible. Experience made instant evaluation of the situation easier. The forming of the correct decision to try for a grab from the cockpit and the execution of that decision, which brought Roger and the cockpit close enough together, lasted less than two seconds. I acted like a musician, a ball player, a doctor, who prepares, practices, and acts over and over again in similar but not identical situations. It was not a reaction to an entirely novel situation. Everything I did had been done before under other circumstances. Having retrieved lost fenders, sponges, and hats made the rescue a natural. Yet with a child, the stakes were higher and I might not have had a second chance. The lessons learned have been at some emotional expense.

Set the highest possible standards for your basic judgment and seamanship. If you imagine every sponge and fender as a child, you

The boy

learn a lot as it drifts astern. Take every opportunity to make and execute decisions under varied conditions. If you are not satisfied, find out why, throw the sponge overboard, and try again. A disaster is not bad luck but the inability to recognize and act upon unpredictable events. Preparation and practice are as indispensable to the expert as they are to the beginner.

Stay Aboard

For falling overboard, surely the best cure is prevention. The books are full of good ways of making yourself fast to your vessel, and race committees of the principal ocean races publish lists of required gear to keep crews aboard their yachts. Safety harnesses properly clipped on, pulpits, life lines, and solid handholds have certainly forestalled many desperate adventures and some tragedies before they happened.

However, most of us are not racing offshore under survival conditions. We are going on a picnic or a pleasant sail down the bay. We expect to be back for tea. Few of us on a moderate summer day are going to get harnessed up and clip on every time we leave the cockpit. Who wants to take a sunbath in a safety harness? Yet these are the times someone tries to wing out the jib with the boat hook and flops overboard, or two kids get to fooling on the foredeck and forget they are on a boat, or a trusted friend drops the anchor with a turn of the line around his ankle.

Protection against such perils is not physical but mental. You must find a way to wing out that jib and still keep a hand on the shroud. Any coil of line may whiz out without warning. Don't you be standing in it. If you must unsnap the spinnaker from its pole, an action requiring two hands, embrace the headstay as you do so. Never let anyone tow astern in the dinghy. Even becalmed, seated in the cockpit, beer and sandwich in hand, there must always lurk in the back of your mind the awareness that you are surrounded by a hostile element in which man can live unsupported but a brief time. Keep one hand for the ship but the other for yourself.

Unwrapping a Spinnaker—
The Easy Way
Capt. Paul Wolter

There they fly, the spinnakers, the picture-book sails with wild colors, emblems, patterns, hanging over the waves like balloons over the lawn of a garden party. Who has not seen a racing fleet rounding the windward mark when the spinnakers pop up like flowers in a speeded-up botanical movie?

Suddenly there goes the bubble, twisting, billowing, turning and wrapping itself around the headstay. With only one twist you are lucky. It is then a four-story-high hourglass on a big boat. It costs time in a long race and may force you to give up in a small race. I have seen bad wrap-ups where the whole thing looked like a multicolored band with a little bubble in the middle the size of a football.

How do we get that thing out? Cursing and vigorous leech tugging does not help. Looking in horror at the devilish thing only makes the skipper raise his voice. "Let go the halyard, down with it!" Easier said than done. The halyard is loose but nothing happens. "Let go sheet or guy!" "Unshackle them!" You cannot unturn it from the bottom. The middle is wrapped over top and bottom.

I have read stories from heroes who have been up there in the middle at the bubble. The crew on deck must have sometimes feared that the battle between man and sail was being won by the spinnaker when there were already enough loose folds to plug the man out of the chair, cover him up, and eat him.

A knife, cutting the sail to ribbons, would be another last resort.

A spinnaker net will reduce the possibility of a wrap, but not eliminate it altogether. But nets have their shortcomings. On an ocean race I have seen a wild spinnaker eating up the net while wrapping itself around the headstay. We could only stare at the seven monstrous bubbles with little bits of net looking out here and there.

The net itself can be in such a snarl that the impatient skipper will yell, "Get the kite up!" And you will drop the net and set the kite. And before the net is cleared and hoisted, the finest wrap has occurred.

Only a headsail set inside the spinnaker will be a sure defense. But you cannot always have a sail there without disturbing the air for the spinnaker.

All this shows that wraps will always be with us. If it has not happened to you, you have not lived or sailed long enough yet. Maybe this summer already the beauty up there will turn against you and turn and turn . . . . Read on and find out that there is a way to de-wrap it without a man on the mast or the knife.

To untwist the monster you need only use the very same forces that wrapped it around in the first place: wind and momentum.

The man in command now needs to know how the spinnaker is wrapped around the headstay. As an answer he does not want to hear "pretty badly"; no, he wants to know whether the spinnaker is turned right or left around the stay. He should send a scout forward. This man should know the difference between left and right or clockwise and counterclockwise.

If the spinnaker is wrapped to the right—clockwise—the boat should be put onto the port tack. If the spinnaker is wrapped to the left—counterclockwise—the boat should be put onto the starboard tack.

Once on the appropriate tack, the boat should be well off the wind, with the spinnaker pole carried wide and the mainsail all the way out to the shrouds. Any slack should be taken out of spinnaker sheet and guy and these should be kept manned in expectation of the de-wrapping success. A preventer must be rigged from the end of the main boom to the stem. This is most important, as the de-wrap success depends on the mainsail staying where it is even when the vessel is driven off quite a bit by the lee. The preventer should be made of nylon, for stretch.

These preparations done, the de-wrap now rests with the helmsman. On big boats, where the helmsman at the wheel cannot lean far enough to windward to see what happens at the headstay, a man must stand at the windward shroud. He must know the procedure, watch the spinnaker, and give orders to the helmsman. The man at the helm must concentrate on steering.

1. The vessel is driven sharply off a point or two by the lee. New air, backcurrents behind the mainsail, and momentum all combine to drive the spinnaker bubbles forward around the stay toward the pole.

2. Quickly but smoothly, the vessel is brought up again a point or two above "dead before it." Momentum and air from windward

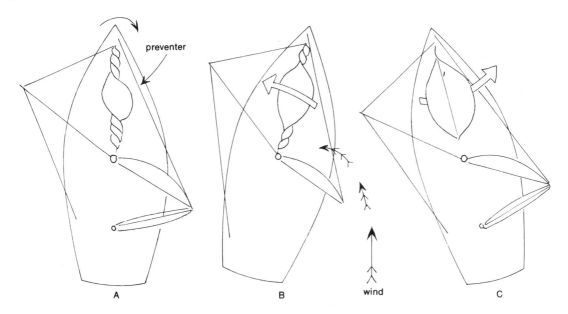

A   B   wind   C

combine to swing the bubbles back around inside the stay.

3. Each repetition of this pattern removes one turn from the wrap. How far up or down the boat must be steered depends upon wind and sea conditions and the tightness of the wrap. Far enough to get results.

The helmsman must steer firmly and show the boat who the master is. And he must be aware of what's happening forward. He must not be afraid to sail by the lee. The main is secured by the preventer. A very few attempts will show how far to swing the boat to each side, and after that a sustained rhythm will accelerate the de-wrapping. And de-wrap it must.

This method has a number of advantages. It requires a minimum of men. The watch on deck does not have to call the watch below and thereby avoids having to listen to some inappropriate comments from the off watch. Although some distance is lost in steering a snakelike course, boat speed is kept up and the sails do not have to come down.

Remember that the very same forces that wrapped up the spinnaker to begin with are the very forces that can be used to de-wrap it successfully. The key lies in the understanding of these forces and a firm hand on the helm.

Reefing

When the wind gets over twenty-five knots, most of the lovely little sailboats that glide around so smoothly begin to act frantically. Here is a little eighteen-footer, flat to the water in a heavy puff, then rounding into the wind, her sails shaking madly, only to lose way and be smashed down again by the next puff, proceeding in a series of terrified swoops. Here is another, her skipper a little more experienced, with his jib sheeted flat and only the after quarter of his mainsail full, making his way cautiously home. Over yonder is a yawl, her mainsail furled, sailing serenely under jib and mizzen. As she passes, we see that her engine is running. Between those overpowered under full sail and those undercanvassed, we see one vessel, three feet of bare

spar showing above her mainsail, snugly reefed and working well to windward.

Why reef? It is a matter of efficiency as much as of safety. When a modern yacht with a tall rig and a fin keel heels far to leeward, two things happen. The lead, deep down on her keel, becomes more and more effective as a force to right her. Also, the wind, deflected upward by the high side of the hull, strikes the narrow top part of the steeply heeled sail at an oblique angle and skids *up* off the top of it instead of passing *across* it, as it would if the boat were more or less upright.

The harder it blows, then, the harder it has to blow to heel the boat further. Consequently, the yacht will probably not lay her masthead in the water, and unless her rigging parts and she is dismasted, she will probably be safe enough.

However, the wind blowing more up the sail than across it robs the sail of much of its forward drive. Also, dragging her rail through the water slows the yacht, and the shape her steeply heeled hull presents to the water is far less efficient than its shape upright. The boat, instead of driving forward, is pushed bodily to leeward by wind and sea and makes very slow progress in spite of considerable splash. A dispassionate look at the angle of the wake and at the speed of passing bubbles will prove convincing.

Reefed, the boat will sit more on her bottom, presenting her designed shape to the sea. Her sail will again have the wind passing across it, and if well cut, will set flatter than her full sail. Her keel, more nearly vertical, will prevent excessive leeway. People can take off their oil clothes, relax, and enjoy the day instead of feeling like the statue of the Gloucester Fisherman.

There are three common ways of taking a reef.

Roller Reefing

Here the boom is rotated by a ratchet or worm gear to roll the sail around the boom like a window shade. It is a flexible arrangement, for one can roll in as many turns as he wishes. It is important to take the weight of the boom on the topping lift in order to keep it perpendicular to the mast so the sail will roll smoothly. Also the sail must be kept pulled aft as it rolls up. The main sheet must be watched too, lest as the boom turns the sheet turn with it. Usually the sheet is attached to the after end of the boom on the same fitting as the topping lift, and the opposing strains should keep both of them out of trouble. See also the discussion on Roller Reefing and Furling on page 112.

Reef Points

A sail cut for this conventional method of reefing will have a row of short lines sewn through the sail parallel to the boom. At each end of the row in the luff and leach of the sail will be an eye or "cringle." First heave to, or at least trim the jib flat. Then support the weight of the boom on the topping lift and lower the sail so there is plenty of slack in the luff. Tie the cringle on the luff firmly to the gooseneck. This is "passing the tack earring." Next pass the clew earring, hauling the new clew of the sail, the cringle in the leach, both out and down. This should produce a snug tension along the row of reef points. Now tie in the reef points, passing the lee one between the boom and the sail and tying each pair together in a single bow. Be careful to avoid grannies. Next hoist the sail again, put the usual tension on the downhaul, and go on your way, efficiently and under control.

It is much easier, especially on boats with long booms, to attach a cheek block to the boom just outside the point at which the leach cringle comes down. Tie your reef pennant around the boom just outside the cheek block, pass the end up through the cringle, down through the cheek block, and forward to a cleat or winch. Thus, you can stand inboard and pull strongly down and out on the clew earring.

On sails that hoist on tracks, be sure that the track is strongly attached to the mast where the head of the sail will come when it is reefed. Also, lash the top slide to the sail well, for the halyard cannot hold the sail tightly against the mast when it is reefed, as it can when hoisted right against the sheave.

Be sure the sail is not pinched between the reef point and the tabling in the foot of the sail or the reef point will quickly chafe a hole.

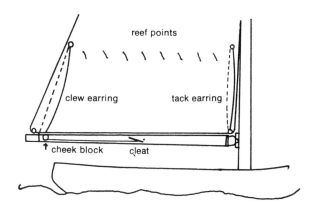

Slab Reefing

This is essentially a quick variation on the conventional method. Both clew and tack earrings are rigged as described above for the clew earring. First the clew earring is hove taut, cocking the boom up. Then the halyard is slacked off as the tack earring is hove down on a winch. If the cringles at luff and leach are properly reinforced, the sail can stand the strain without reef points. On larger boats, the weight of the boom is taken on the topping lift, the tack earring is passed, then the clew earring is hove down with a winch. It is well to tie in the reef points if the boom is long, because the strain on the sail cloth is enormous.

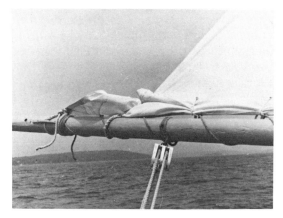

The clew earring pulls out *and* down.

A gaff-headed sail can be quickly shortened by "scandalizing" it, that is, by lowering the peak so only the forward lower corner of the sail draws.

For no clearly accountable reason except perhaps because of stories written by people who never reefed, reefing has come to be regarded as a cowardly act. Yet the hard-driving skipper "unafraid of a devil, a witch, or a gale of wind" who drove his vessel hard through squall and gale might have arrived sooner with his gear intact had he shortened sail when his vessel labored hard and set it again as soon as conditions permitted.

More on Roller Reefing and Furling

Simply rotate the boom, rolling the sail around it, and thus instantly reef the sail. This fundamentally simple idea at first glance should provide a quick and safe way to shorten sail with no one risking his life to pass a clew earring. However, there are a few points to be considered in perfecting the scheme.

First, the worm gear of lever-and-ratchet to turn the boom must be of the heaviest construction. Under reefing conditions there will be heavy and complicated strains on the boom and it will not turn easily.

Second, before turning in a reef, the topping lift supporting the end of the boom must be set up just enough so that the boom forms a right angle with the mast. Otherwise the sail will roll too tightly at one end of the boom and too loosely at the other. Even if the topping lift can be perfectly adjusted, on some boats a man must be stationed at the outer end of the boom to stretch the sail out along the boom as the boom turns to be sure that it rolls smoothly. He is no more secure doing this than he would be if he were passing the earring to lash down the clew in a conventional reef.

Another difficulty in getting the sail to roll smoothly around the boom lies in the cut of the sail. A sail achieves the fullness or draft in its forward area partly by a slight convex curve in the luff. This means that as the sail rolls up, it will creep forward on the boom and

the roach in the leech will cause it to creep aft at the after end of the boom. Furthermore, in modern sails some of the fullness in the sail is achieved by curving the seams so that the sail cannot be laid out flat. This is sure to make a wrinkle.

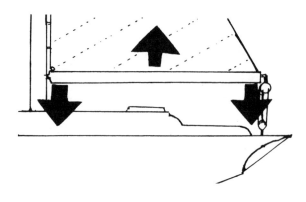

Consider, too, the problems of main sheet and vang. The sheet is usually fastened to the after end of the boom on a bolt centered in the spar and rigged so the boom can turn freely without winding up the sheet. On a sail with a long foot, this concentrates the load on the spar at the gooseneck and turning gear on the forward end instead of spreading it along the spar by attaching the sheet and its blocks at different points. Consequently, a heavier and stiffer spar is needed and the sail must be attached not by means of slides and a track but by letting the bolt rope into a groove in the boom.

The vang must be attached to the boom with claws having rollers on their ends so the boom can turn within them. This is a heavy and expensive fitting and can chafe the sail badly, particularly where the leeward claw bears against the sail. Note too, that the shape of the sail will be slightly different on one tack from what it will be on the other, for on one tack it will be pulling over the top of the boom and on the other under the bottom of it.

Finally, it is a neat trick and takes some rehearsing to slack the halyard as the boom is rotated. It cannot be slacked first and then rolled, because it must come down smoothly and under some tension, and the slides must

112

be kept from rolling into the sail and causing wrinkles and chafe. At worst, it may take four men to roll in a reef in a big sail. One must steer in such a way as to take some of the weight out of the sail but not to let it slat and shake wildly. Another must stretch out the foot from the after end. Another must ease the halyard and another rotate the boom. At best, two skillful men who are familiar with the rig and have done it before can roll in a smooth reef quickly. One yachtsman swears by roller reefing, and at least one widely experienced ocean-cruising skipper discarded his roller-reefing gear in favor of jiffy reefing.

In any form of reefing, however, beware the main halyard winch, which reels up the wire on a drum and holds it with a friction brake. The incautious seaman will fit the winch handle to the drum, hold it with one hand and release the brake with the other. The wire, under tremendous tension from the strain of the downhaul and the pressure of the wind, snaps the handle out of his hand and on its next revolution may break his arm or knock him cold with a blow on head or jaw. Never pick up the winch handle before slacking the brake to take the heft of the strain off the drum. After slacking a foot or two, the strain can be taken on the winch handle without undue difficulty. Hal Roth recommends a winch so constructed that the brake comes under the winch handle so that it cannot be released with the handle in position.

Headsails

Roller furling and reefing of headsails presents all the problems of a window shade, with a few complexities. The principle is simple. The luff wire of the sail is free to rotate at top and bottom. A reel is attached to the bottom, around which is wound a light line. When the line is pulled and the sheet slacked, the luff wire rolls the sail around it and the sail is instantly furled.

This assumes, of course, that the luff of the sail is bar tight. This is achieved by hoisting the sail on a wire halyard and setting it up hard on a winch. To resist this strain, there must be a permanent backstay, also set up

hard. In light and moderate conditions, roller furling works very well.

If there is a forestay in addition to the luff wire on the roller jib and if either gets a bit slack under the strain of the other, in heavy winds and seas the sail may flog about enough to wind up the stay inside the sail. This, of course, jams the next turn and the sail must be unwound and wound fairly. Also, under great strain the luff wire twists, thus rolling the lower edge of the sail more tightly than the upper edge. Wrinkles develop, and in order to furl the sail completely, the sheets will be wound several times around the sail, a clumsy arrangement at best.

This is overcome to a large extent by using a rod luff instead of a wire luff. This does not twist so much, but it still twists, and it makes changing jibs a far more difficult matter. Hood has developed a hollow luff rod with a C section so the luff rope of the jib runs up inside it. This twists very little and rolls the sail evenly but still makes shifting jibs a slow business and is an expensive rig.

Theoretically a roller jib can be rolled up halfway to thus reduce the area of the sail in the same way a mainsail is roller reefed. However, unless the sail is cut with the miter and sheet lead perpendicular to the luff, the sheet will have to be led farther forward. If the yacht is equipped with adjustable leads, this is no problem. Also, however, the wire may twist under heavy strain, causing the sail to roll unevenly and loosening the leach so it flutters badly. The luff of the sail where it is cut with a belly in it to provide draft will be rolled up first, leaving a sail with little or no draft and putting a heavy strain on the exposed part. This may stretch a light sail completely out of shape because it has been built of light sailcloth for light winds and cut to be fully set. It is far better to change to a smaller and heavier jib that has been cut for heavier winds.

Finally, a roller jib should have the leach and foot lined with sunproof cloth so that when the sail is rolled up, the sailcloth is not deteriorated by ultraviolet rays.

An interesting application of the roller furling principal is found in a few yachts that have applied it to the mainsail. The stay or rod on which the sail is rolled is stretched tightly inside the hollow mast and emerges through a longitudinal slit in the after side. The mainsail is set by simply releasing the reel line and pulling on the clew outhaul. The sail, set loose-footed, at once runs to the end of the boom and the yacht is underway. It can be furled as quickly. The yacht is shot into the wind. As she ranges slowly up to her mooring, the skipper pulls on the reel line. The sail disappears inside the mast instantly. He walks forward, picks up his mooring buoy, and is ready to go ashore.

Roller reefing and furling, simple and foolproof in principle, have a few problems, difficulties, and drawbacks, all of which can be overcome by intelligent thought and more or less expensive equipment and thus are not the answer to prayer but are competitive with older and more conventional rigs. The man contemplating installing roller gear would be well advised to sail with the rig on a friend's boat in heavy weather before making the rather heavy investment involved.

Caught Out

What do you do when you are caught out? The best you can with what you have! Here are a few suggestions.

On a warm, muggy day you might notice a brassiness, a darkness, in the haze to the westward, then the top of a thunderhead over the haze. From this point the weather develops with startling speed.

The thunderhead grows, flattening on top into the familiar anvil shape described in all the books. The sky rapidly darkens. The wind drops, the haze clears somewhat, thunder begins to bump around inside the cloud and lightning flickers. A veil of rain sweeps down.

As you sit in front of this tremendous development, feeling like a nail waiting for the hammer, you may notice that the bottom of the approaching cloud is ragged and swirling or you may see an arc of hard-rolled cloud advancing above the rain. Now it is too late to run for shelter. What can you do?

If you have an engine, use it to get away from dangers east of you, for the wind will surely come out of the west or northwest. Douse all sail and tie everything down tightly. Be sure to pass a stop around the head of the jib or it will slat its way up the stay and perhaps be damaged. You may need it later. Get the crew below or into oil clothes and keep them away from mast and rigging as best you can. With forestay, shrouds, and a permanent backstay, you can't get very far. If your rigging is not grounded, shackle a short length of chain to an upper shroud and hang it overboard. Anyway, throw a bucket of water on the turnbuckles and let it run down the side; it can't do any harm, and it may help to ground the system.

The old wind dies; the rain and the new wind rush across the water.

"If the wind before the rain, soon you may make sail again" is generally true.

When the wind strikes, it may blow unbelievably hard for a short time, the rain may really sting, and the thunder and lightning may snap all around. Or there may be just a capful of wind and a splash of rain. Probably you will soon see light under the clouds to the westward, the sky will clear to a hard blue, and the northwest wind right from Hudson's Bay will blow the haze right out of the sky.

If it blows really hard, you may have trouble beating back to America against it. Of course, if you can reduce sail to fit the wind—jib and jigger, foresail and staysail, #2 genoa alone or whatever dress suits your particular boat—you will have no difficulty. If you find yourself in a small boat not equipped to reef, set the jib and sheet it in hard. Set the mainsail and slack the sheet enough to keep the boat on her feet, holding just enough wind in the leech of the sail to force the bow to windward against the pressure of the jib. Forward drive is provided by the full jib, for there is no drive in the mainsail when it is all a-luff.

If it becomes evident that you can not get to windward against the rising sea, make distress signals at once before you are driven off so far that they will not be noticed.

Keep people as warm and dry as possible and keep your courage up. It is only an adventure, and these things usually blow themselves out at sunset.

Notes from the Sailmaker:
Heaving To
Nathaniel S. Wilson

Heaving a vessel to is usually thought of as a precaution against breaking seas during a heavy gale. However, it is not necessarily a heavy weather maneuver. In ordinary weather with all working sail it can be a convenient way to reef, change sail, eat a meal, or get some rest.

By learning how to heave your boat to under a variety of conditions, you can develop a better understanding of her qualities. Knowing how to handle your boat in heavy sea conditions will relieve anxiety in your crew, in your wife, and in yourself. When hove to, most vessels will lie easy and more or less dry from the seas.

Heaving to is a maneuver in which you want the bow of the vessel to lie somewhat head to the seas with little or no way on. There is no true and fast rule for heaving to, for every boat will vary in different conditions of wind and sea. Many techniques must be tried and adjustments made until one is found that works for your boat.

In ordinary weather with most of your working sails set, you round up to the wind slowly, back the jib or staysail to windward, and slack away the main sheet some. The boat will lose way. At this point, lash the tiller to leeward. As the bow pays off down the wind under the pressure of the backed jib, the slack mainsail will begin to draw. When the main fills, it will drive the boat ahead slowly against the pressure of the jib, giving the rudder a little steerage. The bow will come up toward the wind again. As the mainsail loses driving power and luffs, the vessel stops, the bow falls off, and the process begins again. With the proper balance between sails and helm, the vessel should lie about six points (67°) off the wind and drift slowly to leeward, rising to the seas as they come.

In heavy weather, heaving to is usually done with storm canvas. You are dealing with much greater forces now, and to achieve a balance between sails and helm may take experi-menting. Heavy seas breaking against the bow will increase the tendency of the bow to fall off. Boats with deep forefoots and long keels have a better grip on the water than boats that are cut away forward. The latter have a tendency to pivot on the short keel so that some-one may have to stay at the helm and con-stantly trim the rudder.

Some yawls and ketches can be hove to under mizzen alone. The mizzen in this case acts like a weather vane, keeping the bow to the wind. A small jib may still be needed to keep the bow from coming through the wind or to prevent her from lying so close to the wind that she drifts backwards and puts an un-due strain on her steering gear. Most sloops can be hove to under some combination of try-sail and storm jib. Another method that may work on a sloop is to run a very small jib up the fixed backstay, leading the clew forward to a *strong* cleat. This gets sail way aft and may help to hold her bow to the wind.

With the addition of a sea anchor, some of the problems of heaving to can be eased.

Sometime when you are out on a fair day, try to heave your vessel to. You will gain more knowledge of the way she handles and of her balance, and some day that knowledge may be indispensable.

Coastal Storms

Most storms are heralded well in advance by radio forecasts. The National Weather Service broadcasts are carried by many commercial stations and also are broadcast continuously on VHF. Hurricanes are tracked carefully and even a line of thunder squalls is followed with care and accuracy.

Even without radio, you can usually see a storm building up in time to get under cover from anywhere up to thirty miles offshore. The mares' tails, thickening overcast, falling barometer, heavy look to the approaching clouds, and deep roll should provide adequate notice.

The projected path of the storm is of great significance. If it is to pass west of you, the wind will start in the northeast and shift clock-wise through east to southwest. If it is to pass east of you, it will begin in the southeast and shift counterclockwise through east and northeast to northwest. This is true of all cyclonic storms but is especially noticeable and important in hurricanes. The skipper seeking shelter should calculate on the probable shift when selecting an anchorage.

When you get into a reasonably well protected harbor, there are some further considerations. Remember that in the event of a really heavy gale, it will be difficult even to move around on deck, and therefore everything possible should be done in advance.

First, seek a big mooring. Do not plan to lie alongside a wharf or float as a general rule. The very high tide that comes with a storm may endanger the mooring of a float or even destroy a wharf by floating the platform and raising the pilings. Those who saw the Eastport waterfront disintegrate in the Ground Hog Day gale of 1976 or who witnessed the damage in Scituate and elsewhere along the Massachusetts coast in February 1978 will prefer a heavy mooring to a berth alongside.

Second, mooring or not, seek a location in shallow water well clear of other vessels. There is no known defense against a dragging ferryboat or a barge adrift. If the prediction is for winds in excess of forty knots, get your best ground tackle on the bottom where it will do the most good. Lay out your anchors in a V facing the expected gale.

One problem of lying to anchors in a gale is that the yacht will swing a little, present one cheek to the wind, and sail herself ahead and out to one side. Then the strain on one anchor line will be enough to turn her through the eye of the wind. She will turn the other cheek and drift sideways bodily to leeward, to fetch up hard on the second anchor and sail herself ahead again. This can partly be prevented by dropping a small anchor out abeam on the side *away* from which the wind will shift. A strain on this rode will provide a hammer lock to prevent swinging. Another device is to stream from the stern a big old tire or two. This will tend to hold the stern steady yet permit the yacht to swing as the wind shifts.

Once your vessel is well moored, be liberal with chafing gear.

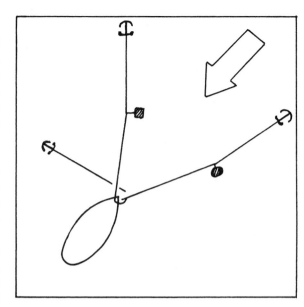

The "Hammerlock"

Next, remove as many sources of windage as possible. Get all loose gear off the deck. Boat hook, fenders, deck mop, buckets, whatever will move except man-overboard gear should be sent below. Unbend sails, especially jibs. They have a bad habit of climbing the stay in a heavy wind and accentuating swinging until they slat to pieces. Lash halyards to the mast to prevent their slatting, wearing themselves out, and damaging the mast. This may require a trip aloft if the lower spreaders are low and the wind has not yet got up. The alternative is to tie the halyards out to the side, but they will still slat some.

Tie down booms in gallows frames. If you use a scissor-type boom crutch, lash it sideways as well as down, or it will capsize. Get the dinghy on deck if possible and lash it upside down. If it must lie astern, lead a painter to each quarter of the yacht, attaching one of them to the dinghy's forward thwart.

Be sure the engine is ready to turn over slowly. This will ease the strain in the heaviest puffs and provide a current of water by the rudder to permit some control over wide swinging.

Finally, fire up the stove and have a good hot lunch. Have your oil clothes ready, and sit it out. The most savage storms seldom last very long, but the "tale end of the hurricane" grows as the years pass.

116

If you doubt the accuracy of your aneroid barometer, borrow the trusted instrument of a friend and put both barometers in a plastic bag so that both dials are visible. Tie up the bag tightly and roll up one end so the pressure in the bag increases. If your barometer changes in the same amount as the other, be reassured. No expensive repairs are necessary. If there is a serious discrepancy, take your instrument to an expert.

Avoiding the Worst

September Wreck

The sloop *Second Sight* entered Monhegan harbor on the afternoon of September 24 and was directed to a vacant mooring by a passing fisherman. The harbor is tide ridden and open to the south, with a sandy bottom. The harbor is used in the summer by local fishermen, seiners, yachts, and excursion boats and is the pilot station for steamers bound up Penobscot Bay. In the winter it is the center of an active and rugged lobster fishery. In a southerly gale it can be very rough indeed.

About dark the wind breezed up from the southwest, and as the flood tide made, it increased. About 9:00 P.M., with a big chop running up the harbor, the skipper of *Second Sight* came on deck, checked his mooring line against chafe, went below, and turned in. Sometime after ten, as high water approached, the wind rose to thirty-five knots and a three-foot sea was running up the harbor. *Second Sight* dragged her mooring and went ashore on the rocks stern first. She swung around, smashed her dinghy under her, drove her bow hard aground, and pounded on the ledge as each sea lifted her and dropped her. Her skipper and crew got safely ashore, and as there

was nothing they could do for her, left her for the night.

In the morning, a cradle was built around her to protect her from pounding as the tide came. At high water a powerful fishing vessel tried vainly to haul her off. A little later she was joined by the mail boat. The nylon tow line parted, fortunately without hurting anyone, for it snapped back violently. Finally, with a new and stronger tow line, *Second Sight* slid off.

Such leaks as could be reached were patched with duct tape and the boat was towed to Hodgdon Brothers yard in East Boothbay.

As the photos (p. 118) show, the yacht was severely damaged. Not only did she have a number of holes pounded through her fiberglass sides, but her keel appeared to have been started away from the deadwood. Also, the pounding had sprung bulkheads and damaged the seal where the bulkheads are fastened to the sides of the boat.

What useful conclusions can the Sailor draw from this misfortune? First, do not take a mooring without checking it out. The owner of *Second Sight* is not much to be blamed. First, because of its exposed location, one would reasonably suppose that any mooring at Monhegan would be strong enough to hold a heavy boat in a southerly winter gale, hence plenty strong enough for a little yacht on a quiet night in late summer. Nevertheless, the wind and sea coming just on the top of the high water were enough to move the mooring rock over the soft sand bottom. It would be well, of course, before leaving the boat or turning in for the night to find out what is on the bottom and how frequently the gear is checked. Rust and chafe are dangerous enemies, and even shackle pins well moused may unscrew themselves. Usually the harbormaster can tell you what you are lying to.

Second, whenever it comes to blow, no matter how stout the mooring, give her some extra scope. Just bend your own anchor line to the bight in the mooring line and slack off a few fathoms. The easier angle and the extra stretch of the nylon rode may make all the difference. Give it all the scope you can and then run a weight down the line. A second anchor would probably help, but once it begins to blow in earnest and the chop builds up, bending on another anchor, making it up, and taking it out in the dinghy might be a major project. Being overboard at night from a capsized dinghy in the company of a seventy-five-pound anchor and chain could be perilous.

Once the vessel struck, not much could have been done unless the engine started at once and was powerful enough to push her to windward against wind and sea. The vulnerable detached rudder must have been damaged almost at once.

The Sailor suggests that the skipper and crew did well to get ashore when they could. There was no way in which they could have got an anchor out to windward, as their dinghy was stove in and it was too rough to row an anchor out anyway. Attempts to move the vessel while she lay pounding on the shore could have met with little success and could have led to injury. Once the tide started to ebb, there was nothing to be done until morning.

Pulling her off the ledge by main strength the next morning was questionable. The morning tide was about five inches higher than the night one, according to the tide table, but the night tide was being driven by a heavy southerly wind, and besides, the vessel was driven up the ledge by wind and sea. Therefore, a considerable amount of her weight was resting on the ledge. Certainly some of the damage was caused by dragging her across the rock.

Note the value of a roll of duct tape. It is

wide, strong, and will stick to almost anything. Builder's supply stores carry it.

One might question the construction of the boat in the first place. Her topsides seemed very thin, consisting of a layer of cloth, a layer of roving, a layer of either cloth or mat, and then the gel coat. The roving appeared not to have been well saturated with resin, for it was quite loose and silky. Still, as the yard foreman pointed out, when a hull is pounded so, the resin often turns to powder and parts company with the glass fibers. Granted that the boat took violent punishment, one might reasonably expect the bulkheads to hold. Apparently they were installed tightly against the shell of the boat.

Fortunately, the accident happened in a community inhabited by law-abiding and sympathetic citizens. In another community the boat might have been utterly stripped by morning.

Finally, anyone who works around the water all year will tell you that winter winds are heavier than summer ones. A twenty-knot breeze in December will raise a bigger sea and make a boat pull harder on her ground tackle than will a twenty-knot breeze in July. Late September and October are well on the way to winter.

What Can We Learn from the Loss of ''Aquarius''?

The thirty-eight-foot converted lobster boat *Aquarius* left Portsmouth, New Hampshire, on the morning of December 20, 1975, bound for Boston via the Annisquam Canal and Gloucester. The weather was fair, cold,

and calm. The run to Annisquam was uneventful and the passage of the canal was routine to the point where a bridge did not open to Captain Gorman's signal. He turned back and landed at the Cape Ann Marina, called the bridge tender, and also telephoned for a weather report. The weather report predicted an easterly gale to commence that evening with snow beginning in the afternoon. Captain Gorman realized that if he passed through the canal and headed for Boston, he would run right into the gale during the evening. He elected to run back for Portsmouth, an easy four hours away.

It was snowing lightly when *Aquarius* left Annisquam about 4:00 P.M. Darkness shut down, but the vessel was on course. The watch below started supper, and all seemed under control. By eight, the wind had breezed up from the northeast and a sea rapidly rose

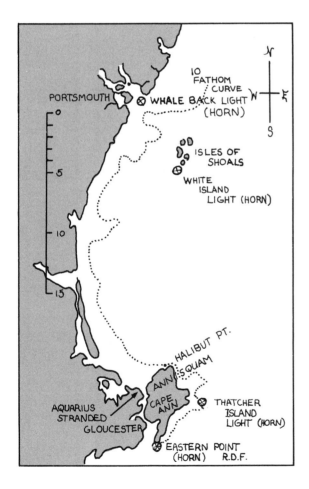

with it. At eight there was no light visible in the driving snow and no fog signal audible. By nine the skipper was aware that he did not know just where he was. Instead of driving ahead into the snow and rising sea, ignorant of his position, he slowed his engine, held *Aquarius*'s bow to the wind, and rigged a trysail to steady her. The mast carried away, so maintaining steerageway with the engine, Captain Gorman and his crew of five planned to ride out the night.

Because it was cold and blowing hard, one-hour watches of two people each were set. All but the skipper were seasick, but each did his part, nevertheless. Between two and three A.M. a fire started in the galley. The well-trained crew responded and put it out at once. Gorman nearly fell overboard, but one of the crew grabbed an ankle until he could get aboard. All hands wore warm clothes and life jackets. At dawn visibility was still poor, but about nine Paula Paquette, on watch, saw a flashing buoy. Gorman edged *Aquarius* toward the buoy and identified it as one of those on the Annisquam bar. However, the sea was breaking all across the bar and *Aquarius* had worked into the steep seas in front of it. Her cabin windows were broken and she began to ship water heavily. The power pump could not handle it. All hands started to bail. Then the engine stopped. Gorman got it going again, but it was flooded out. *Aquarius* was drifting back on the lee shore of Wingaersheek Beach.

Gorman got an anchor over the bow. The crew fired flares and launched the life raft. Gorman had each person tie on another life jacket. A sea rolled *Aquarius* over, trapping two people below and several others on deck beneath the capsized boat. The two trapped below and the woman who had been on the bridge were drowned. The other three fought their way ashore through the breakers, almost exhausted by cold and wet, and two of them made their way to an occupied house, whence help was called. The three were warmed up and revived, but the other three, two women and a young man, were lost.

Aquarius drifted ashore on the beach and in a matter of hours was completely looted by the local residents.

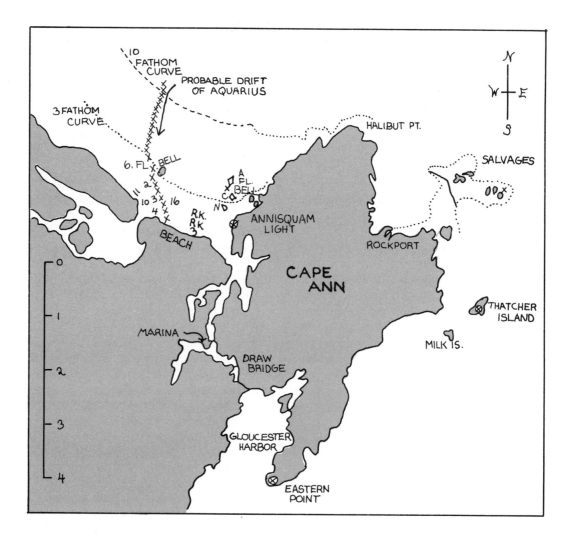

What conclusions can be drawn from this tragic story? Sitting comfortably at home, warm and dry, we can think things out far more lucidly than could Captain Gorman at sea in Ipswich Bay in a northeast gale. Where did he go wrong?

First, *Aquarius* was a sound vessel, a big, able lobster boat built only ten years before. She was what we call a Novi or a Scotia boat designed for winter lobstering in the Bay of Fundy. She had big windshields in the forward end of her cabin, but this is standard practice. Unlike lobster boats, she had a bridge over the house, but there is no evidence that its weight made her unstable.

She had a reliable engine, which died only when it was flooded. The skipper was an expe-

rienced seaman. He had trained his crew carefully and they had made several trips together with him in the boat. They never gave in to panic and were able to carry out Gorman's orders intelligently and effectively. Not only did they respond to fire as they had been trained to do but rigged jumper cables to the engine when they were half underwater, bailed as long as they could, burned flares as ordered, and launched the life raft—all this after a night of cold, seasickness, and uncertainty.

If we can raise a question on Captain Gorman's judgment after the fact, it is at the point where he decided to run back for Portsmouth instead of lying over at Annisquam or Gloucester. It was already 4:00 P.M. on the shortest day of the year and snow was begin-

120

ning to fall in advance of the storm he knew was coming that evening. The snow was not then heavy and visibility was probably not badly limited, but long before he made Portsmouth it would be black dark and thick of snow even if the storm had not yet begun to raise wind and sea. If he failed to make Whaleback Light or its horn, he would be on a lee shore twenty-five miles long with no available harbors. What few gaps the rivers have cut in the beach are impossible in an easterly. Escape to seaward would be obstructed by the Isles of Shoals, and the shoal water around York Ledge could be a danger to the north.

On the other hand, as long as it did not blow hard or snow a lot harder than it was snowing when he left, he would be able to see Whaleback or hear the horn and make his way up the familiar river. Many yachtsmen take worse risks than this and get home safely, not knowing enough to be scared. When we consider the fools who navigate from maps on the backs of bus schedules, Captain Gorman looks sound indeed. Running for Portsmouth is a chance most of us would take if there were a good reason for it—not just for fun perhaps.

Given this decision, Gorman's judgment during the night and the next morning seems to have been unexceptionable. When he realized that he did not know just where he was, he decided to ride out the gale at sea under trysail and engine. Certainly that was better than to try for any harbor to leeward. Perhaps one could claim that he should have known the mast was inadequate, but the loss of the sail was not a key factor in the ensuing tragedy. Employing the 20–20 vision afforded by hindsight, we might have advised Captain Gorman to work easterly as much as possible with the hope of clearing Cape Ann; but Cape Ann is a rugged coast in a northeaster and had he struck anywhere from Annisquam to the Salvages, no one could have survived.

Until Paula Paquette sighted the buoy on the Annisquam bar about 9:00 A.M., *Aquarius* was really all right. At that point a series of misfortunes struck about which no one could do anything, and everyone did what he could.

From offshore, seas breaking to leeward look far less dangerous than they are, for the observer sees only their backs, not their steep faces. The Monday morning quarterback sees at once that getting into shoal water near the buoy was dangerous. Yet it must have looked "not too bad," and identification of the buoy seemed important.

First a breaking sea stove in the windows forward. The windows had lasted through the night in the longer offshore seas, but the short, hollow seas on the bar came over the bow much more heavily. Logy, heavy in the water, *Aquarius* took several more seas and flooded her engine. She was now fairly into the shoal water. The only hope was to get the engine going again and get out. However, the engine ran only briefly and was flooded again. What next? The only hope, and a dim one at best, was to anchor. Apparently the anchor did not hold in the sandy bottom against the weight of the steep seas. What hope remained? Signal for help and strike for the beach. Red flares were burned, extra life jackets issued, and the raft inflated. When a sea capsized the vessel, everyone did the best he could.

When asked for the key to the disaster, Gorman blamed the lack of a radio. His was ashore being repaired. Yet for generations people have made their ways along shore and across vast oceans without radios. Had he been able to call the Coast Guard after 9:00 P.M., it is doubtful if a rescue craft could have found *Aquarius* anyway, for radar between two small boats in seas higher than either would be ineffective, and visibility was zero. In the morning, no rescue craft could have come out of Annisquam or Newburyport, and a boat from Gloucester would have been too late. Nevertheless, something might have been done. All one can say, and it must be said in charity, is that nothing must be left undone to ensure safety, and taking a radio is one of those things.

One can speculate on whether careful attention to a fathometer could have told Gorman his position without closing on the buoy and thus getting into shoal water. He might then have realized that his best bet lay in working offshore around Cape Ann and going into Gloucester in the lee. Certainly, any attempt to cross the bar in that sea could have led to nothing but disaster. This is at best a speculation.

RDF would have been of little service, for the only station near enough to be of use was Eastern Point, across the land mass of Cape Ann. It would have told him only that he was in Ipswich Bay, which he knew very well already. Sometimes events combine against a good man such that in spite of good preparation and wise decisions, disaster ensues. Afterward it is easy for others to see clearly what should have been done and to pontificate over the glasses about what would have happened if . . . . We must recognize that under the pressure of the event a decision that looks sound at the time can turn out to be disastrous. We must respect the decision for we might not have done so well ourselves.

And look at all the damned fools with shoddy equipment who make it nonetheless!

A ballad by William Henry Drummond, "The Wreck of the *Julie Plante*," concludes: "You can't get drown on Lac St. Pierre/ So long you stay on shore."

True, but maybe staying ashore is too high a price to pay. Your chances of being lost in a well-found yacht are so dim that it may be better to go to sea and live your life than stay ashore because you are afraid of losing it.

Hulling

An article in an old *National Fisherman* reminded the Sailor of a sentence from Frank Robb's classic *Handling Small Boats in Heavy Weather*. The thirty-foot sloop *Snowdrop,* Dutch built and nearly thirty years old, was caught off the Gulf coast by Hurricane Eloise. Her crew set no sail, towed no warps, wrestled with no sea anchor—but lashed the tiller, went below, and prayed. Although *Snowdrop* lost twenty-five feet of her mast in a bad knockdown, she survived and sailed in, jury rigged.

Frank Robb wrote: "You strip your boat, lash everything firmly, and leave her to fight her own battles while you curl up below with a good book. . . . It seems to be as safe as any of the other defences. It has additional merit in that it leaves the boat free of a lot of human

beings badgering her to do something she probably doesn't want to do."

Towing

Suppose you wish to tow your yacht with the outboard-powered skiff. You make fast a tow line to the bow of the yacht and pass the end to the boy in the skiff under your port bow. He makes it fast to the stern seat and puts the power to her. The line comes taut (Fig. 1A) before the skiff is directly ahead of the yacht and yanks the skiff's stern to starboard, her bow to port (Fig. 1B). The boy in the skiff puts the tiller hard to port in order to steer to starboard (Fig. 1C). The propeller, of course, goes to starboard and drives the stern of the skiff farther to port against the pull of the tow line, which pulls the stern to starboard, letting the bow of the skiff fall off farther to port. If the yacht has any way on her, she ranges up on the skiff, increasing the angle and further confusing the boy in the skiff.

Figure 1

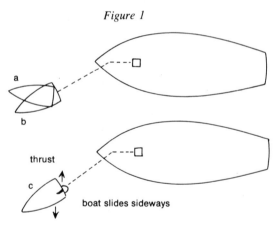

The boy then eases the throttle, gets slack in the tow line, reverses his tiller, and if he does not get the propeller fouled in the tow line, crosses the yacht's bow and performs the same evolution to starboard.

There are two solutions immediately obvious when the problem is sketched on paper.

1. Make fast the tow line in the skiff around the rowing seat, or tie it to the bow

painter, pass it under the rowing seat, and seize it to the middle of the seat (Fig. 2). Now the skiff, with the force of the propeller acting astern of where the line is fastened, can swing the stern to port or starboard in the usual way and the skiff can take station ahead of the yacht.

2. The preferable solution in quiet water is to lash the skiff alongside, making fast with bow and stern lines, and applying the power on a spring line (Fig. 3).

Figure 2

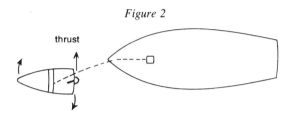

Figure 3

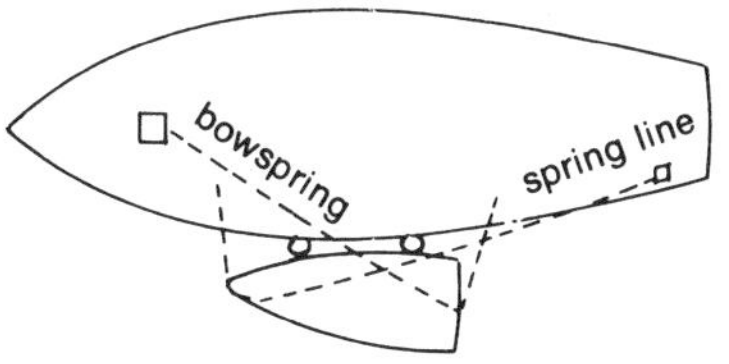

The bow line will be slack most of the time and will simply prevent the skiff's bow from swinging away from the yacht should a passing wake or a change of course incline it to do so. The stern line resists the tendency of the skiff's stern to swing away from the yacht in response to the pull of the spring line on the skiff's starboard side. The spring does all the work. It is made fast in the forward part of the skiff to the painter or bow thwart and around a winch or solid quarter bitt on the yacht.

The outboard motor can now be wound up to a moderate speed and the yacht steered with her own rudder. Should one be maneuvering in restricted waters, rig another spring from the stern of the skiff to the mast or forebitt. Of course, adequate fenders should be used between the skiff and the vessel.

You may see commercial sailing vessels pushed in calm weather by a yawl boat under the stern. Yacht sterns are usually not built for this treatment, nor is provision usually made for rigging heavy lines to the quarters of skiff and yacht. Should a sea catch the bow of the skiff under the overhanging stern of the yacht, the skiff might well be swamped.

Towing One Yacht with Another

This operation must be approached with caution, for heavy strains may be involved and unwary people can be hurt.

First, unless it is a case of desperate emergency, ease up as near to the distressed vessel as possible and tell her skipper your plan. Have only one person talk and be sure you are clearly understood.

Next, coil your tow line on deck forward, lead it aft, and pass it to him from your lee quarter to his weather bow. If the line is not too heavy and you can get quite close, just take the first five or six coils in your right hand and lay a few fathoms more on deck loosely at your feet. Swing the coils toward the target and back to get up momentum and finally heave them as high and far as you can, pointing your arm directly at the target. Grab the loose line and ease out slack until the crew of the tow signals that the line is fast.

Take a turn with the tow line around your mast or forward bitt. Ease the tow line as the tow picks up speed. For towing at sea, use as long a line as you can to take advantage of its elasticity and the effect of the sag. Make fast with a tow-boat hitch.

Should it be impossible to pass the tow line directly to the tow, use a light heaving line with a weight of less than lethal mass on the end of it. Another dodge is to make your heaving line fast to a life preserver, slack it well out astern, and tow it under the bow of the distressed vessel so it can be gaffed aboard.

Towing puts a heavy strain on the tow line and anything to which it is fast or with which it comes in contact. Use the heaviest line you have—nylon is the most elastic—and protect it with chafing gear wherever it touches anything.

The strain is much increased as you approach the tow's hull speed. The rule-of-thumb formula for hull speed is $1.5\sqrt{LWL}$. A boat twenty-five feet long would have a hull speed of 7.5 knots and certainly should not be towed faster than 4 knots.

Do not fail to consider the strain on your engine, shaft, propeller, and thrust bearing. Take it easy.

If You Need a Tow

The usual distress signals may work. Try everything from hoisting your ensign upside down to calling for help on the radio. DO NOT USE MAYDAY unless there is a real danger to life or vessel, and remember that aid voluntarily offered and accepted may render you liable to a salvage claim.

Be sure you understand what the towing vessel plans to do. When the line is heaved to you, don't just shut your eyes, hold up both hands, and miss it. As it snakes toward you, look at the part of it coming nearest and try to catch it like a ball. If you miss, grab for the specific part lying across your deck.

Quickly take a turn around the most solid fixture in the forward part of your vessel. Wave your arm to signal that the line is fast. Ease out slack as the strain comes on and make fast with a tow-boat hitch.

Keep everyone clear of the tow line as much as possible. A line, parting under heavy strain, snaps back with savage force.

Keep a sharp knife available in case of a jam.

Steer directly along the tow line.

Keep the weight in your vessel amidship or aft.

Do not let yourself be towed fast enough to cause a quarter-wave behind your vessel.

Beware of a coil of line on deck. Never let anyone sit or step on it.

If Your Propeller Gets Wound Up

How easy it is to get wound up in a lobster-trap warp, a dock line, or your own dinghy painter! It happens so fast and seems so final. The engine suddenly stops and the dinghy floats, outraged, under the quarter with its nose in the water and its tail in the air. Or a pot warp leads deep underwater from your wheel. One yachtsman wound up his genoa sheet in

the propeller and tore the clew out of the sail before the motor choked to death. What do you do?

The first move is to care for the safety of the yacht. Usually the quickest and safest move is to anchor, for these contretemps usually develop in the shoal water of harbors and narrow channels. Then fish up the line and address the problem—gently at first.

1. With the clutch in neutral, pull from different angles. This probably won't work, but it is worth a try. The shaft might just turn over and roll the line off.

2. If she wound up going ahead, put the clutch in reverse. Apply a strong steady pull to the fouled line and have someone hit the starter button with the switch off. As the shaft turns over slowly, the line may unwind at least a turn or two. If it does give you a little slack and then jams again, try it in forward. Maybe you can twist and jiggle it clear.

3. If these measures fail, take a careful look under the stern. It is difficult to see the propeller in many auxiliaries because of the refraction of the water and the position of the wheel under the overhang of the counter. Still, if someone will hold the skiff steady, maybe you can work off a turn around the blade with a boat hook.

If these three steps have not succeeded, more heroic measures are in order. You will have to go overboard. You will need a sharp knife. Take time to sharpen it. You will also need a ladder with which to get aboard again and a line around your shoulders so the mate can pull you to the surface if you should get wound up in your work. If you have a face mask and a pair of flippers, the job will be much easier.

Now get overboard with the knife tied around your wrist. You will probably find that there is a turn of line around a blade right next to the hub and then that the two ends of the line forming the bight have been wound tightly around the shaft in overlapping and interlocking turns. As the engine turned its last, it hove those turns down very hard. If the line is nylon or polypropylene, it has stretched considerably and hence become smaller and much harder.

Cut off both ends of the line a foot or so from the snarl. If it is a pot warp, try to save the buoy and tie it to the line again. That trap is worth money to its owner, who set it where you fouled it, not from personal malice but from economic necessity.

Now you will have to submerge and do the best you can. Start at the end where the line is slack. Cut the top turn and try to unwind it and come up for air. Just butcher away at it, but don't try to stay down as long as you can, and take plenty of time between dives to get your breath. If the line is wound so hard that it turns the edge of your knife, try a hacksaw blade. Sometimes two men, one on each side of the boat, can help each other, but the chances of cutting your helper as well as the line are not negligible.

After fighting it for a while, you will finally get to one of the turns that is locking the rest together and the line will come off all at once. You may need help getting aboard, especially if the water is cold.

Now proceed with care. Start up the engine and cautiously put it in gear at slow speed. If it runs without undue hammering and vibration, it is probably all right. Pull your anchor, go ahead gently, and slowly accelerate to cruising speed. The danger is that you may have bent the shaft. If the deformity is so great that the propeller hits the rudder or the bottom of the boat, you will have to stay right where you are and call for help. If it is just sprung, it may vibrate badly enough to damage the strut, stern bearing, or stuffing box. Proceed as slowly as you can.

You may be able to avoid getting wound up by taking some precautions. Note that a lobster-trap warp leads from the trap on the bottom to a toggle (a float or empty bottle) on or near the surface and thence to the buoy. Because nylon sinks, the warp will sag to about propeller depth and the buoy will lie down the tide from the toggle. Notice how the buoys are lying and pass down the tide from the buoy, never going between the buoy and the toggle.

In harbors and wherever you expect to proceed slowly with the possibility of reversing, tow the dinghy on a very short painter.

Back away from your mooring or let the wind set you away from it before you start on your way.

Fishermen often install a cage of steel rods around the wheel to protect it, but this slows down a boat too much to make it practical for most yachts.

Finally, keep a mask aboard, for sooner or later you can't avoid getting wound up.

How often has Cautious Conrad, seeking to avoid one peril, rushed headlong into another? He bent a trip line to the crown of his anchor, buoyed the end of it, and dropped the buoy overboard as he ranged up to anchor. When he reversed the engine to take the way off her, the wheel fouled in the trip line.

Moorings

If you rent a slip in a marina or can hire a yard to set your mooring off, you will save yourself a heavy, dirty job. If you set 3 off your own mooring, you will save considerable money; and when it comes on to blow, you can sleep soundly, knowing well what is under you.

You won't find an ideal site for a mooring unless you are very lucky and live far from human habitation. Protection from heavy seas is of course the first consideration, for it is the sea, not primarily the wind, which breaks out an anchor. A real summer gale or a September hurricane can raise a nasty chop with even a short fetch. The second consideration is swinging room. A crowded anchorage is a dangerous one, for not only must you lie to short scope yourself, but so must everyone else. When one boat drags, she will foul others and pile up the lot on the beach. Swinging room is partly a function of depth, for the deeper the water, the wider circle must your boat swing in. Yet water too shoal is obviously dangerous. A fairly soft mud and clay bottom is ideal, but a good mooring can be set on almost any kind of bottom except smooth ledge or very hard, slippery clay. Finally, you must be able to approach your mooring from any direction and leave it in any combination of wind and tide without getting ashore or entangling yourself with your neighbors. You cannot find the perfect site; compromise where you must.

In purchasing anchor and chain, ignore the tables in the marine hardware catalogs and buy the heaviest gear you can handle—within the limits of reason. Remember that all bodies weigh less in water than they do in the air. Iron loses less weight than granite and granite much less than cement. A mushroom anchor on any kind of soft bottom is ideal. It has no fluke to foul and, left to itself, will soon work its way down through the mud almost out of sight. A big flat rock is the next best bet, and a cement block is the least satisfactory but will do, especially if large amounts of scrap iron are embedded in it. An ordinary man with a tackle consisting of a double and single block can handle a 150-pound mushroom anchor without difficulty. A boy with a come-along can lift a 400-pound anchor.

Next buy chain. Use galvanized proof chain as heavy as you can handle and afford. For a boat of over twenty feet I suggest at least three-eighths-inch chain. True you can lift her out of the water with three-eighths-inch chain, but after five years it will not be so strong or so heavy. The weight is significant, for the boat must lift the weight of the chain before it pulls on the anchor, and even then it will pull along the bottom and not up. No matter how restricted the anchorage or how heavy the chain, you will do well to have at least twice the depth of water in chain.

Finally, you will need a pennant of nylon line. Nylon has great elasticity and tends to absorb jerks on the chain, which might break out the anchor. Small-diameter nylon lines are strong enough, but a large-diameter line is easier to grab and to pull on, more elastic, and more resistant to chafe. Some yachtsmen shackle a heavy post to the chain and use just a short pennant to connect the vessel to the post. The post must be pulled out nearly

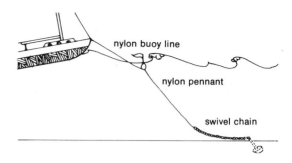

straight to exert much strain on the anchor. Others attach the pennant to a buoy and attach a short painter to the buoy. Here again, the buoy must be pulled under before much strain is exerted on the anchor. The mooring pennant to the boat should be attached below the buoy in case the rod through the buoy breaks.

All connections must be solidly made, for you will not see any of them until September. The best way to attach a chain to an anchor or a block of granite is to have a ring welded to the end of the chain. Pass the end of the chain through the staple in the granite or the ring in the anchor, then through the ring on the end of the chain, pull the chain through, and work the ring right down to the anchor. This avoids all shackles and makes certain that nothing will come adrift.

Next attach a swivel to the end of the chain. Make it bigger than you need. The weakest point in a swivel is the top of the shaft on which the upper part turns. This should be about the size of the chain. The pin through the jaws is usually held in place by a small cotter pin. Substitute the heaviest galvanized nail that can be driven through the hole and bend it so it cannot possibly move either way, even if the head of the nail rusts off.

Then spring a stainless steel thimble around the eye of the swivel and splice the nylon pennant tightly around the thimble. Nylon line stretches so much that unless you fit the splice very snugly, the thimble may capsize under the strain and leave the splice chafing against the swivel. I have never seen this happen, but it could. Fishermen used to soak mooring pennants in tar or copper paint, but synthetic ropes do not rot and weeds and mussels do them little harm.

On the upper end of the pennant, splice the buoy and lead the mooring line from under the buoy to the boat so the strain will not come on the buoy. Finish with a neat eye splice just big enough to fit over the bitt or mooring cleat. Parcel the mooring line with canvas or split rubber hose where it bears against chock or bobstay, attach a pick-up buoy to the loop at the top, and you are ready to set the assembly off.

Of course, if you use a post instead of a buoy, you will shackle the eye at the bottom of the post directly to the swivel. The iron on the post should be bolted right through the post and should be much heavier than the chain.

If you must use a shackle anywhere in the assembly, grease the pin liberally, set it up with a wrench until a thread or two on the pin comes clear through the shackle, and peen the last thread down. Then mouse the pin with stainless-steel seizing wire. As a boat swings and jerks on her chain, she tends to unscrew shackle pins.

Setting off can be done quickly, easily, and safely if properly planned. First cover the rail, deck, and topsides with a tarp or old sail. A rusty scar inflicted now will be with you all summer. Then by means of halyard winch, tackle, shore derrick, or come-along lower the anchor overside between float and boat abreast of the main rigging. Pass a short, stout line through the anchor ring, over the rail, around the mast, and tie it to its other end with a square knot. Lower away until the weight of the anchor hangs on the line.

Now tie a link of the chain through a scupper with a piece of light marline to support its weight. Tie another link through another scupper as you work aft with the chain and then coil the line on deck with the buoy underneath. Keep everyone on the other side of the boat.

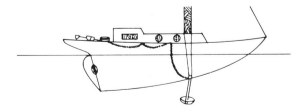

Get under way and motor gently off to the spot where you want the anchor. Move slowly and be sure you are just where you want to be. Then, cut the line around the mast. The anchor will drop to the bottom, parting each marline stop in turn, and pulling the chain after it, but not under it. Pick up the buoy and hang on.

It is particularly important to keep people away from the chain and line, for a mooring can twitch a man overboard quickly and irresistibly.

If you want protection at anchor, whether you are in an "anchorage area" or not, you will need an electric anchor light. On a quiet night, an oil lamp in the rigging looks picturesque, but the oil lamp has never been made which, despite its inside chimney and special oil, will not blow out in a hard rain squall. And who is going on deck to relight it with pajamas flapping wetly around his knees?

Dinghy Seamanship

Dinghy Adrift

Never swim after a drifting dinghy. You probably won't make it.

Sooner or later almost everyone lets a boat go adrift. You pick up a line out of the bow, make it fast, and turn to find that it is not the painter but an odd rope's end. Away down the harbor goes the boat.

Or you are bringing aboard a line—a mooring pennant, for instance. You pass it aboard and forget to tie the dinghy because you have already passed a line to someone aboard. Or your wife catches a fine fat mackerel on a line trolling astern. You haul the dinghy alongside to get it out of the way of the fish and the bowline flips off the bitt. You don't notice it until too late in the excitement over the fish. All three possibilities happened aboard my sloop this summer.

The temptation to make a quick dive for the drifting boat is enormous, but don't do it. You will be surprised at how slowly you swim with clothes and shoes on. Even in swimming trunks you don't cover ground very fast, while a light dinghy will skid off down the wind like a bubble. The longer the race goes on, the greater lead the dinghy gains over the tiring swimmer. Then when he gives up, having tried his best, he is a long way from the yacht, breathless and cold, and he has a tough swim ahead of him against the wind and waves.

Should he finally catch the errant dinghy, he must somehow get aboard. If he comes over the side, he may capsize the boat. If he tries to climb over the stern, his feet will slip under and he will find it difficult indeed. Perhaps the best he can do is to hang on and yell for help.

One yachtsman this summer saw a Boston Whaler adrift at sea with no one aboard. Sailing over to investigate, he found a man alongside clinging to the gunwale and trying feebly to get aboard. He had been picnicking on an island. The rising tide had floated his boat off. He swam after it, caught it, and would have drowned alongside it had not help come in time. The rest of the party marooned on the island could do nothing to help him.

A family on an anchored catamaran lost the dinghy painter. The father swam after the boat and drowned right in front of his helpless family, who could not get under way in time to save him.

Instead of yielding to the temptation to take a quick dive, start the engine. That is what you have it for. Or yell for help—ignominious as that may be. Or give the CB radio a whirl. Anything is better than swimming for it.

Going Off in the Dinghy

On a quiet day someone may want to row off a way in the dinghy to take a picture of the yacht, drop a fishline over the side, or visit another vessel. This can be done neatly and without anyone's getting wet.

The vessel is first hove to with the jib backed or sheeted down hard, the main sheet slacked off, and the tiller hard to leeward. Not until she loses way is the dinghy hauled along-side to windward where she will be clear of the main sheet and will lie in the little slick the yacht makes as she sags sideways and slowly moves ahead. With the boarding ladder and fenders rigged, the dinghy is held alongside by a man forward with the painter. The oarsman drops into the after part of the dinghy, all at once, not one foot at a time, and lets go of the side of the yacht. His camera and other impedimenta are passed to him, the man forward drops the painter into the bow, and the dinghy floats astern. The occupant may now get the oars out from under the seat, start the outboard, or take whatever action he likes.

When he is ready to be picked up, he should stow the oars under the seat and sit still. He should never under any circumstances go forward in the dinghy to pass the painter to a man on the yacht.

Bring the yacht up to leeward of the dinghy and heave her to as before. A man on deck with a boat hook catches the bow of the dinghy so she lies alongside. The camera and the fish that have been caught are passed to someone aboard. The man in the dinghy climbs aboard and *from the deck of the yacht* reaches into the dinghy and picks up the painter. The man with the boat hook casts off and the dinghy drops astern.

The secret of success is to keep the weight aft in the dinghy. If she trims by the bow, she will take a sheer and may tip over. Also, if the man in the dinghy tries to hold on to the rail of the yacht from the middle of the dinghy when the painter is cast off, she will swing sideways and either pull him off-balance or tip over.

Be careful not to get the dinghy under the counter as she is hauled alongside, either with a man in her or without. As the yacht's stern comes down on a sea, it could crush the gunwale of the dinghy and would certainly mar the stern.

In a power yacht the maneuver is carried out in the same way, the motor providing just enough forward motion to keep steerageway. In the event of an accident, though, the motor must be stopped at once. If the yacht has a boarding stage on the stern, the dinghy must be towed on the quarter so the occupant can step to the stage without going forward in the dinghy. Presumably an adequate handhold is provided for him.

Sea Breeze

From New York to New Brunswick the southwest wind blows in a broad steady sweep most of the summer, pumped northward from the Bermuda high. The skipper should consider what happens to this moving mass of air as it strikes the land along the coast he cruises.

First he might notice that along shore the force of the wind is affected by the changing temperature of the mass of North America. The land heats up by day and cools off by night much faster than the water or the air over the water. By day the warmer air over the land rises. About ten o'clock we begin to see puffy little cumulus clouds with dark bases forming inland and almost certainly the hot morning calm is broken by the strong, cool southwest wind coming in off the water to replace the thinner, warmer air over the land.

Then, in the late afternoon, as the land cools the clouds disappear as the pressure builds over the land. It seldom builds enough during July and August to produce a reverse flow of air against the steady drift from the south, but it will kill the wind near the shore. In September and October there will often be a northerly draft at night, but in the summer the night is usually almost calm. However, offshore ten miles, beyond the influence of the

land, the southerly is likely to air along all night. The skipper headed down east will do well to take advantage of this by running at night from Cape Cod or Cape Ann to the Maine coast, thus doing overnight what might take two or three days. Bound west, if anyone still beats "up to Boston," he would stand offshore from around 3:00 P.M. to midnight and then tack in shore, bringing the sea breeze with him in the morning.

Notice what happens to this sea breeze when it hits an island. This mass of air has been moving unobstructed over the surface of the ocean. The air on the bottom has stayed on the bottom, for there has been nothing to overturn it. This air has been slowed by friction with the water so the upper air is moving faster than that below.

When this stable air mass strikes an island, the lower air must rise over it. This, together with the convection engendered by the heat of the island, mixes the lower air with the faster-moving upper air, imparting the speed of the latter to the whole mass. Then the accelerated air swoops down the lee side of the island, in the case of a really high island becoming denser as it goes, and rushes over the water, usually in strong puffs.

Close under the weather shore, especially if it is a high and steep shore, the oncoming wind will pile up a cushion of more or less dead air and the rising air will slide up over it. Either that or the wind close to the shore is blowing straight up, either way providing very little motive power to a vessel under sail. Consequently, one does well to stand a mile or so outside a steep island or promontory. Numerous examples of this can be found. Cape Ann off Gloucester can be pretty sloppy. The weather side of Cape Small, Pemaquid Point, Otter Cliff on Mt. Desert, and Southwest

Head on Grand Manan demonstrate the same phenomenon.

On the other hand, the lee side of an island, after one gets far enough off to be clear of the dead air close under the shore, is likely to provide a brisk working breeze and a quick passage. As one approaches Nantucket's northern side, for instance, one will often find a very fresh southerly blowing off the land. One yachtsman, storming into Nantucket harbor single-reefed and dripping wet, asked if it often blew this hard in the summer and was answered in the affirmative by an unimpressed native. Ipswich Bay, the Maine thoroughfares, and the waters north of Grand Manan show the same characteristics.

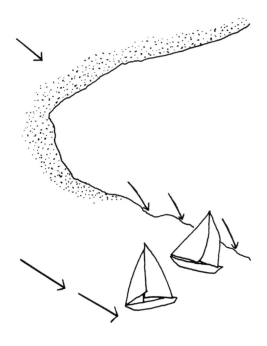

The sea breeze behaves in the same way, of course, as it crosses a point of land as it does over an island. We have noticed that if it comes down off the land at an angle, it usually tends to swing offshore, blowing more from the westward off the easterly side of a point lying north and south. Thus, by crowding in close under the land, one often gets a favoring slant off the land so one can fetch almost straight up the shore in smooth water on a course that would be nearly a dead beat offshore in lighter air and a sloppy sea.

Competition among sailors is endemic. Fishermen used to race to market, and a fast boat made money. Yet weatherliness and the capacity to carry a trip of fish were also important. Now, racing has become among yachtsmen not only endemic but epidemic. In order to win, one must increase the expense and decrease the weight of a yacht to the brink of disaster; and even then, only one boat wins.

Yet who can so admire the grace of another yacht sailing through his lee that he will not have a pull at the main sheet and observe that every boat is a compromise?

The Waves in Your Wake May Be Expensive

It is hardly necessary to remind a considerate yachtsman that the wake raised by his boat may be anything from an annoyance to a serious hazard. The afflicted have had heretofore little recourse. Curses are inaudible. The boat raising the wake is seldom within missile range by the time a suitable missile can be found, and the authorities, except in isolated cases, have been reluctant to take action.

Some years ago a small yacht was anchored in the mouth of the Huntington River in Long Island. The two young men aboard were contemplating the sunset in anticipation of a dinner of new green peas, even then boiling on the stove. Just as the peas were in transit from stove to table, a fast motor launch sped up the river and spilled the peas. The irate cook seized a shotgun from its hooks on the bulkhead and sent a blast after the retreating launch, unfortunately already out of range.

Knowing that what goes up the river will almost inevitably come down, he sat in his cockpit with the gun across his knees and as the launch drew abeam, fired both barrels loaded with birdshot. The motorboat owner was stung and astonished but not severely damaged.

Presently, through the gathering dusk appeared a rowboat manned by three policemen. One in the stern held a pistol, another rowed, and the man in the bow protected the others with a shield improvised from an ash-can cover. The young men invited the policemen aboard and explained the situation, but as the law forbade the discharge of firearms in the town of Huntington, the man who had fired the shotgun was taken to jail for the night.

His friend spent the evening making the rounds of the anchored fleet, telling the story, and easily raised enough for bail. However, time had passed swiftly, bail seemed hardly worthwhile, and the rest of the night was spent in spreading the story to the New York newspapers.

At the arraignment the next morning, the courtroom was crowded with yachtsmen and reporters. The youth admitted to having fired a gun in the town of Huntington, was judged guilty and fined one dollar. Yachtsmen vied for the privilege of paying the fine. One reporter had had a medal struck overnight and pinned it to the shirt of the guilty man. By unanimous vote he was awarded the money collected the night before and was escorted from the court in high procession.

The judge then turned to the motorboat operator and threw the book at him—everything from disturbing the peace to assault with a dangerous weapon—and hit him with a heavy fine. The unfortunate and unimaginative man could not understand why he, the aggrieved party, who had been attacked by a maniac with a shotgun, should suddenly find himself the guilty party while his assailant was feted through the fleet.

Since then we have all heard of people who have been burned, bruised, fractured, or drowned by irresponsible skippers. One summer, Roland La Branche, anchored at the mouth of the Saco River, was badly burned when a pot of steamed clams was spilled on his legs by a passing motorboat. The York County Superior Court awarded him $18,000 damages. That kind of money talks with a loud voice.

6

Navigation and Piloting

Selecting a Compass

Edgar J. White

"Truth lies within a little and certain compass," wrote Henry St. John, Viscount Bolingbroke, 250 years ago, "but error is immense." This English statesman, associate of Alexander Pope and Jonathan Swift, was in no way referring to the navigational instrument, but his lament for his isolation from his native land readily translates for the sailor who has been less than thorough when buying a compass for his sailboat.

The compass, foremost accessory to any craft that strays out of sight of her anchorage, is marketed today in so many varieties and brands that the conscientious boat owner must do his homework if he is to skirt Bolingbroke's frustration. All compasses, at any price, sitting on display in the showroom will point magnetic north within acceptable tolerances, but what will happen to that reading when you're hard to the wind (force 6) ten miles offshore in a sloppy sea?

"A compass is nothing but insurance," says Robert White, distributor for navigational and weather instruments in Boston, "and its expense should be commensurate with the risk." Therefore, a thirty-foot yawl that may weekend two or three times a summer in Cape Cod waters would require a different compass if she were cruising five days a week up and down the Maine coast.

As a general rule, one should remember that the larger a compass, the more accurate it is in holding a reading during the four different motions encountered in sailing—roll (heel), pitch, yaw, and surge. Stability of the card under these conditions is a function of the mass of the compass liquid in proportion to the mass of the card assembly. Obviously, the liquid in a six-inch compass will provide greater stability than will the liquid in a three-inch compass. The wrinkle is, of course, that larger compasses are more expensive than smaller ones (note: a typical Danforth eight-inch Constellation retails at more than five hundred dollars, a five-inch one at less than three hundred dollars. Also, the larger compass is easier to read at greater distances. For the large bluewater cruising sailboat this extra insurance may be worth the extra cost, but for those of us with more modest ambitions and less time a smaller compass will be suitable. Whatever the circumstances, compasses between three and one-half- and six-inches apparent card diameter will meet the requirements of just about all sailboats. Rare indeed is the craft that demands the extra measure of security offered by an eight-inch instrument.

After size, the next important consideration is type. Compasses are internally and externally gimbaled, flat-top, spherical, and truncated spherical; they come with conventional open-face dials (flat cards), or hemispherical, "aft-reading" dials. They are flanged, binnacled, and bracketed for different mounting systems. The cards themselves may be in increments of one, two, or five degrees, in quarter points, or in quarter point and degree combinations. Corrector systems may be built-in, or external. All these factors, and others, are worthy of the careful buyer's consideration.

The true spherical compass is the best design for almost all sailboats. Since the fluid does not swirl within the sphere, boat motion has little effect upon the stability of the card assembly within. Some cheaper compasses appear to be spherical but actually are truncated at the bottom, out of sight. In this configuration the fluid circulates irregularly and, of course, reacts with the card accordingly (Fig. 1). Also for the sake of stability, the compass card should be perfectly centered in the sphere, its plane bisecting the fluid and hence subjecting itself to equal resistance on both sides. Some cards are "dropped" on the pivot so that they rest in the lower half of the sphere and react to unequal pressures.

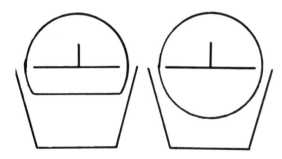

Figure 1

In some few cases, a flat-top box compass is acceptable for light-air, calm sea sailing in small craft, but normally these attractive and "antiquey" items are better suited to bookshelves and coffee tables.

Almost any boat that expects to encounter choppy waters or angles of heel more than thirty degrees should be equipped with an internally gimbaled compass, where the gimbal rings move within the sphere of fluid, providing greater stability. Externally gimbaled instruments, since there is no fluid to offer resistance, may actually "flip-flop" with violent

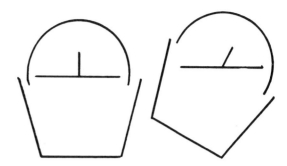

Figure 2. Powerboat compass, externally gimbaled

motion. Maximum's Polyaxial is unique with its extra gimbal ring, allowing for installation in nonvertical places.

It should be noted that some types of powerboat compasses bear an almost perfect likeness to their sailboat counterparts, and the unwary buyer will be hard-pressed to tell the difference. The problem is that the common medium-priced powerboat compass is not internally gimbaled, even though it may appear identical to the sailboat compass. To find out which is which, lift up the compass and tilt it. If the lubber's line stays the same in relation to the compass housing, it's a powerboat model (Fig. 2). If it moves with the card, it's a sailboat compass, internally gimbaled (Fig. 3). Several sailboat manufacturers have been cheating their customers by supplying the boat with a powerboat compass, and undoubtedly they will continue to do so as long as the customer doesn't know the difference.

Choosing a compass with a suitable card is a matter of common sense rather than special knowledge. Most sailors need nothing

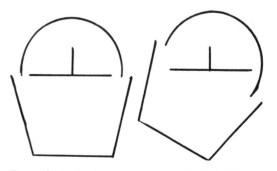

Figure 3. Sailboat compass, internally gimbaled

more detailed than a card in five-degree increments; the five-degree card is now fairly standard on all but the very large compasses, where one- and two-degree intervals are offered for those running long courses in open seas. But try a long trick at the helm with a one-degree card and see how long it is before you come down with Excedrin headache #38: "Helmsman's Hypnosis."

Hard to understand is the availability of aft-reading dials — the hemispherical dial with the lubber's line on the side facing the skipper. One retailer suggested that this style of compass is for people who are used to the little compass on the dashboards on their cars. But what's good on the road is "all wet" at sea, at least for the sailor who knows the difference. One advantage inherent in the spherical design is that the fluid is shaped into a meniscus lens. You can see the same effect with a spoon in a glass of water. If you view through the glass at eye level, the image of the spoon enlarges as you move it from the near side to the far side of the glass. The conventional open-face card effectively uses the magnification properties of the meniscus lens, but the hemispherical aft-reading card does not. In addition, the fluid in the sphere is not as good a stabilizing element on the aft-reading card. Omni, Aquameter, Airguide, and Ritchie's Explorer series all offer this kind of dial, but we suggest that the money you save isn't worth it—unless the compass is to go on your car dashboard.

All good sailboat compasses are available with at least three lubber's lines—one forward, and two forty-five degrees off-center for easier reading by the helmsman, who shifts sides when tacking. Maximum's Polyaxial comes with four (one aft), Ritchie's with three, and Danforth's with three (but as an extra option on their Constellations). Unless your helm position is always directly aft of the compass, as on a pedestal, you'll want these extra lines.

How about compass correctors? There is considerable controversy as to whether a sailboat compass should have built-in correctors, external ones, or none at all. Most sailors like the convenience of a built-in system, with easily accessible adjusting screws, rather than fussing with deck magnets, but there is no surefire way of knowing if built-in correctors will do a better job for your particular boat than deck magnets without hiring a first-rate adjustor. And no matter how fancy your arrangement of various compensating magnets, no matter how finely tuned your compass is to all sources of error on your boat, your compass just won't read completely accurately *all* the time, under all circumstances. For many years sailboats have run straight courses—and long ones, too—with primitive correcting systems or even none at all. More than one book-length dissertation is available for those who want to understand the numerous varieties of deviation and the possible remedies. In light of all that knowledge and opinion, it's almost a moot consideration whether or not your compass comes with built-in correctors, except for the question of convenience.

Compasses can develop problems over the years, like anything else, and should be readily reparable. A common problem, despite the touting of the catalogs, is bubble formation in the sphere. A quality compass is an assembled unit and can be taken apart to have the bubble removed. Many cheaper compasses, like Danforth's Lodestar, are fully sealed units whose inner workings are utterly beyond the reach of compass repairmen. A bubble in a Lodestar and similar inexpensive instruments means, in effect, time to throw it out and buy another.

Before you buy, know where you're going to install your compass.

Most good compasses come variously equipped for bracket or pedestal mounting, deck, or bulkhead flush installation, but costs vary.

This brings up some general observations on expense. If all the foregoing advice seems reasonable to you, then you'll have to spend close to one hundred dollars or more for a quality four-inch compass, with prices increasing for extra goodies and larger sizes. A suggested retail price lower than that certainly means sacrificing some important quality—one that may be important to your own needs and tastes. But every boat owner should know, dollar for dollar, exactly what he's getting for his money, in hopes for the most "truth" from his "certain compass".

Mounting Your Compass

Edgar J. White

Probably the most important piece of equipment you will ever buy for your cruising sailboat is your compass. Consider a number of factors before buying: the size and use of your boat, legibility and accuracy of your compass, its stability under surge, pitch, and roll, ease of adjustment, inherent quality, and, of course, cost. But in turning your attention to these things, you may overlook the end result of all your hard work: where are you going to put your compass, and how are you going to put it there?

Archetypal navigational instrument that it is, the compass tends to act as the spiritual focal point of the cockpit, and so it is natural that many a yachtsman prefers to assign it the central position. Pedestal mounting has impressive visual appeal. Horizontal or vertical flush-mounting in deck, wooden console, or bulkhead imparts a sense of built-in solidity and emphasizes the pure shining curve of the dome. And yet, by mounting his compass in any of these attractive ways, the cruising sailor may discover that he has sacrificed practicality for appearance.

Bracket mounting, by comparison, may not win high marks for beauty, but it will for common sense. The fully exposed bracket-mounted compass is far more visible than one half buried in the bulkhead. Relatively little light reaches the forward edge of the card in a bulkhead-mounted instrument, and that tiny red compass light you use for night navigation isn't worth much during the daytime when glare can be a real problem.

The compass mounted on a bracket is, of course, eminently portable. It can be stowed for day trips, it can go home with you for the winter, and it can be easily removed for cleaning or repair. Undertake that with a flush-mounted compass and you have some work ahead of you—not to mention a gaping hole in your deck or bulkhead. For those who like to have a compass in easy view when they're bunking down below or "dog-watching," easy portability is essential. (However, one manufacturer offers a model for deck mounting with the card printed on both sides so it can be read simultaneously by the helmsman and by the skipper in his bunk.) And for taking bearings—imagine using a vertical bulkhead-mounted compass for finding the bearing of a mark two or three points off your bow! We suspect that the recent resurgence of hand-bearing compasses is at least partly the result of yachtsmen's dissatisfaction with the inflexibility of their flush-mounted instruments.

Pedestal steering compasses appear to have one distinct advantage over bracket-mounts in that they are nearer the helmsman and therefore more easily read. There is danger, however, in such proximity. Any sailor not stationed directly aft of his compass is going to have varying amounts of difficulty with parallax, depending on how much he moves to one side of the compass's fore-and-aft axis. Forty-four thousandths of an inch (the sine of an angle of one degree on a four-inch card) is all it takes to miss a mark by three hundred yards on a ten-mile run. Better be five or six feet directly aft of the compass rather than a foot behind it and a foot to one side.

Also, pedestals come in standard heights, usually low enough for adequate reading when you are sitting but not particularly good when you are standing at the wheel staring down over a hooked lubber's line at a card that is not optimally magnified. The hooked line, of course, increases the parallax error significantly. For many of us the pedestal is just one of the more glamorous ways to bang a knee, bruise an elbow, or strain eye muscles looking back and forth between compass, horizon, and the set of the sails.

The vibration factor is another consideration in compass mounting. How long would you like to keep your compass before having it repaired? Boat vibrations—mostly from your auxiliary—amplify when they travel vertically and therefore are especially hazardous to the sensitive pivot and jewel of many nonbracket-mounted instruments. Vibration is especially wearing on compasses that sit atop a pedestal mounted directly over the engine's drive train.

Mounting on a spring-plated bracket receptable should greatly increase pivot and jewel life, since most of the vibrations are absorbed between the bulkhead and the compass.

What now remains is choosing the best place on your boat for mounting the compass. Because of all the relevant variables—size, rig, predominant use, cockpit space—there can't be a definitive answer for all sailboats, but you should be satisfied with your choice if you keep the following general rules in mind.

The fog shut down thick as tar. The old man, having hauled his last lobster trap, soaked a woolen mitten overboard, set it on the engine box, and carefully set his compass on it. This, he explained, was to prevent deviation. Then he headed straight for home. At first the compass read west northwest. Slowly it turned to northwest, north, and northeast. Then it turned back all the way to southwest. The wake stretched straight astern, and soon we broke out of the fog at the harbor entrance.

The romantic put it down to a mysterious sixth sense of direction either inborn or acquired through long association with the sea in all seasons. No one claims that the compass, with or without the mitten, had anything to do with it. Some of us know that on soft summer days there is always a slow ground swell making up the bay from the south . . .

The old man says nothing.

Where to Mount a Compass

First, avoid the engine. Compass deviation is a complex phenomenon; we politely defer to those who have made it their life work to understand it. However, you should keep your compass as far as possible from ferrous metals and from anything that sets up an electromagnetic field. The alternator, when it is charging, is an especially nasty influence. Remember that the effect of a magnetic field decreases as the square of the distance. If your compass is six feet away from the engine, it is four times better off than if it is three feet away. Don't forget other demons like propane storage tanks, heat-exchange pipes, and electrical equipment.

With the recent development of aluminum engine blocks by leading inboard-outboard manufacturers, the engine should become less of a deviation factor; but as long as you have the old iron-block auxiliary, keep the compass away from it.

Second, mount the compass at a distance from your usual steering position that will give you readability of the card without the risk of excessive parallax. Between three and six feet is fine viewing territory for a four- or five-inch compass. In any case, before buying a compass, try it at various distances to see what's comfortable for you. (NOT in the showroom with all that fluorescent lighting! Take it outside in the bright sunlight and try it in different directions.) The ideal angle of view is fifteen degrees to twenty degrees below the horizontal. At this angle you get a good clear look at the whole card and benefit from the greatest magnification.

Third, be aware of traffic patterns. Cockpits are busy places. Expect occasional collisions between the animate and the inanimate. No man is transparent. One must wonder about the wisdom of flush mounting a compass in the cockpit deck six inches aft of the companionway, but we have seen it done. Also, if bracket-mounting on the bulkhead of your sloop or catboat, watch out for halyards and sheets that may lead into the cockpit.

You may conclude that the best arrangement is to mount two bracket receptacles, one on each side of your bulkhead. On which side will it be best to have the compass compensated? While you are likely to get different deviations on different sides of the boat because of heeling error and asymmetrical deviational influences, it is good to know that on one side at least your compass points north (magnetic). Many yachtsmen prefer the starboard side for the following reasons:

- Under power it is preferable to sit to starboard to have the best view of the "dangerous quarter" in right-of-way situations.
- On most auxiliaries the alternator is mounted on the port side of the engine.
- Abstruse as this is, it is worth considering: For those who steer on the windward side, on the East Coast, chances are you will be leaving harbor more often on the starboard tack, since prevailing summer winds are southwesterly and most New England harbors face south or east to the sea. On a short run, fetching a seaward mark may require more compass work than heading home, when you're likely to rely on familiar landmarks.

Unless you are ketch-rigged (where mounting on the mizzenmast may be best), or you have an unusually long cockpit, or you are in the habit of ocean racing, we recommend bracket-mounting port and starboard. You'll save time, labor, and irritation; you'll reduce the risks of theft, excessive parallax, damage from engine vibration, and poor legibility. And compared to the other two forms of installation, you'll save money.

Compass Correction
Winslow Palmer

Most articles on compass correcting on small boats perpetuate the mistaken notion that it is *necessary* to know magnetic north and east *precisely* in order to correct the compass.

Actually, no external magnetic reference whatever is required. The only external reference needed is some means of knowing when the boat is turned exactly 180°, which can be provided more or less conveniently with a rudimentary sun compass—a pencil stuck in a perpendicular hole in the center of a square block of a two by six.

The procedure is to turn to a heading of 0° by the compass, without regard to the actual heading, and position the block so that the shadow of the pencil lies across one corner. Then, keeping the block fixed in position on deck, turn the boat exactly 180° so that the shadow falls on the diagonally opposite corner.

Adjust the athwartship corrector to re-move one-half the amount the compass undershoots or overshoots the 180° turn. Then turn to 90°, reposition the block, turn the boat 180° so that the shadow again falls diagonally opposite, and adjust the fore-and-aft compensator to remove one-half the error.

Two or three rounds of such adjustment, first N–S and then E–W and repeat, converges to the state wherein the corrector magnets exactly cancel the horizontal component of the boat field at the compass location, which is all that can be achieved with only two correctors.

Another convenient way of getting the exact 180° turn is to tie the boat bow and stern between two points on shore bearing approximately N–S and E–W respectively, winch the lines up tight, and read the compass. Then swap bow and stern lines, winch up tight again, and adjust the appropriate compensator to remove one-half the overshoot of the compass indication. The headings do not have to be exactly N–S or E–W, nor need they be exactly at right angles. If they are within a few degrees of the cardinal directions, the procedures converge to the correct adjustment within two or three rounds.

Actually, it doesn't take any profound mathematical knowledge to understand these principles. The point is this: It is NOT the purpose of correcting a compass to make it point in any particular direction. The purpose is to cancel the magnetic field attached to the boat so that the compass can respond freely to the earth's field. Therefore, we must devise a test that separates the boat's field from the earth's field so that we can cancel out the former. This is accomplished by simply turning the boat 180°. The overshoot or undershoot will be twice the deviation.

WITH THE DIAGRAM on page 138, the Sailor works it out on paper thus: First we head north by our erroneous compass. We do not know how much the error is, but let us suppose that it is 10° easterly. That is, our actual magnetic heading is 10°. Now we turn 180°. The deviation is now 10° westerly, because all influences on the compass are reversed. Our north point on the compass is now 10° west of

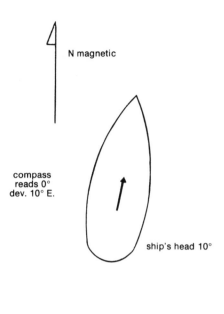

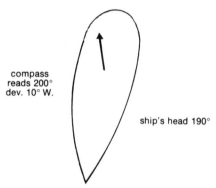

Chapman has a section on halving the deviation by running reciprocal courses. Bill Rice of Maine Compass Services uses a portable gyro compass that works the halving method. A company, I believe "Direcktor" is the name, makes and sells a sun compass that uses the same principle. I would not use an object the size of a pencil for a shadow. It would be about 5° wide, therefore not very precise. A block of two by six would be pretty loose if not properly secured.

I feel that it is better to make all conditions as close to reality as possible, such as run a course as near to magnetic north and south, and east and west as possible with the vessel running as close as possible to speed (vibration) as would exist in a real fog condition. No matter what method is used, running back and forth is necessary and halving is always done.

A *brief* discussion on compass compensation is dangerous. There is too much to cover and it can create more problems than intended . . . . Briefly, Mr. Palmer is not wrong, but he does leave some things out, and I would never feel that a compensating job done this way would be good enough.

IT OCCURS to the Sailor that this scheme is built on the assumption that the deviation is symmetrical; that is, that a reversal of course produces an exact reversal of magnetic influences. If the compass is not in the middle of the boat or if there is a tank, for instance, on one side of the boat and no tank on the other, an error will creep in. This would happen by any other method too, but if you have a magnetic north reference, at least you will know what it is. Also, one must remember that the sun moves about a degree every four minutes. If one is steering by the shadow while the adjuster is moving magnets, a small allowance might have to be made. Captain Brown points out also that Bowditch is the ultimate authority on compass adjusting. Bowditch observes, "It must be borne in mind that the compensation of the compass is not an exact science and the only safeguard is unceasing watchfulness on the navigator's part."

the magnetic north, and, although our real heading is 10° plus 180° magnetic or 190°, our compass reads 200°, because the north point is pulled 10° to the west of north. Our "overshoot" is thus 200° minus 180°, or 20°. Half of that is 10°. We remove 10° of deviation so that the compass now reads 190°. If we now head north, by our compass, our 10° of athwartships deviation has been removed and we are heading magnetic north. Of course, having no external reference point, we don't know it; but if we turn 180° again, inasmuch as the deviation has been removed, we will be heading south 180°, and there will be no overshoot or undershoot.

CAPTAIN TED BROWN, an experienced navigator and compass adjuster formerly with the Kittery Navy Yard, wrote us as follows:

Practically no one carries a compass in his dinghy and practically no one gets lost in the fog while rowing off to his boat at night; but a practical man knows that if he can see his breath before sunset, he better take his compass ashore with him, for the fog will shut down black as tar at dusk.

First Aid for the Compass

If your compass card begins to turn yellow and then brown from the effects of sun and age on the white markings, take out the plug and put in a few drops of hydrogen peroxide, which you can buy at a drugstore. Shake well and watch the brown bleach.

If your compass develops a bubble, turn it on its side and take out the screw plug. Sniff the contents. It will probably be fine kerosene or alcohol. Turn it so the bubble is under the hole and fill it up with a medicine dropper.

Compasses are filled either with a mixture of alcohol and water or with a highly refined oil something like kerosene. When the Sailor suggests that you sniff the contents of the bowl, it is to help you determine which of the two liquids is used in your compass. An alcohol compass can be topped up with distilled water. If the card is yellowed, a few drops of 3 percent hydrogen peroxide will indeed bleach it white again. Don't use much of the hydrogen peroxide, however, because it liberates oxygen and will form a new bubble of oxygen instead of air.

If your compass is oil-filled, don't put water or hydrogen peroxide in it. The hydrogen peroxide has a water base. The water will not mix with the oil but will form what looks like a bubble, but instead of rising to the top it will lie on the card, posssibly unbalancing it, for water is heavier than oil. You can probably remove most of the water by turning the compass so the plug is down and starting it enough to let the water leak slowly out.

To remove an air bubble from an oil-filled compass, at least temporarily, take off the bottom plate. Turn the compass so the plug is up and the bubble floating just below it. Start the plug just enough to let the air leak slowly out as you gently squeeze the expansion bag. If this doesn't work, use the compass with the bubble in it until you can get to a repair center.

The Bearing Compass

A good hand bearing compass is a valuable aid to the precise navigator, but carelessly used, it can be very misleading. The principle is simple: it is a compass with a sighting device across the top. Sight across it, read the bearing, and plot it on the chart. However, there are several sources of error to consider.

First, this compass, like any magnetic compass, aligns its magnets to the very faint terrestrial lines of force. Any local magnetic influence will cause deviation exactly as it will in the yacht's steering compass. Because the steering compass is permanently installed, it can be compensated for local influences like tanks, engine, and ballast, which are also permanently installed. However, the bearing compass, which is used in any convenient place on the boat, is subject to varying deviations. The worst place to use it is in the cockpit, for here it is subject not only to the influences working on the steering compass but also to the compensating magnets and to the magnet in the card of the steering compass. Furthermore, the bearing compass's magnet will influence the steering compass.

The thoughtful navigator will choose a clear, quiet day and establish himself near a charted buoy, whence he will have a good view of several distant charted objects like lighthouses. The farther away these are, the better. He will then take bearings on them from different parts of the boat until he finds a place where all the observed bearings agree with the charted bearings. The Sailor found errors of five to ten degrees on his boat from the cockpit, the stern, the companionway, and the top of the house. By standing far forward at a maximum distance from the ton of iron on the keel and the engine, which weighed hundreds

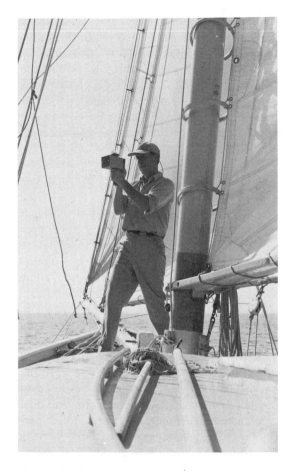

of pounds, he was able to get accurate bearings. Stainless steel rigging is ordinarily nonmagnetic, but some grades of rigging wire will affect a bearing compass significantly. Note that an error of five degrees in a bearing on an object five miles distant introduces an error of nearly half a mile (.436 miles).

Another consideration affecting the accuracy of bearing compass readings is the angle at which the compass is held. The instrument is designed to be held vertically with its top horizontal. The compass card pivots on a sharp pin on which, in the finer instruments, rests a jeweled bearing. If the pin is not vertical, the bearing may catch. Also, the optics involved in prisms and mirrors for reading the bearing introduce errors if the instrument is not held vertically. Most bearing compasses have a line etched into the sighting prism indicating the exact point of aim. This line should be vertical as nearly as you can judge. Rock

the instrument from side to side slowly around the line of sight to get a sense of when it is most nearly verical.

Take time enough to let the card settle down. The liquid in the compass bowl is intended to damp the violent motions of the little card caused by the motion of the boat and the changes in bearing. When the compass is held steadily on one bearing, it takes up to half a minute on a lively boat to get an accurate reading. Even then, you may get readings several degrees apart. Take the average as nearly as you can estimate it.

The accuracy of the compass is affected, too, by the care it receives. It should live in a padded box or rack either permanently installed in the boat or chocked off so it cannot slam around. It is better carried vertically than laid on its side so the card sits properly on its bearing and the pin cannot be bent by shocks. We used to be told to carry a compass upside down so the card did not rest on the pin, but that seems to be less emphasized with modern compasses. However, even a good jeweled bearing can be cracked by a sharp jolt, and the less durable plastic bearings are damaged even more easily.

Carefully cared for and wisely used, a bearing compass is much more accurate than sighting across the steering compass with a ruler. The only better scheme is a proper pelorus permanently installed and gimbaled. This, however, is not convenient on a small boat, and is seldom used.

Box the Compass

The world's navies and merchant services long ago gave up steering by points of the compass and adopted degrees as the way of defining direction. Their reasons are doubtless compelling, but to the yachtsman piloting and steering by a four-inch compass with an inexperienced crew, there is something to be said for the old way.

The circle of the card is divided into thirty-two points, each named in a clearly logical way.

Consider the northeast quadrant bounded by North and East. Halfway between them at

A point is 11¼°. This obviously is not a small enough division for fine steering; therefore, each point is subdivided into quarter points, each logically named. Remembering that nothing follows a three-letter point, the nomenclature is obvious. Anyone who can steer a small boat within a quarter point each way is a very good helmsman indeed. No smaller divisions are needed.

Boxing the compass is traditional and salty, but what can be the objection to the simplicity of a 360-degree card? Anyone who can count can read it. The objection lies partly in the similarity of the numbers: 260 at a distance looks very much like 280. Many modern cards for yachts use few numbers, print them in large characters, and indicate the divisions between them by unnumbered and undifferentiated lines at 5° and 10° intervals. Ten degrees is about the same as a point, but the card so marked lacks the clearly defined pattern of the card graduated in points without affording the accuracy that degrees suggest. Yet no one can steer within a degree anyway, even if the card were so marked.

Another objection to the old-time card is the time and effort required to learn the names of the points. Anyone who can remember the names of the Elizabeth Islands, the stops on a suburban railway train, or the thirteen original colonies can learn to box the compass by following the simple pattern.

Another practical reason for maintaining the ancient nomenclature is that, to people

45° is Northeast. Halfway between Northeast and North is North Northeast at 22½°, and at 67½° is East Northeast. In each case the name of the point is the combination of the names of the points it divides in half.

To continue the system, however, would become cumbersome. The next subdivisions are all "by" points. Translate "by" as meaning "1 Point." The first point east of North is North by East—North 1 Point East. The point following North Northeast, between that and Northeast, is Northeast by North. It might have been called North Northeast by East, but there has developed a principle that nothing follows a three-letter point. One never says North Northeast by —— or South Southeast by ——. With this in mind, the thirty-two points of the compass can be easily named.

The markings on the card accent the pattern. Big, clearly marked triangles mark North, Northeast, and East. Long thin triangles mark NNE and ENE. The "by" points are marked by smaller triangles. Thus, if the helmsman is asked to steer NE × E, he can see clearly and at a considerable distance from the compass the small triangle between the big triangle at NE and the long, thin diamond at ENE. The navigator, checking the course by the dim red nightlight, can easily see what part of the quadrant the course lies in. The very name *point* defines its place in the pattern.

A modern compass card

unaccustomed to speaking accurately of directions, 135° does not mean very much, but *southeast* carries a clear meaning. To be sure, the meaning of W X S½S may not be at once evident to the uninitiated, but he would guess quickly that it must lie somewhere to the south of west, whereas 253° has less significance until one performs some mental arithmetic.

A compelling reason for marking a card in degrees and for using degrees in chartwork appears as soon as the navigator drops the land below the horizon and takes in hand his sextant. All navigational tables are read in degrees. Azimuths, bearings of celestial bodies, are stated in degrees, and these bearings are used in plotting lines of position on the chart. The traverse tables used in figuring dead-reckoning positions are given in degrees, although old editions of Bowditch give them also in points. In offshore work, the use of points to the exclusion of degrees would be cumbersome indeed.

Therefore, the practical seaman might well develop a familiarity with both methods, using points for steering and piloting and degrees for celestial work. If all else fails, the neophyte can be told to steer for the left-hand end of that island or for the star on the end of the Little Dog's tail.

The Chip Log

Coasters, fisherman, naval officers, and clipper captains relied on the chip log as a simple and accurate measure of a vessel's speed through the water. While we now have sophisticated electronic instruments to measure speed instantly to the second decimal place, the chip log is still sufficiently accurate for the ordinary cruising man, is much less expensive to build and maintain, and does not depend upon electric current.

The chip log consists of a pie-shaped piece of wood, the chip, weighted to float upright, a length of line wound on a reel and punctuated with knots at regular intervals, and a sand glass or stopwatch. Drop the chip overboard, let the line run off the reel for a predetermined number of seconds, and count the number of knots that have run out.

Traditionally, either a fourteen-second glass or a twenty-eight-second glass was used and the distance between the knots determined as follows:

$$\text{Feet between knots} = \frac{14 \text{ sec}}{3600 \text{ sec}} \times 6080 \text{ feet/nautical mile}$$
$$= 23.64$$

To prevent your timekeeper's being taken by surprise, about thirty feet from the chip tie a rag to the line and about ten feet beyond it another rag. Drop the chip and let the line run off the reel. When the first rag goes out, say "Ready." When the second one goes out, say "Turn." After ten seconds, he will count down the last four seconds to fourteen so you can stop the line at exactly the right instant to count the number of "knots" you are sailing.

You will probably part the line and lose

About to stream the log. The wedge is not yet engaged in the clothespin.

your chip when you try to reel in unless you rig the chip so it will feather when you stop the line. Bore a hole in each corner of the chip and run your line through the top hole. Seize a clothespin to the line about three feet from the chip. Rig a bridle through the other two holes with a wedge of wood to fit snugly into the clothespin in the middle of it. While the wedge is jammed into the closespin, the chip will float upright and draw the line off the reel. When the line is checked, the wedge will pull out and the chip will skitter easily along the surface.

Constant Bearing

The navigator knows that when another vessel approaches on a course converging with his own, there is imminent risk of collision if the bearing of the approaching vessel remains constant. It is assumed, of course, that the careful navigator will constantly check bearings of other vessels even if he must continually crawl over the other people in the cockpit to sight across the compass.

If distant land shows behind the approaching vessel, there is an easier way. If the other vessel appears to be moving briskly ahead against the background of the land, she will pass ahead of you; if astern, you will beat her to the crossing. If she moves very slowly or she does not move at all, it will be too close.

The bearing of a house on the distant land is, of course, constantly changing as you sail past it. The farther you are away from it and the more slowly you sail, the slower will the bearing change. For instance, if you are four miles offshore and sailing at four knots, the bearing on a house abeam of you will change about 1° per minute. Another yacht appears 500 feet to windward sailing 30° freer than you and hence converging on your course. If he is sailing 4.61 knots, you will collide in 2.14 minutes if no one changes course. During that time, his bearing relative to you will have remained constant and the bearing on the house will have moved aft only 2°. In the fifteen seconds during which you watched his progress along the land, the bearing of the house changed a mere ¼°, an inconsiderable dis-

tance. He will appear, then, to have practically remained stationary relative to the land.

Suppose, however, that he is sailing at five knots and you are still sailing at four knots. In 1.97 minutes he will pass 67 feet ahead of you. Your bearing on the distant land will have changed a mite less than 2° and his bearing will have changed 90° from abeam to dead ahead in less than two minutes. In the fifteen seconds during which you watched him, the house will have moved aft about ¼° and he will have moved ahead about 11°. Clearly, he is moving ahead rapidly against the land.

In actual practice, how reliable is this device? The more distant the land and the closer the other boat, the more reliable it is; but if the other boat is definitely dropping back over the land, you in your port tack yacht can roar with assurance at the starboard tack yacht, "Hold your course," with the confidence that you have him in your pocket. If he is holding even or going ahead, bear off early or tack ship and let him go. It is possible in close quarters for a man forward on your boat, watching the stern of the converging boat moving ahead over the land, to believe that you have it made, whereas the man at the wheel of your boat, watching the approaching bow, will see that it is gaining. In that case tack at once. You are scheduled to hit him amidships.

The technique is useful too when you are approaching a buoy, just fetching it with wind and tide setting you down toward the shoal. If the buoy is moving to leeward against the land behind it, you will clear it; if it is moving to windward, you won't.

The old man could tell about where his sloop would fetch on the other tack. He closed his leeward eye and turned so the shadow of his nose was on the bow. Then he opened the leeward eye and closed the other. The new shadow showed the new course.

Approaching the Current Problem Using Hindsight and Foresight

L. Charles Hughes AP

The principle involved is obvious if we look at Figure 1. Assume boat speed equals 5 knots, current speed equals 1 knot, and course from Buoy #1 to Buoy #2 is 090° magnetic.

Without current, if we left Buoy #1 for Buoy #2 steering 090° on our ship's compass, the boat would travel on the line shown between the buoys. Under these conditions a magnetic bearing of Buoy #2, if it were visible, would read 090°.

With current, if we left Buoy #1 for Buoy #2 steering 090° on our ship's compass, the boat would travel on the line shown between Buoy #1 and Point A. Under these conditions a magnetic bearing of Buoy #1 would read about 260°. In fact, if we look astern we see Buoy #1 off to the starboard of the boat's center line and staying the same angular distance off this line. Let's use this observation to correct for the set of the current. Note that this correction, if properly done, would keep us on a line where our hindsight (magnetic bearing) of Buoy #1 would always read 270°.

The Procedure upon Departure from First Mark

We take departure from Buoy #1 for Buoy #2 steering 090° on our ship's compass in such a way as to leave from a position on the desired course line and close to Buoy #1, say about six boat lengths away. Check your timepiece and note the time. Our boat will travel along the line shown from Buoy #1 at Point A as a result of our steered course and the current set.

At the end of five minutes' run, several things should be done. Assume this run places us at Point A in Figure 1. We have been taking hindsights on Buoy #1 and noting them down. We find that they will be unchanging. We determine what the difference is between the hindsight we are reading at Point A and what the hindsight would be if we were on our desired course line. This latter hindsight would be equal to our desired course line magnetic plus 180°. In our example we would read about 260° hindsight taken near Point A. The hindsight if we were on our desired course line would be 270° (090° + 180° = 270°). The difference between hindsights is 270° − 260° = 10°, which is a "boat to left" of our desired course line error, as evidenced by Buoy #1 being to the "right" of the aftward extension of the boat's center line.

The difference in hindsights found above is our error. Multiply the error by two and add or subtract it to the original ship's compass course given to the helmsman so that the boat will aim back toward the desired course line. In our example we take our error of 10° and multiply it by two to get 20°; to bring the boat right we *add* it to the original course of 090° to get 110° as the next course to steer. This new course will move us on the line in Figure 1 from Point A to Point B.

As this second run begins to near five minutes' duration, further hindsights taken of Buoy #1 will indicate that the readings will approach the hindsight reading that we determined would be seen if we were on the desired course line, in our example 270°. When Buoy #1 gives a hindsight of 270°, we should be ready to give the helmsman a new course to steer. We will take the original error read at Point A and apply it to our original course to oppose the effects of the current observed; i.e., the error determined at Point A was that the boat was 10° to the left of our desired course, so we will apply the 10° error to the

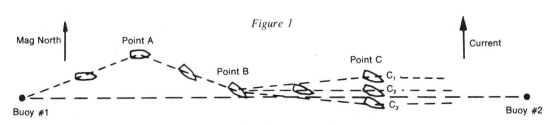

Figure 1

Mag North   Point A   Point B   Point C C_1 C_2 C_3 Current

Buoy #1   Buoy #2

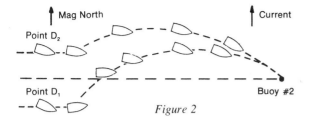

Figure 2

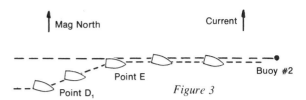

Figure 3

desired course to take the boat to the right (090° + 10° = 100°). This will be our new course to be steered from Point B.

At Point C, representing the end of another five-minute run, we determine by the hindsight of Buoy #1 what, if any, new error has been generated by the run from Point B to Point C, comparing our readings to 270°. If no error is found, we are on our desired course line and on our way toward Buoy #2, as indicated in Figure 1 by Point C.

If at Point C we find an observable error in the hindsight; i.e., the hindsight reading that would be read 270° if we were on the desired course line, we will correct our present course using this new error. Since our ship's compass and helmsmen can only operate in 2½° "notches" between courses, we will give a 2½° correction to our course steered to Point C to counter the observed new error. In our example we steer 100° from Point B to Point C so that if we determine through comparing hindsights that we read less than 270° we know we are at C_1 and would add 2½° to 100°, equaling 102½°, which would probably be our last course correction. We would sail on until we pick up Buoy #2. However, the process of checking the hindsight can continue as long as Buoy #1 can be seen.

The Procedure upon Sighting Second Mark

Our lookout reports seeing Buoy #2 ahead, which is reassuring. This is represented in Figures 2 and 3 by Points D_1 or D_2. Don't have your helmsman relax and aim for Buoy #2 or you will generate a "closing arc," as shown in Figure 2. This "closing arc" represents the considerable distance off our desired course line that can be generated by "aiming at the mark."

Assuming we find ourselves at Point D_1 as shown in Figure 3 and our foresight (magnetic bearing) of Buoy #2 is 085°, we are obviously to the right of our desired course line and in need of some corrections to get back on the desired course line, also probably in need of a changed course to stay on it. Since, as we noted previously, 2½° was the smallest course change we could give our helmsman, we will figure a new course to steer that will take us back toward the line. Let's change course by two "notches." We will change course by 5° to the left to get back on the desired course line. When our foresight reading is changed to read 090° as shown at Point E we will back off one of those corrective "notches" by which we changed our course at D_1. From Point E on we use the one "notch" to the left corrected course as compared with the course that took us to Point D_1. From Point E on we use our foresights to make sure that we are still in our desired course line.

Some Additional Thoughts on the Run from Buoy #1 to Buoy #2

Our helmsman should know that the boat must be steered so that the compass readings average out to the course requested. Perhaps it would be well if he learned to steer looking at the clouds or distant objects up ahead, if visibility permits, while still checking the compass every eight to ten seconds. We find this produces smaller course variations and also allows the helmsman to spot drift and/or arriving waves.

The magnetic bearings of the buoys are taken with a hand-held magnetic compass designed to give a reading by looking over it through two sighting vanes. Of great help for use at greater ranges are attachments that are applied to a pair of binoculars to allow magnetic bearings to be taken of objects farther than the naked eye can see. There are also, for the affluent, binoculars available that have built into them a magnetic pelorus. Be careful not to hold your magnetic pelorus or bearing compass near magnetic influences, which will affect its accuracy. Keep it away from the steering compass, for each will affect the other. The alternator on the engine and vertical steel rigging of material other than nonmagnetic stainless steel are particularly dangerous.

The hindsight-foresight corrections found and applied as previously shown also correct for leeway and windage. They are useful when under either power or sail.

Currents can vary because of the influence of obstructions such as islands and outlets from bays. In long runs we will find that the tidal currents vary both in direction and magnitude as the time of day changes. Also, the effect of the current will vary as the boat speed varies, which is a common experience under sail.

If you leave Buoy #1 with some sort of correction already applied to your desired course you may use the hindsight method to check that it is the correct one. If corrections are necessary, they are applied to the helmsman's course at Point A just as we did in our example.

As you pass an aid-to-navigation buoy or those ubiquitous lobster-pot buoys, look for the effects of current. With practice, by careful observation, you can get information about the direction and magnitude of the current from these. This information can be used if you are using a vectoral system to find a cor-

rection for current. At the least this information will help give you a "feel" for the current action.

If, by the time you get between Point A and Point B, you find Buoy #1 is beginning to disappear because of haze, you may want to return to Buoy #1 to make a corrected departure. This is done by sailing the reciprocal of our desired course line from Buoy #1 to Buoy #2, corrected to offset the current by using the initially found "error" in hindsights. In our example 090° + 180° = 270°; 270° − 10° = 260° would be our ship's compass course t return to Buoy #1. Note the direction previously given under "The Procedure upon Sighting Second Mark." We would then again leave Buoy #1 steering 090° + 10° = 100° and proceed as before.

We found this hindsight approach accidentally while leaving Buoy #1 and looking astern, and hope that if you practice it you too will find it a necessary part of "the craft" of piloting a boat.

The Vertical Sextant Angle

Theoretically, the calculation of one's position by vertical sextant angle is as simple as a problem in a geometry text.

BC is the height of a lighthouse. Angle A is observed with a sextant.

$$\text{The tangent of } A = \frac{BC}{AC}$$

$$AC = \frac{BC}{\text{Tan } A}$$

A quick look at a tangent table and a bit of

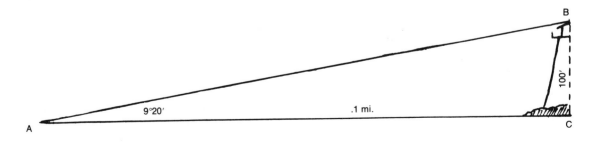

9°20'   .1 mi.   100'

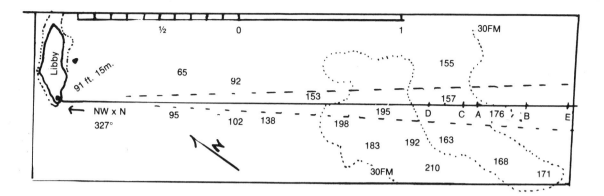

long division gives us AC, our distance from the lighthouse in feet. Divide this by 6080 and we have our distance from the light in miles.

The navigator can beat this process by referring to Bowditch's *American Practical Navigator,* Table 9. From this table we find that if we observe a light 100 feet high at an elevation of 9° 20′, we are distant from it .1 mile.

However, in actual practice, the solution to the problem is somewhat less precise. Suppose we are crossing the Bay of Fundy and make Libby Islands on a hazy day with nothing else in sight. We seize our sextant to take the elevation of the light and at once run into a problem. The chart gives the elevation of the light, BC in our drawing, as 91 feet. This is the height of the lantern, not the height of the tower, above high water. So we guess that it may be 6 feet from the lantern to the top of the tower, making the lighthouse 97 feet high. As it is about half tide, we must add another 7 feet because the height was measured with reference to mean high water.

Now we measure the angle of elevation with the sextant and find that because there is a sea running, we can't tell just where in the band of surf around the island the true water level lies. We take a guess, but we may be a foot or two off.

Because there is a sea running, we find it difficult to hold the sextant steady and vertical. We brace ourselves against the mast, about 9 feet above the water. We must remember to subtract that from whatever figure we come up with for BC. Also, as we go up and down 4 feet more or less on every sea, we must take our angle when we are about halfway if we are to refer it to sea level.

Anyway, after all these guesses and estimates, we come out with an angle of 20′ after making a correction for the instrument error of the sextant. We then calculate BC:

height of lantern	91
height of tower above lantern	+6
	97
allowance for tide	+7
	104
height of eye	−9
Therefore BC =	95

Table 9 in Bowditch gives us a distance of 2.6 miles, which places us at A, the light bearing NWXN.

Suppose now that because of the variables, unknown quantities, and guesses in BC that the figure should have been 100 feet instead of 95. We would then be at B, 2.9 miles from the light. If we have erred by 5 feet the other way and the height of the tower is really 90 feet, we would then be 2.5 miles from the tower at C.

The angle above is about 20′. An error of 10 percent in such a small angle is not inconceivable in view of the difficulties under which the observation was taken. If we have an error of 2′ so that the angle is really 22′ and the height is 90 feet, we will be at D, 2.3 miles from the light. If the errors are compounded in the other direction, we could have an angle of 18′ and a height of 100 feet, putting us at E, 3.2 miles from the light.

147

Because we took our bearing over the steering compass in the cockpit without an accurate pelorus, we are likely to have a possible error of a point (3°) either way. This places us somewhere between the dotted lines and somewhere between 2.3 and 3.2 miles from the light. Our fix now looks a little less precise.

Fortunately, in this case our depth sounder will give us a little help. A sounding of under 30 fathoms, corrected for tide, will put us roughly between A and D. Over 30 fathoms and under 35 puts us probably inside D, and over 35 fathoms puts us out near B or E. On some parts of the coast, off Highland Light, for instance, the soundings are more accurate than a sextant angle in determining distance off the beach.

A sextant angle, unsupported by other evidence, is a most uncertain method of obtaining a fix, useful where only one mark of known height is in sight. A cross bearing or a horizontal sextant angle is much to be preferred. Even doubling the angle on the bow beats a vertical sextant angle.

John S. Kaufman of Scarsdale, New York, writes: "At night it is particularly hard to tell if one will pass clear of another boat. If one observes the other boat's light in relationship to a convenient star, a constant bearing can be determined. If the ship's light does not move relative to the star, there is trouble."
The idea is excellent, much better than using a shore light, for the star is moving at only 15° an hour, an imperceptible amount in half a minute.

The Depth Sounder in Deep Water

The depth sounder is most useful not in shallow water where there is danger of running aground but offshore in the fog or at night.

For instance, going west in Grand Manan Channel one must hug the American shore to keep out of a three-knot flood tide. Yet that shore is a cliff with jagged outcrops that extend far enough to make it perilous to follow it by the loom of the shore in the fog.

As you converge with the shore, the bottom comes up to meet you. At the 100-foot mark, turn to the southwest to parallel the cliffs. If the bottom drops away, come westerly a point; if it comes up, stand off to the southward. Presently you will run into choppy water. That is the rip off Long Point. Soon you will find that in order to maintain 100 feet you will have to turn far to the west.

Shortly after that, you will pick up the bell outside Cutler, whence entrance is easy.

A steady eye on the depthfinder will keep you off the beach on the back side of Cape Cod at any distance you choose, for here the bottom drops off evenly. You can run up Buzzards Bay or Vineyard Sound on the depth finder, hanging to soundings on either shore.

The most sophisticated instruments record depths on a roll of paper, indicate something of the character of the bottom, and even show schools of fish. However, one that gives accurate readings to 300 feet costs close to two hundred dollars. Surf Rider and Seafarer have given good accurate service.

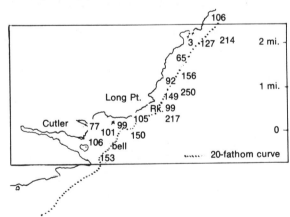

You May Be a Target
Arthur H. Walker

Often when cruising in the fog, yachtsmen find the noise of a foghorn so offensive that they

148

will use it only when they hear another horn or have other reason to believe another boat is near. Even a bow watch is often neglected for the relative comfort of the cockpit or cabin when it is foggy and cold. Yet the advent of lower-priced radar systems and relatively inexperienced users suggests that more noise and more watching and listening is essential.

This fact was brought home during a run from the Schoodic whistle, past Petit Manan and on toward Mistake Island. I was employing a Whistler, a depthfinder, and a highly reliable compass as we made contact with Egg Rock and the smooth string of islands and ledges that run from there to Moose Peak and the Cows Yard. We were sailing along easily when suddenly a white yawl appeared under power heading right for us with four excited people on the bow. They asked us if we knew where the buoy was, and I pointed confidently into the fog. Off they surged. Within five minutes another larger vessel lurched out of the fog, again under power, and came right to us. The person at the helm pointed to my radar reflector and said, "We had you on our radar and we thought that you were the buoy!" Then it struck us. Our radar reflector was being heard or seen as the buoy and they were homing on it with no noise to tell them otherwise.

While I cannot fathom how either boat could have thought that we were the buoy west of Egg Rock (we were well south and east of it), nevertheless, the fact is that they did and we were in fact their target. This brought home to us the necessity of posting a watch at once and blowing the horn each minute in order that others might not interpret our presence as something other than another vessel.

From the other standpoint I have found that experience is essential in using radar, either visual or audible systems. In my first year of use, I managed to confuse a freighter at anchor with Partridge Island off Saint John, New Brunswick. Only the banging of a dishpan by the cook brought me to my senses. One can be lulled into a false sense of security by assumptions about the meaning of the images or signals being received. On the other hand, pru-

dent use can be invaluable at times when passage might have been impossible.

All of this says that the advent of electronics has increased, not decreased, the need for constant vigilance and the frequent use of a horn to further identify yourself to others.

The Double Sextant Angle

Most methods of taking a fix depend upon the accuracy of the compass, whether the ship's compass or a hand bearing compass. Both are subject to deviations, for one reason or another. The double sextant angle is entirely independent of compasses and is far more accurate than the vertical sextant angle.

With your sextant held horizontally, take the angle between Freeman Rock and Moose Peak Light in the map on page 149 and apply whatever instrument correction is necessary. One need be accurate only to the nearest degree. Suppose we get an angle of 15°.

The locus of points at which we can get an angle of 15° is a circle that touches Freeman Rock, Moose Peak, and our position. To establish this circle, draw a line from Freeman Rock in any direction, let us say due south. Lay your parallel rules across the center of the compass rose through the 15 mark. Walk the rules across the chart to Moose Peak and draw

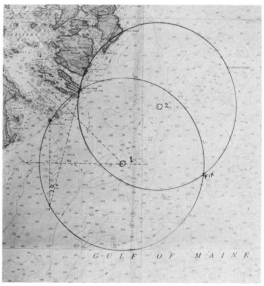

100 mm = 4"

60 mm = 2⅝"

a line from the light that intersects the north–south line. The angle formed will be 15° and the intersection will be a third point on the circumference of the circle.

Connect Freeman Rock and Moose Peak with another line. Now bisect two sides of the triangle thus formed. Put the point of your compass on the intersection and, with a radius sufficient to reach any one of the three points, describe a circle. It will touch all three, and you are somewhere on that circle, for from that circle and only from that circle can you observe an angle of 15° between Freeman Rock and Moose Peak.

In order to find where on that circle you are, take with your sextant the angle between Moose Peak and Black Head. It comes out, let us say, to 25°. Perform the same construction as before and draw a circle touching Moose Peak and Black Head. The two circles will intersect at Moose Peak and at one other place. We are not at the lighthouse, so mark the other intersection FIX with confidence.

In practice, of course, the two angles should be taken almost simultaneously. A three-arm protractor makes the whole process much easier and eliminates many opportunities to make mistakes. Simply set one arm on 15° and the other on 40°, the sum of 25 and 15. Move the protractor around until each arm touches the appropriate mark. Drive your pencil down through the center hole, for that is

your position unaffected by possible compass error and unlikely to be affected by an error in observation of less than 30 minutes or feet, an accuracy well within the reach of even cheap "practice" sextants.

Cruising Information Center

Where can a yacht buy gasoline in Suva?

Can one safely leave his boat in the Azores?

What conditions of wind, sea, fog, and ice prevail in the summertime on the north coast of Iceland?

These are the kinds of questions to which one can get answers through the Cruising Information Center at the Peabody Museum in Salem, Massachusetts, and Mr. Frederick Johnson, a deep-water sailing man of long experience, is the man to talk to.

In three small rooms adjacent to the museum he has assembled a fascinating store of practical information. To answer your questions he has access to the up-to-date nautical library of the museum. Then he has a large and growing collection of published cruising guides to many different areas of the world, from New England to New Zealand. He is building a collection of government Sailing Directions, most of them published by the United States government but some by the British, Danish, and Swedish governments. There is sometimes a translation problem. Other published material includes carefully selected articles from magazines. Those describing the beauties of the waving palm trees are omitted in favor of those describing the ranges for entering the pass in the reef. *The Flying Fish,* the journal of the Ocean Cruising Club, is another valuable source. The newsletter published by the Seven Seas Cruising Association consists of letters written by itinerant cruising men who live aboard their boats most of the time.

There is also a wealth of unpublished material in the form of letters, logbooks, journals, and miscellaneous information from clients, friends, and friends of friends.

Beyond the factual information is a bibliography file of over 4,000 titles—none of it ordinary tourist travelog material but solid, useful information based on firsthand knowledge. This file is kept constantly up-to-date as new books are published. There is also an index to *Flying Fish,* from which one can find references to recent visits in most unusual places.

In the chartroom is a growing collection of charts, most of them given by voyagers recently returned. These are bulky to store and awkward to handle, so only the most useful are accepted. The collection includes parts of the world about which many inquiries are made, such as the west coast of Scotland and both coasts of Spain, as well as the pilot charts, which give prevailing weather conditions in the oceans of the world.

Inquiries come from three general categories of yachtsmen. First is the man of considerable experience in foreign cruising who knows what he needs but has no time to assemble the material himself. Second is the man of considerable experience in sailing who has done very little transoceanic voyaging. He doesn't know what he doesn't know. For instance, he may be taking for granted the customs and immigration regulations in a certain port, regulations that are interpreted differently and administered differently in different parts of the world and in different ports in the same country. Last is the man who is situated in a nautically barren part of the country. Very little cruising information is available in the midst of Arkansas or Texas, for instance.

One inquiry came from a man in Maine bound for England. He wanted to know the best route, the facilities in different ports, what charts to buy, where to buy them, where he could leave his boat, the frequencies on which to expect the best weather forecasts, the radio rules for communication between ships and between ships and shore stations on the high seas and in various countries, how far LORAN was effective, and the usual information on supplies and fuel. This sort of inquiry can be quite readily handled, but the same questions about the islands north of New Guinea are more difficult.

If you want information for a contemplated cruise, write Mr. Frederick Johnson, Cruising Information Center, Peabody Museum, East India Square, Salem, Massachusetts 01970. Tell him as specifically as possible where you plan to go and what you want to know. In some cases he will be able to answer your question directly. In other cases he will tell you where and how to get the answer. It may take some time to collect the information, because people who know the answer may not get their mail frequently on Pacific islands or may not answer the telephone. However, he will put together the best information he can find. You must remember, of course, that the Cruising Information Center cannot guarantee the accuracy of the information. It assembles and coordinates facts but cannot be responsible for verifying them. You must use your own judgment. If a correspondent speaks of a "snug anchorage," you may find when you get there that his standards and yours are not at all in agreement.

The cost of his service is, of course, quite high. In the past the charge for a simple letter on an Atlantic crossing or a short Caribbean cruise on which information is readily available has been about fifty dollars. For a longer cruise in less frequented waters the cost runs to two hundred dollars or more. However, the center now contemplates charges based directly on the time involved in finding the information requested. Something on the order of thirty dollars to forty dollars per hour is contemplated.

The center was established by members of The Cruising Club of America as a nonprofit operation to serve the needs of all cruising men. It is entirely independent of the parent organization. However, it is not yet self-supporting and is still dependent upon gifts of information and money. The Peabody Museum is one of its chief benefactors, for it provides office space, connection with its telephone system, and use of its valuable library. Gifts to the center will be much appreciated and are deductible in the usual manner of gifts to educational organizations.

NOTE: *Mr. Johnson has retired since this article was written, but the center is being carried on by a new director.*

The Mathematician and the Pilot

Mathematician and pilot, cruising in company, awaken to the drip of fog dew on the deck. Both are wise enough to stay a while in the sack, but after breakfast and a walk ashore, when the fog has scaled up enough in the harbor to consider making a move, each gets his own vessel under way. Their attitudes diverge as they face the same problem indicated on the accompanying chart—to get from North Haven to Isle au Haut.

The fog in the Thorofare has scaled up—indeed, there is a little watery sunshine—as the two yachts leave the bell off Channel Rock. The mathematician lays his course for The Brown Cow whistle, 126 degrees, 3.5 miles. At six knots it will take him $t = \frac{q}{r}$ or $\frac{3.5}{6} = .583$ hours. The tide is flooding 11 degrees at .25 knots, he supposes. Therefore, .25 miles per hour $\times$ .583 = .146 miles. He lays this out on the chart as shown and at 1033 leaves Channel Rock bell, having allowed three degrees and .146 miles for tide, on a course of 129 degrees to run 3.5 miles. His ETA (Estimated Time of Arrival) at the whistle is .5833 hours later or 34.99 minutes later, which is at 1107.9. Watch in hand, off he motors into the fog, which is lying heavily in the middle of the bay.

The pilot's mental processes work a little differently and a little less precisely. He lays his course for the whistle, but makes no allowance for tide. He guesses it is running about N or N $\times$ E at around .25 knots, but he does not know exactly how much to allow—and he knows he does not know. He figures the tide will "set him up the bay some." He knows that he does not know exactly how much, because the force of the tide and the speed of his boat are both variable. He does know that he will make somewhere to leeward of the whistle, where he can hear it, and probably somewhere close to the bold ledge on which the surf will be breaking noisily. He is sure of finding the whistle, the rock, or both, depending on the strength of the tide and the wind. He knows that at six knots he will go a mile in 10 minutes or 3½ miles in about 35 minutes. As he leaves Channel Rock bell, he notes in his log the time, 1033, and the course, SE 3/4⁴E. For the first quarter-mile the fog is up off the water as the landmass to windward dries it up. There is a moderate little breeze with a smell of spruce and hay in it, so he sets his sails, shuts off the engine, and before he plunges into the fog, looks back at the bell, still just visible astern. It is almost dead aft, so he figures that in under the shelter of Calderwood Neck the tide has not affected him much and probably a quarter knot is a generous allowance where it is not a moon tide. A glance at a passing pot buoy leads him to guess a speed of five knots, and a mile in 12 minutes.

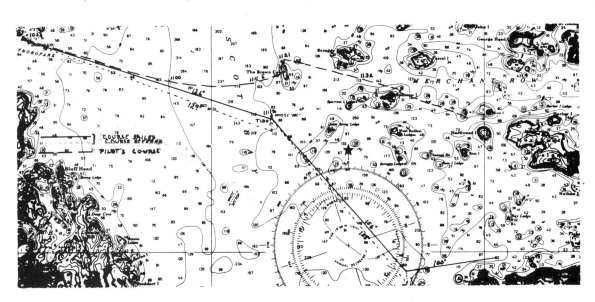

The mathematician is rumbling along ahead through the fog, Penobscot Bay falling into the wake at a steady six knots, the clock ticking along regularly. At 1042 the sounding machine shows a sharp increase in depth from 64 feet to 78 feet and continues to drop off slowly, fluctuating up and down. Unable to find a 78-foot sounding on the chart close to his course, the mathematician assumes that at least he is over the 60-foot curve, but he worries about it. At 1055 the depth increases sharply again to 230 feet and continues to drop sharply. The mathematician is now over the 120-foot line and is behind schedule by one minute. He revises his ETA to 1109. On he goes, watch in hand. At 1105 he begins to be itchy, asks the lookout if he hears anything, and goes forward himself to look. The lookout reports a pot buoy. The mathematician ignores it but at 1107 stops the engine to listen. Close on the starboard quarter comes the gentle moo of the Brown Cow whistle. He starts the motor again and the whistle presently emerges from the fog, the great white letters 2BC on the red buoy identifying it for certain. Time is 1112.5.

Let us return to watch the pilot as he too plunges into the fog. He passes a pot buoy, guesses the tide at about a quarter knot, and as the breeze may have eased a little, figures maybe 13 minutes to the mile instead of 12. The wind smells colder and wetter with no more hint of spruce in it. His depthfinder shows a drop to 12 fathoms, so he figures he is over the 10-fathom line and, as he sees no more buoys, it seems reasonable. Far off to starboard he hears the intermittent motor of someone hauling traps. There is no other sound but the bubble and swish under the lee bow and the occasional squeak of the main sheet block. The helmsman holds the course, the cabin clock ticks on, the lookout listens.

At 1100 the pilot tries the depthfinder again and watches the bottom drop off from 16 fathoms to over 40 fathoms. He figures he surely went over the 20-fathom line and notes that he must be a bit north of his course to get that steep a drop.

The helmsman turns over the wheel to the pilot for a bit and takes a spell at lookout while the former lookout goes below to warm up. Still the gray seas roll up the bay, rippled on the top with the light southerly breeze. There is no sound but the bow wave and an occasional snap from the nylon ensign on the leach of the mainsail.

The pilot glances at the clock, 1111, calls the man below to take the wheel, and goes forward to listen. Almost simultaneously the lookout reports the distant moo of the whistle to starboard and the pilot hears the swash of surf to port. He knows he is between the whistle and the ledge, chooses the ledge, and heads for it on a course of East. Sheets are eased; the lookout sharpens up. Presently a pot buoy appears, apparently rushing off to windward at a brisk pace. "Reckon that tide is running more like three-quarters of a knot out here," thinks the pilot. The wash is louder. The water suddenly looks choppy, there are more buoys, the pilot runs her off before the wind, and the rock shows through the fog, its tawny back dripping as the sea drops away from it. The wind has the sour smell of surf and weed.

Watching the compass, the pilot swings away from the rock, keeping it just in sight.

At 1121, "Steer SE × E," he tells the helmsman. He is running for the lee side of Sparrow Island Ledges and Sparrow Island, sailing a course to strike very close to them, figuring the tide will set him off but that he will be close enough to see them. At 1132 the breeze freshens a little, the sound of surf is heard on the weather bow and the screaming of gulls in concert. As it draws aft the water smooths out, the breeze freshens more and smells of guano. Sparrow Island appears wreathed in fog and bringing the smell of sweet fern. Then the course is SE × E for Hardwood Island, but before it appears the breeze increases, the sky turns blue, and the sloop steps out of the fog like walking out a door, the islands ahead serene in the sunlight and the bulk of Isle au Haut showing misty to windward.

"Most usually get a scale-up under Isle au Haut if the sun is shining over the fog," observes the pilot.

The crew had a lunch and a pleasant beat among the islands in smooth water with good visibility. They rafted alongside the mathematician in mid-afternoon.

The mathematician swelled with achievement. He had hit the whistle "right on the nose," then run 158 degrees for 27.9 minutes, which included an allowance of two degrees for a flood tide running 11 degrees at .25 knots. Then he had turned and run 100 degrees, making no allowance for tide behind Kimball Island and planned to run for 22.5 minutes to make the can off Flake Island. Miraculously, the fog had lifted and he had been almost right on; a neat cross-bearing showed him a little north of his course. He had anchored before 1300. It had been a tense and harrowing experience but they had made it.

"What happened to you?" asked the mathematician.

"Oh, we had a good sail," replied the pilot. "Let's go ashore and walk up to the store."

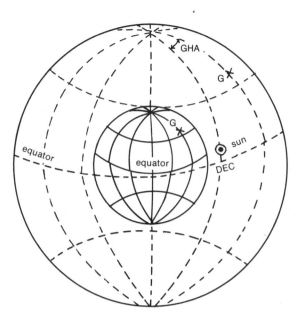

Figure 1

Celestial Navigation No Mystery

Anyone who can balance a checkbook or look up a number in a telephone directory can navigate by the sun and stars. For generations a mystique has surrounded the process, but computerized tables have simplified the mathematics, and the fundamental concept never has presented great difficulties.

Imagine that the universe consists of the earth at the center with a sphere of "infinite radius" surrounding it. The inside of that sphere is the sky with all the stars stuck into it like pins. This outer sphere is called the celestial sphere.

Imagine that the earth stands still and that the whole celestial sphere rotates on its axis, a projection of the earth's axis, from east to west at an almost constant rate of 15° per hour—a complete rotation every twenty-four hours. The sun, moon, and planets move on the celestial sphere in relation to the stars in predictable courses.

If the poles of the earth, the equator, the parallels of latitude, and the meridians of longitude are projected to the celestial sphere as in Figure 1, they will be stationary, as is the earth; thus any given star, and the whole ce-

lestial sphere with it, will move across 15° of longitude every hour. The *Nautical Almanac*, published annually by the Hydrographic Office in Washington, tabulates the positions of the celestial sphere and the latitude and longitude of the sun, moon, and principal planets for every hour, minute, and second of the year.

A heavenly body's latitude, its distance north or south of the equator, is called its declination; its longitude is called its Greenwich Hour Angle, GHA. This, strictly speaking, is the angle at the celestial north pole between the meridian of Greenwich and the meridian on which the body is at the instant. It is measured westward from Greenwich through 360°.

If we know what time it is, we can look up the location of the sun, for instance. If we can work out our relation to the sun, we can determine our own position. Historically, it was done by "meridian Altitude" and "time sight" in this simple way.

Meridian Altitude

Imagine the sun in the morning having passed Greenwich, proceeding westward at about 15° per hour, approaching our position off the coast of the United States. As it ap-

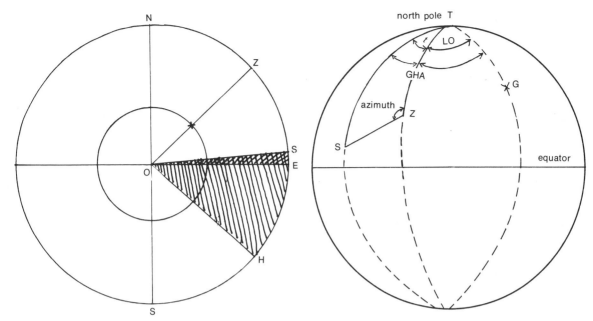

Figure 2

Figure 3

proaches, it climbs higher in the sky and its azimuth, its compass bearing, becomes more southerly. Presently it is, for an instant, due south (true) of us and at the same instant reaches its highest point in the sky for that day. It is on our meridian. We seize our sextant and measure the sun's altitude in degrees above the sea horizon.

Now if, at the same instant, we slice the celestial sphere from pole to pole, the knife running right down our meridian and through the sun just as it crosses our meridian, we will have a picture like that in Figure 2.

In this picture, Z is our zenith, the point directly over our heads where a line from the center of the earth through us would strike the celestial sphere. S is the position of the sun on a day in late summer, a little north of the equator. H is our horizon, 90° from our zenith. It is drawn from the center of the earth, not tangent to the earth at our position, because, the drawing being far out of scale, it makes very little difference in the angle. This small difference is tabulated in the almanac under parallax and included with the other corrections to be applied to an observed altitude of the sun.

Our latitude is angle ZOE.

We have measured angle SOH with our sextant and applied the necessary corrections.

We can look up angle SOE, the sun's declination, in the almanac.

If we subtract SOE from SOH, we have left angle EOH.

If we subtract EOH from ZOH, which is 90°, we will have left ZOE, our latitude. T0his process is expressed algebraically.

$$\text{Latitude} = 90 - (\text{alt.} \pm \text{dec.})$$

We perform this simple calculation and plot our latitude on the chart.

For years navigators had to stop there, for determination of longitude depends upon accurate knowledge of the time. Nevertheless, Columbus, sailing west on the latitude of China, discovered America, returned to Spain, and made three more voyages to the Caribbean, finding each time the landfall he sought. Magellan and Drake circled the globe, and indeed, most of the world was explored before navigators learned to calculate longitude.

The Time Sight

All navigational problems except the meridian altitude involve the solution of a triangle

155

on the surface of the celestial sphere. The solution to every possible triangle has been worked out in tables so that nothing more than simple arithmetic is needed to arrive at an answer. Figure 3 shows the triangle as it would look about three hours after our meridian altitude observation at noon. Then the sun was precisely on our meridian as indicated by Z at our zenith. Since then it has traveled about 45° west to S.

If we know three sides of the triangle STZ, we can calculate the angles. If we know two sides and the included angle, we can calculate the other side. We would like to find our longitude, angle GTZ.

What can we find out about triangle STZ?

We can take the altitude of the sun with our sextant and simultaneously note the time. By subtracting the corrected altitude from 90° we can determine SZ, the angular distance from the sun to the zenith.

We determined our latitude at noon so we can subtract that figure from 90° to get TZ.

We can look up the declination of the sun in the almanac, and subtract it from 90° to determine ST.

We now have three sides of the triangle. By looking in the proper tables we can find angle **t**.

We find the sun's Greenwich Hour Angle in the almanac, subtract **t** from it, and we have our longitude. Crossed with our noon latitude sight, this will give us a "fix."

The Sumner Line

Unfortunately, this is a mathematically difficult way to solve the triangle. Capt. Charles Sumner developed an easier way.

We assume we are at Z, assuming a latitude and longitude somewhere near our true position. Using this latitude, we determine TZ. We calculate angle **t,** using our assumed longitude, and we look up the declination as before to determine TS. We now have two sides of the triangle and the included angle.

We go to the table for SZ, 90° minus the altitude, and calculate the altitude. It will be the altitude we would have read from our sextant had we actually been at Z, our assumed position. However, we were not at Z. Our sextant reads, let us say, 10' *less* than it would have read had we been at Z. Therefore, the sun is a little *lower* in the sky than it would have been at Z. We draw a line through Z in the direction of S, taking the angle at Z from the table. We move 10' of arc, that is 10 nautical miles along this line, *away* from the sun to make it drop *lower* in the sky, and there draw a line perpendicular to the azimuth line. We are somewhere on this line. Where it crosses our latitude, which we determined at noon, will be our "fix."

This explanation is perhaps oversimplified, having omitted corrections to be applied to observed altitudes and the relationship between sidereal and Greenwich time, but these do not affect the fundamental concept. You will have to study the details in any simple navigation text, but once the principle is clear, the rest is easy.

However, navigating a vessel across a wide ocean to the landfall on a tiny island involves more than calculating a position and plotting it on a chart. What book or lecture will tell you how to balance yourself on the deck of a small boat, catch the sun in your sextant through flying clouds, and bring it down to a horizon now fifty yards away and then five miles? Where will you learn how much to allow for a boat's tendency to "climb" to windward on a reach? How do you account for a consistent difference between your dead-reckoning position and your sights? Has the temperature of the water changed?

Any well-written textbook can teach you celestial navigation if you read it as carefully as it was written, but you will earn the title of navigator only by going to sea and practicing the art. When you have learned the craft, you will know wherein lies the mystery.

7

Living Aboard

Pre-Cruise Countdown for the Absent-minded Skipper

Hugh G. Williams

"Where did you put that package of steak that we're having tonight?"

"What do you mean, where did I put it? If it didn't come aboard with the other perishables, then it's probably home in the fridge."

"Oh, well . . . look in the port locker and throw me out a can of beef stew."

"You mean, the port forward locker? Uh . . . sardines, canned boiled potatoes, peanut butter . . . where did you say?"

And so supper, the first night out, left something to be desired. Even so, it's a good thing this conversation wasn't about charts, toilet paper, cooking fuel, or an extra anchor line.

If you're going to be living on your boat for a few weeks, either at sea or along some fairly thinly populated coast, it's demonstrably helpful to have a routine, fairly rigid and extremely comprehensive, to keep track of the hundreds of items whose presence will keep annoyance and inconvenience to a minimum. A cruise won't crumble to pieces if mayonnaise, extra plastic bags, toothpaste, or your reading glasses are missing and presumed forgotten; but a cotter pin of just the right size, or a pair of binoculars, or an extra can of freon for the foghorn, not available when called for,

could help to produce a wish-you-hadn't-come situation.

Several volumes on small-boat cruising do include helpful checklists, but their chief value lies in providing a basis for the compilation of your own. Each boat is different in her needs from every other, as are the needs and the tastes of every individual party or crew. Also it is well to have many copies of your list, as you may wish to mark it up quite severely, or to divide responsibility for filling it among several other crew members. Mine is run off on three sheets of duplicator paper. Items not hitherto included are written in longhand and each year's list is saved for use in revising next year's.

This all sounds very bureaucratic, and the apparent proliferation of paperwork will evoke a knowing sigh from disciples of Professor Parkinson. The fact is, however, that many years of cruising, one of which found us the first night out without any means of lighting the cabin, have produced a nearly foolproof system, knowledge of which is sure to help at least some people. Let me describe it.

Page one of our Pre-Cruise Checklist contains four smaller lists:

1. INDIVIDUAL: Includes such items as work gloves, toilet articles, heavy socks, birth certificates, cameras, knapsack

2. CABIN: Flashlights, Kleenex, medicines, mosquito nets, and such

157

3. MOTOR : Engine spare parts, lubrication, funnels, cotton waste, and so on

4. TOOLS AND BOSUN'S SUPPLIES: Sail needles, spare oarlocks, hatchet, WD-40, and the like

Page two bears lists:

5. NAVIGATION: Instruments, publications, various licenses and documentation

6. BOAT GEAR: Anchors, safety equipment, dinghy, rigging

Page three contains lists:

7. GALLEY EQUIPMENT AND SUPPLIES
8. STORES AND PROVISIONS

On each list, every individual article is mentioned specifically. "Cabin-cleaning equipment" is the kind of item that leaves far too much play for a scatterbrained memory to do its worst.

Since the list is on three pages, it can be farmed out, page by page, to be filled by various members of the crew. The fewer items one individual has to focus on, the less scope for one's powers of forgetfulness and the less legwork per person.

Items fail to reach their place of stowage because (a) they weren't purchased in the first place; (b) they were known to be in the kitchen cupboard, down cellar, or in the bathroom cabinet or the trunk of the car, and each crew member thought someone else had brought them aboard; or (c) the checklist was either neglected or incorrectly marked. We have four ways of marking the list. In the first scanning, any item not needed for this particular cruise is marked with the letter *N* before it. A circled item indicates that the article is available somewhere at home and won't have to be purchased. A horizontal dash before any item means that it must be bought. A single line drawn through any item means that that article is aboard the boat now, that someone will swear to having seen it there, and also that he could put his hand on it immediately.

One of the last acts before getting under way should be for the skipper or his appointee to make a final inspection of the whole list—all three pages—and see that every item is either run through with a single line or marked with an *N*—even the previously circled ones. None should remain unmarked.

It's well to save each list, with any annotations you may have made, to use in preparing for your cruise next year. This way, lots of work and inconvenience is avoided. After a few years you may want to put out a revision; items that have been written in year after year may want to be added permanently, and those marked consistently with *N* can of course be dropped.

Perhaps you'll feel that constructing a list of this sort is a franker confession of weakness than you care to make and that you'd just as soon not, personally, be found using one. But you'll also be impressed by the number of visitors alongside during a season to borrow just such trifles as this catalog stoops to. And the embarrassment is certainly greater when you yourself have overlooked something important. It was dusk, that evening twenty-four years ago, when we made port, lightless and consequently supperless. A kindly building contractor bade us take one of the lanterns from an excavation he'd just completed. We have it yet, and for several reasons cherish it.

> "We are going to just *love* staying all winter," bubbled the new owner of a year-round house to the old man, "but there *are* a lot of funny people around here."
>
> "Yes," he replied without a flicker, "but they'll all be gone by Columbus Day."

The Galley

The Stove

In northern latitudes, even in summer, a stove burning coal, wood, or briquets is a great source of comfort and a great convenience to the cook. If the skipper contemplates coming to anchor late in the day, the cook will do well to torch up about an hour and a half before dinner time. Building a fire under way presents no problem. The easiest and cleanest way to do this is to make "cartridges" before you come aboard. Wrap a double handful of briquets in several layers of newspaper and seal with freezer tape. Drop one of these into the firebox, tear open the paper on top and bottom, and *before* you light a match pour in half a cup of kerosene. The briquets will absorb it thirstily, like the soapstone on a fire-lighter.

Set the smoke head in place on deck, pour a little water into the deck iron, and be sure all drafts and dampers are open. If the smoke head is to leeward of the mainsail, the stove will draw famously. If it is to windward of the sail, in order to prevent a smoky back-draft, invert a bucket over the smoke head.

Now shove a lighted match into the ash pit and up through the grate. The paper, stimulated perhaps by some of the kerosene that percolated through the briquets, will catch easily, and the briquets themselves, after a smoky start, will settle into a quick, hot fire.

If your stove is well bolted down and you keep the ash pit clean, there is little danger of your setting your yacht afire. If the fire does escape from the stove, a bucket of water will extinguish it. True, this stove will not boil water from a cold start as quickly as a liquid- or gas-fueled pressure stove, but it will live a long time without attention and will cook your dinner for you, either in the oven or in a pressure cooker lashed on top, without supervision.

Such a stove can be purchased from The Portland Stove Foundry, 57 Kennebec St., Portland, Maine; from Paul E. Luke in East Boothbay, Maine; or from Shipmate Stove Division of Richmond Ring Co., Souderton, Pennsylvania. The price will depend on size and finish.

The Pressure Cooker

Thoughtfully selected, frequently cleaned, and wisely used, the pressure cooker can be the best tool in the galley. For four people the two-quart size is adequate, gets up steam quickly, and maintains its pressure better than the larger sizes, which radiate a great deal of heat very quickly. Look for the kind with a rigid lid arranged so that the pressure forces the lid against the gasket. The top should be as big as the bottom with no lip to catch the contents as you dump them out or to make a difficult corner to clean. Be sure that there is a safety valve or fusible plug and that the pressure is maintained by a weight that cannot roll or jump off. Should it do so, your dinner will be forced suddenly through a very small hole and be spattered on the overhead.

Potatoes, carrots, onions, and other tough vegetables can be cooked in only seven minutes at fifteen pounds pressure. Because very little water is used, the goodness is not boiled out.

After a little practice you can make very good bread in a pressure cooker—better than store bread, anyway. (See the following section on bread.)

A fine stew can be made in a pressure cooker in half an hour—stew with chunks of real meat in it.

Once you get steam up on the front burner, you can set the cooker on the back of the stove or even on a can of Sterno to sizzle along while you prepare the rest of the meal.

A pressure cooker is not likely to tip over and cannot spill. You can use it safely at sea. It is usually easy to wash because food seldom burns on to it.

A few precautions:

• Be sure the hole is clear before you put the lid on.

• Carry a spare safety valve and gasket.

• Never try to open the lid with the valve in place. You may get a puff of superheated steam in the face.

• Never remove the valve weight without letting the cooker cool down. If you do, you will suddenly lower the pressure inside without as quickly lowering the temperature. The contents will boil faster as the vapor pressure drops. This makes steam very quickly and may blow the safety valve.

• Select a heavy aluminum cooker and keep it away from salt water as much as you can. An aluminum pot is quickly corroded and pitted, but a heavy one will last a long time anyway.

• When the cooker is not in use, keep the rack and the valve weight inside where they cannot be lost, and leave the lid ajar so it will not get musty inside.

Most cookbooks fail to do justice to a pressure cooker. Follow the little book that comes with the pot and improvise from there.

Bread

Capt. Paul Wolter

One of the world cruisers in small boats invented a way to bake bread in a pressure cooker on top of a stove. I don't know who it was, but the recipe goes from mouth to mouth, in the true sense of the word, you may say.

The common type of pressure cooker is wider on top than on the bottom. That is the better one, since you can dump out the bread much more easily.

The normal size of four quarts is right for the following ingredients:

4 cups of flour (plain flour, not the self-rising kind)
1½ cups of salt water (out in the ocean, seawater is just right; otherwise, make salt water)
1 tablespoon of sugar
1 envelope of yeast

Dissolve the yeast in some of your salt water. Throw all the ingredients together and make a dough.

If you are a good cook you already know how to do it. If you are my type of cook, some hints about making dough may help. I throw all the ingredients together into a large salad bowl: that is, the flour, the sugar, the dissolved yeast, and the remainder of the salt water. Then I take a large spoon and stir it. It becomes a heavy paste. Now I sprinkle some dry flour on a wooden board and plop the mixture on it. With some more flour on my fingers and some on the dough I start kneading. As soon as it sticks to my hands too heavily, I sprinkle more flour on the dough, the board,

and my hands. Soon the thing can be shaped and you really can do now as the bakers do: push it out flat, fold it over, and flatten it again. Does the dough stick to the board again? Hands? More sprinkled flour stops that.

Knead the dough until it does not stick to the palm of your hand anymore when you hold the glob there for a while.

Now grease the inside of your pressure cooker—I use salad oil and smear a thin film on. Then throw some flour into the pot and roll and turn it until the flour covers the oil.

Throw your dough in, cover the pot with a towel, and let rise for two hours. Choose a warm spot. Don't put it under a hatch where a cold down-draft will hit it. The warmer the place, the better the rising will be.

After two hours take the towel off and put the cover on, but leave the steam valve *off*. Then put the pot on medium flame. Yes, I also wondered, "What is the medium flame on an alcohol stove?" There are no graduations as on your range at home. I find the medium flame by guessing: Turn the burner up; that is, high. Now turn the flame down; that is, low. Now the middle. Go through it once more, and you will swear there has never been a more medium flame than on your stove right there.

On this "medium" you leave the cooker for fifteen minutes, then fifteen minutes on low heat. After this, take the pot off and open the cover (there is no danger, since the valve is off). Dump the bread onto a plate and put it back into the pressure cooker upside down. Put the cover on, again leave the valve off, and let it bake for another half hour on low heat. Through the steam hole, not covered by the valve, comes that wonderful aroma of freshly baked bread.

After the proper amount of time, take the bread out. There it is, slightly steaming, giving off a heavenly aroma and looking like the picture in a food advertisement. You can eat it right away, and you probably will. Contrary to your grandmother's predictions, even if you eat too much of it so fresh, you won't get a stomach ache, just a very satisfied feeling there.

On board *Palawan,* we don't buy bread

before a trip anymore—we bake our pressure-cooker bread once a day and sometimes twice. There is no more pleasing way to wake up the new watch in the morning than the aroma of freshly baked bread wafting through the cabin.

Coastwise Provisioning

Many successful cruising people set up menus for the first week of the cruise and then build a list based on the required ingredients. There is an obvious wisdom in this, a sort of Puritan forehandedness, but it carries with it a Calvinistic sense of predestination about the fare for the coming week.

There is another approach. Make your shopping list of known and proven staples. Add enough canned meat, fish, fruit, and vegetables for emergencies, and live off the country.

Troll a line astern. Fresh mackerel is hard to beat. If you are lucky enough to get a blue-fish, you will have the excitement of getting it aboard and a gourmet dinner. If the wind lets go, try the cod jig. A fresh cod steak is superb. Or you can build a chowder if you carry salt pork, potatoes, onions, and canned milk. However you cook it, it is pretty hard to ruin a fresh fish. Just don't cook it too long.

You may see a local fisherman jigging codfish or hauling lobster traps. Heave to and send a boat aboard with a few dollars and a six-pack. You may make a trade. One day when it was too rough to send a boat, we sailed close under the stern of a fisherman and got a ten-pound codfish, airborne. Some of the beer cans fell overboard because of the extreme range, but we parted the best of friends.

Fresh summer vegetables are too good to miss. When you take a walk ashore, you may pass a farm. See if you can buy a mess of peas or string beans. A tomato just off the vine still warm from the afternoon sun is so much better than the hard pink little golf balls that come from the supermarket wrapped in plastic. The lettuce and spinach may have some sand in it, but washed in salt water it has added snap. Use your judgment, though, on the matter of pollution.

If you cruise in less populated regions, wild berries are worth scrambling around the

brush to get. Strawberries in June and July are hard to find, but of them James Rosier wrote in 1605 on a cruise to Maine, "The Lord could have made, but never did make, a better berry." Sun-warmed blueberries from mountain and pasture make muffins, pies, and pancakes you cannot buy. As the summer goes on, raspberries and, finally, blackberries, ripen in thickets, cellar holes of old houses, burned-over places, and blow-downs.

Besides the good taste of these things, there is a social value. If you go ashore looking for vegetables, you are likely to meet some interesting people and see village stores, farms, and country roads you otherwise would have missed. Try it on a rainy afternoon when there isn't much doing ashore and you may learn some songs and stories that will make the day. Anyway, it is better than staying aboard, getting cabin fever, and dining on canned stew.

Shipmate Bread

A Shipmate stove burning coal or briquets generates considerable heat in the oven while dinner is cooking on top. At the beginning, while the oven is heating up, put canned vegetables in a flat plan and warm them in the oven, rather than taking space on the top of the stove. They will come out as they are supposed to, not overcooked as hard as bird shot.

When the oven really heats up, about the time you are ready to serve dinner, put in two tins of bread and leave them during the heat of the fire and as it dies down. The result will earn you the *cordon bleu*.

Make bread dough in the usual way, knead it up, and set it to rise. Any cookbook will tell you how to do it. However, there are a few problems on a boat seldom encountered by Fanny Farmer. First, you must reduce the quantities in your recipe to fit the smaller oven. Next, the bread must rise in a warm, quiet place. On a reasonably calm afternoon, the best place is under a towel on the cockpit floor where the sun can shine on it and it is out of the wind. Here, though, the cook must stand constant guard. "Ready About" applies as much to the bread bowl as it does to back-stays and jib sheets, for the rising dough must be shifted to stay in the sun and out of the wind and it must not be unduly joggled. One afternoon when it was "all hands and the cook" on the main sheet, the cook herself put her foot in the bowl.

Eight-inch aluminum bread tins fit a Shipmate oven. The oven shelf must be moved down to its lowest position to allow the bread room to rise, or it will hit the top of the oven and burn.

The operation must be timed so that the rising is complete when the oven is hot enough to kill the yeast, or the dough will continue to rise for too long in the oven and make a frightful mess.

About halfway through the baking process the pans must be shifted, because the firebox side of the oven is hotter than the other side.

If everything comes out as it should, you will bring out of the oven two neat, firm loaves of fresh bread to the cheers of the skipper and crew. In view of the mushy texture of most bread available in waterfront grocery stores—bread that cannot stand up to a gob of peanut butter—Shipmate bread is worth the trouble.

When the anchor is down, sails furled, and lines coiled down, all hands gather in the cockpit to reconsider the pleasures of the day. A local man rows by in his punt. Invite him aboard. He may add color to your picture of the region. Ask the people from the next boat. They may have visited islands you have never considered. We have had in our cockpit at different times a New Brunswick salmon fisherman, an essayist, a diver, a machinist, a poet, a schoolgirl botanist, and two physics professors who disagreed as to whether an atomic blast deep in the Pacific would split the world in half. "If it does," concluded one, "I want to be on the half with the coast of Maine."

The Skipper as Host

You can buy one of these signs in any yachtsmans' gift store, and many are the skippers who should heed it. They are not guilty of evil intent; just thoughtlessness. The practical yachtsman can profitably spend at least one of his long winter evenings contemplating a cruise in his boat through his guest's eyes.

Consider the start. All hands are aboard and are ready to back out of the slip. Engines are running, Captain Bligh is at the wheel, and the guests are wondering what to do.

"Cast off forward," shouts Bligh. (It is better through a bullhorn.) "Hold her on the port spring line aft." The quickest of the guests rushes forward to cast off. At least he understands *that* command, but what in thunder is a port spring line aft? The skipper rushes to cast off lines to starboard, which he has neglected to mention, and puts the port spring line in Sam's hands.

THIS IS A SWELL SHIP
FOR THE SKIPPER
BUT A HELL SHIP
FOR THE CREW

"Ease it around the cleat" (you idiot), he orders peremptorily, and leaps back to the wheel. "Stand by to fend off forward." With a rush of decibels, a foaming of water under the stern, and a cloud of exhaust, *MV Tudy II* swings out of her slip and heads down-channel.

"For heaven's sakes, take in those fenders. Do you want us to look like dashed landlubbers?" roars Bligh.

"Fenders," thinks Sam. "What fenders? They aren't my fenders." And we are off for a merry weekend on the water with the skipper enjoying ill-temper and the crew wondering why they came.

How much more fun it would be if the

skipper explained before the engines began to roar that he was going to back out of the slip, turn her stern upstream to port by holding a line on the port quarter, and then go ahead down-channel? Joe could be detailed to drop the bow lines and to stand by to fend off forward. Sam, discovering what a spring line is without having to show his ignorance, could ease it properly after dropping lines to starboard. With the maneuver smartly executed, and with everyone proud of his part in it, the skipper can ask anyone to take in the fenders in the same words Captain Bligh used, but this time Sam will do it proudly, knowing that he is no lubber. And all hands are off for a merry weekend on the water.

A skipper is primarily responsible, of course, for the safety of ship and crew. But a yachtsman, after that, is responsible for seeing that his guests have a good time. The following hints will hear thoughtful consideration.

• Let everyone participate somehow. The skipper loves to steer his boat, but he must be prepared to forego the pleasure once he is in open water. Pass the job around in about half-hour tricks so everyone gets a chance. It may even be necessary to urge the reluctant ones a little. Here a good mate is indispensable, for the mate can sit nonchalantly near the wheel, supervise the careless and help the ignorant so no one is embarrassed and everyone enjoys it. One mate has a neat way of nudging the bottom spoke of the wheel with her foot when a child is steering so he is convinced he is doing it all himself and doing very well.

If you have a Power Squadron member aboard, appoint him navigator. He will be delighted. Lay out charts, parallel rules, and dividers. Show him the deviation card, the fathometer, the RDF. Then let him ostensibly alone. He will have a great time taking bearings and growling about the inaccuracy of the current tables. Of course, you will have to watch over his shoulder, but unless he leads the vessel into actual peril, let him make the decisions. He will probably be a Cautious Conrad anyway.

There is always bosun's work to be done. Show someone how to sew on a sailmaker's whipping and every line aboard will be whipped. A bucket line with a neatly tapered eyesplice on one end and a shroud knot on the other end adds class to any bucket and inflates the craftsman with legitimate pride.

Appoint a galley person who likes the job, and rotate the duty before he or she gets too much. Some people like to shine brass—a little brass. Keeping the log can be a privilege. Setting a spinnaker, if carefully programed, can be an all-hands triumph.

Of course, some people like to be let alone.

• Know enough about the country where you cruise to make it interesting. Did a privateer really hide in this half-tide creek during the War of 1812, her spars cut away and her decks camouflaged with spruce? In this harbor during World War I, five-masted schooners were built, launched, and fitted out. Where did Ragged Island get its name? Who were Charles and Henry, after whom the two capes were named? Did Sir Francis Drake really bury a lead plate in this bay and did anyone ever find it?

You will probably run into the edges of your guests' circles of knowledge and give them the pleasure of adding to your own. It beats talking office politics!

• Plan for the bad day. It has to rain sometime. The leaden skies and hovering fog are not your fault, but if you greet the lowering day as a welcome lay day and, after a leisurely start, plan an expedition ashore for shopping, a visit to a museum, shipyard, sardine factory, or historic site, you may find most of your crew going along and cabin fever forestalled. Just visiting around the fleet in the skiff may lead to a good time.

Some people like cards or books or ball games on the radio. Some go in for drawing or painting or whittling models. Encourage them all, and never growl about the weather.

• If it comes on to blow and rain and the sea gets lumpy, gray, and unpleasant, if for good and sufficient reason you really must reef her down and sock it to her, explain the situation clearly, apportion the work to those best able to do it, try to keep everyone warm, dry, and nourished, and enjoy the challenge.

If this program sounds rather like running a hotel on the water, you may take satisfaction in the number of people who have a good time on your boat. And remember that you will never have much trouble finding a crew.

Helping the Apprehensive Guest

Mary C. Duncan

As your guests climb into your cockpit, there will be some who bring apprehensions with them. Most of their apprehensions come from very natural causes. The alert captain or mate can recognize them and do something to dispel them before they magnify to the point where the trip is uncomfortable for the guest and perhaps for the entire crew.

The most common apprehension for those who have never sailed before or for those who have done very little sailing is the fear of tipping over. They have watched boats from the shore. They have seen pictures and heard tales of capsizing. As soon as the wind fills the sails and the boat heels, they become alarmed. Some will be more comfortable on the high side away from the water. Some will feel more secure on the low side, braced against the coaming. Some will not dare to move at all. In any case, let them shift back and forth as they will or cling to whatever corner they find comfortable. An ideal spot is the seat beside the wheel box where your guest will have support either way until he gets his sea legs. For the brave soul who will try it, sitting on the high side of the deck with feet over the coaming will make him feel like a real sailor and will give him the support necessary.

A logical explanation of why the boat doesn't capsize when it heels is a great help to your apprehensive friend. He will readily understand that as the boat heels, the wind will spill out of the sails and tend to let her up again. He will be interested in the effect of the weight of the keel. The more the boat heels, the more the force of gravity pulling on the keel will tend to keep the boat on her feet.

A friendly, confident word from the skip-per helps, even in jest. One friend, seeking reassurance, said to the skipper, "Captain, this boat won't tip over, will it?"

"Only once," was the reply. It took the guest a moment to think that one over. By the time the meaning was clear, the skipper's nonchalance had won the day. Another friend who, standing in the hatch and clinging with both hands, had taken about all she could, admitted, "You know, Captain, I'm scared."

"My friend," said the skipper, "you know I wouldn't let anything happen to my boat." Confidence was assured.

Little children are often without fear as they come aboard, but when the boat begins to heel, all their instincts are alarmed. They must learn of getting their sea legs and that the boat won't tip over and why. One little guest, age six, was so frightened by the tipping boat that he could only cling to the binnacle and whimper. Once he was told that it was a good thing to hang on to the binnacle until he got his sea legs, he became interested, stopped whimpering, and listened. It was explained to him why it is natural for a sailing boat to tip, that with a good skipper at the helm it would tip only so far, and why. As we tacked back and forth, he found that this was so. Once he understood and the feel of it was in his legs, he moved about the cockpit. Soon he was all over the

164

boat, but still hanging on, and enjoying the trip.

The neophyte is often eager to learn but apprehensive about showing his ignorance and making a fool of himself. Better he is this way, for he will be easier to teach than one who thinks he knows it all. Your apprehensive young learner needs simply to be given tasks at which he can succeed and put into situations where he can figure things out without getting into trouble. Put him at the helm on a windward course with a steady breeze and the boat will soon tell him if he steers too close to the wind. He will not embarrass himself by jibing the stick out of her as he might if asked to steer with the wind astern.

It is always "fun" for some to play tricks on the greenhorn and laugh as he uses the vocabulary of the landlubber. Let the veteran remember that what is second nature to him is a whole new world and a whole new language to the new sailor. The initiate must be given clear instructions, plenty of practice, and plenty of patience.

Sometime there may come aboard a guest who has had a previous traumatic experience on a sailing trip. Such a person accepts your invitation because he wants to overcome his apprehensions caused by the trauma and he wants to be a good sport for you or his wife or his friend. Such a person most likely will speak of his apprehension before he has been long aboard. Do not belittle it or change the subject. Let him talk. You will usually get a good tale and the talker may talk himself out of his fears. If not, he may give a clue that will help you to help him. We once had aboard two young boys and their mother whose father had been lost in a tragic accident. Their dinghy went adrift. The father swam for it, could not catch it, and was too exhausted to swim back. The family left aboard could not tack their catamaran quickly enough to pick him up before he drowned. They were all eager to sail again and overcome this tragic experience. The chance to ask, to learn, and to sail the boat was needed.

A young lady guest once became hysterical in a rail breeze. She wanted us to stay close to the ledges so she could step off if the boat capsized. We could not convince her that the deep water was safer. Her need for solid land was a clue. I took her to the windward side amidships and braced her against the house where she could not see the water rushing by the lee rail. There she calmed down enough to tell me of her first trip at sea in a small boat. They were caught in a wild storm. She was commanded to take the wheel while the men took care of the boat forward. Now she goes only because her husband wants her to, and he loves to sail. She gets hysterical when the going gets rough, much to her own chagrin. Time and understanding may dispel her apprehensions, at least on a pleasant, windy day.

If you are an ardent sailor, you have hit a ledge, been caught in a squall, or managed to get into some kind of jam that will shake up your otherwise calm guests. Often in the heat of the crisis people are too busy to be scared, but fears will develop when it is all over. When this happens, the best you can do is to give your guests time to know that they are really all right after all. We were caught out in a white squall that blew out our jib and tore our mainsail before we could shorten sail sufficiently. Under staysail, the skipper got us under a lee and allowed us to catch our breaths before we patched up, tucked a double reef in the mainsail, and beat home across rough waters.

I was aboard another time when the skipper, running fast before a rough sea, hit a ledge. The wave ahead of us broke. As we

Comfortably reefed on a windy day

165

dropped down hard on the rock, the next wave broke into the cockpit. We bounced over into deep water and were safe but badly shaken. A little girl in the cockpit was scared and soaked down by the wave. After it was all over she quite naturally was still frightened and wished to go ashore. Her parents wisely wanted to continue the trip. Here was an apprehension not easily overcome! She was willing to go below and get some dry clothes. There was little I could do except make her comfortable and talk about little things until she came to realize that the boat was still sailing. The skipper got us into smoother waters, but it was a long time before I could get the little girl to go on deck. Interest in a lighthouse and a lobsterman finally brought her out, but not until she had time to sense that we were all right and it would not happen again.

Miss Penny Whiting of Auckland, New Zealand, may be seen in almost any weather, reefed or under light sails, teaching her crew of yachts-men's ladies to handle her big sloop. An able skipper herself, Whiting is teaching her crews to be of real use on other people's boats—to set spin-nakers, shoot moorings, sail out anchors, and lay courses—but more importantly, she is giving them confidence that women can do these things with precision and grace and that there is pleasure in the doing. Surely someone in this hemisphere could advance the same good work.

Seasickness

There are always some who are apprehensive about getting sick, even on a calm day. This apprehension itself can cause sickness, so it is well to allay it if possible. Once aboard and under way, it is too late for dramamine. The best technique is to talk about something else. If your guest insists on talking about it, make light of it. If you have ever had the prob-

lem yourself and have overcome it, say so with understanding. If one is afraid of seasickness, he often retreats below. This is a mistake. Keep him on deck in the fresh air. Gum or a pilot cracker often relieves the tension, but the best cure I know is a trick at the wheel.

No Cause for Apprehension

The rigors of the day often strain otherwise confident sailors. When it breezes up so the boat drags her rail through the water and feels overpowered, the guests will brace themselves and begin to endure the trip. At this point it is well to reef, but the idea of reefing itself may cause apprehension. Let your guests know why you have decided to reef and just how you will do it. They will become interested in the operation and want to help. Warn them that there may be a good deal of flapping of canvas but the boat will heave to easily. An able guest may hold her in the wind for you as you lower the mainsail. Let your guests help tie in the reef after showing them how. Carefully check their knots and your own. All aboard will feel part of the crew after the shortened sail is set. They will be more comfortable, the vessel will sail more easily, and apprehension will have slipped away.

The elderly and handicapped will be apprehensive about getting aboard and stepping ashore. Move deliberately. Pick a good place in the cockpit where the guest can feel secure. Let him know just where he is going to step before he starts. Point out the hazards, such as the boom that may be swinging as the boat lies to the wind or the spring line stretched across his path. Have someone in the cockpit to help him to his seat. When he goes ashore, let him wait until the boat lies close alongside and have someone on the float to receive him. Our experience has been that such people are most appreciative and help in calming the fears of others. We had one calm old lady who helped an apprehensive young bride from Texas on a day when we had to reef outside in a steep chop. When we remarked that we were impressed by the lady's calm through the rough seas and confusion, she smiled and said that her grandfather had been a skipper in the China trade and she had more than once accompanied him to the Orient. We had a blind guest allay the apprehension of shipmates in a thick fog by being the first to hear the surf on the shore, the birds in the trees, or the sought-for buoy.

Finally, apprehension can be brought on by hunger and fatigue when otherwise there would be no sign of it. Have extra warm clothes aboard. Serve a cup of hot tea and a pilot cracker, chocolate, and raisins. And even if you are tempted to try an extra long sail, head for home in time to get your guests to the mooring eager to go again.

Cruising with Children
Eileen Burt

Every summer for the past five years, my husband and I have packed up our family and taken up the cruising life. We started with a three-week stretch and were up to two months at a time when we sold our boat. Our family consists of three children, currently ages ten, eight, and four. People who meet us when we are afloat often compliment us on our "crew." More than a few have asked how we arrange our cruise so that the children can join in.

Cruising with children is a different kind of cruising from that with an all-adult crew. It can be very rewarding to both the yachtsman and the family, but it does take a little advance planning.

Our boat had to have only one modification to make her safe for our baby. (She took her first cruise at seven months.) I replaced the dacron bunk keeper on her pilot berth with one I made from fish netting bound with folded curtain heading. The baby could then be securely latched in a floating crib seven feet long by two feet wide. She could see us when we were in the cockpit through the hatchway and could follow the play of her older brothers on the cabin sole. She could sit or crawl in the low headroom provided until she was two and one-half years old.

We were already equipped with life lines, about twelve inches and twenty-four inches off the deck, all around the bow, but not in the stern. At one time we had planned to secure fish netting around the life lines, but the children never seemed to need it. In fact, it would have made it easier for them to board from a dinghy, since they usually duck between the life lines to get on board.

We have three safety rules that all small people, our own or guests, must obey. Foremost is that life jackets are worn on deck at all times. The only little people who are exempt from this rule are those who can swim around the boat (*Altair* is thirty-six feet on the water line) three times without stopping. Our second rule, in use whenever we are under way in anything but a gentle zephyr, is that the children must be either in the cockpit with us or below. When there are only two of us to handle the boat, we *have* to know where the children are *at all times,* and this rule helps us do it. Finally, *everyone* on board obeys the captain first and asks questions later.

Within these limits, what do we do with the children to keep them amused? We use imagination, our curiosity, and a few toys from home to expand all our horizons.

When we are underway and the children are in the cockpit, they like to tow things on a length of cod line. The older boys have "batten boats" made from broken battens tied to about eight feet of line. These tow, swirl, plane, and angle through the water as we sail along. My daughter has a fishing line with a sinker but no hook. She likes to drop this overboard and then reel it back in. (Please note: We are a sail-powered boat—none of this goes on under power, for fear of getting such a line tangled in the propeller.)

When the weather is lovely and we are all gathered together on a long passage, we play those old-fashioned parlor word games: Twenty Questions, I'm Thinking of a Word that Starts with the Letter . . . , Pack My Trunk, etc. These can be varied with the ages and skills of the family involved. This is also an excellent time to teach navigational skills: how to read a chart, plot a course, steer by the wind or the compass, and to learn to tie a new knot.

Last resort is a home-made Bingo game consisting of nine or sixteen squares I have filled in with pictures of nautical objects (bells, nuns, cans, etc.) or all kinds of boats. The first one to spot them all or fill in a line wins.

Some of these games are also played below decks, along with a few tried-and-true toys. We never leave our mooring without some unusual coloring books and pencils. Crayons have been banned since our first year when they were trampled, melted, and mashed into the cabin sole, cushions, and sneakers. We also take paint-with-water books, scissors, colored paper, and Scotch tape.

Other old favorites are a deck of cards and a container of dice games. The latter are an old treasure that belonged to my husband as a boy. There are four tubes of dice in a leather container. Each tube contains four or five dice for a game such as golf, put and take, poker, and a slot machine game. The littlest kids enjoy making a tower or a house using the dice as blocks; they also like to fill and empty the tubes. Our older two now enjoy playing the games themselves.

From home we always bring a collection of toys for each child, chosen by the child. These usually include matchbox cars, a cuddly animal, stacking cups, a tiny tea set, paper dolls, and some object that is a treasure only to its owner. We also bring some build-it toy. Our favorite is Tupperware's Build'O Fun, but any toy with large pieces will do (small ones tend to drop down some crack or hole or get underfoot—dangerous on a heeling boat). These can be made into a variety of shapes, and play develops from whatever shape the children put together. Never take a magnetic game—remember your compass!

And last, or maybe first of all, we bring books, usually a mixture of old favorites and new ones, mostly in paperback editions. They are read aloud, chapter by chapter, as we sail long passages, or before naps or bed.

Some of each day is spent doing chores. Each child is responsible for keeping his bunk area neat and clean. This means rolling up his sleeping bag when not in use, folding clothes and putting them away, and having all his personal articles stowed so that they don't fall over when the boat heels. In addition, the older children wash and dry one set of dishes a day. Other, unscheduled jobs come up during the day, such as setting the table, or helping a younger child while both of us are busy on deck.

When, at last, our boat reaches the day's destination, there are other amusements. There is swimming, in warm water, and rowing in any kind. Even the two year old can row. We set her in the dinghy with the painter tied astern and watch while she puts the oars into and out of the oarlocks and rows a stroke or two. The older children now row well, but they learned while tied astern too—with a longer and longer line as they progressed.

Shore time is the easiest time of all, because it represents variety. We try to spend several hours ashore every day to let the children run. Everyone's disposition improves after we have had a long walk or climb ashore.

In rural or uninhabited anchorages, we hike, pick berries, or gather treasures to be saved on board in a coffee can with a lid. Identifying birds, flowers, and trees is a pleasant and educational amusement. If you are not familiar with this kind of wildlife, the *Peterson's Field Guides* are helpful to have on board.

When our destination is a populated area, the children's great delight is swinging at the local playground or schoolyard or exploring the local library. Of course, when some other attraction is easy to reach, we go and visit that too. We have explored old forts, mountain views, shipyards and local museums to the delight of both children and adults.

Cruising with your family strengthens family ties as it introduces each family member to the others as a playmate, teacher or friend. On the other hand, close quarters and long stretches of time make for that cooped-up feeling. A week of rain can be a sore trial. Even with the best of planning, tempers flare. Yet the benefits are real and the experience is fun on balance. I'd advise every cruising family to try it. Modify our methods to suit your family. A musical or artistic family might bring instruments or sketch pads, for instance.

Try it for a weekend or a week at first, but by all means try it!

Cruising with Teenagers
Grandin Wise

The following remarks are based upon thirty-five years' combined experience by two teachers who have taken young people cruising to help pay their boat bills.

If there is one thing a teenager is not, it is contemplative. Whereas you will get joy from a jewel of a Maine island or a perfectly set sail, or the sea-kindly motion of your vessel, a teenager—of either sex—will interrupt your reverie with, "Look at that cool boat over there! I'll bet he's doing fifty. Say, how fast can this bucket go, anyway?" And you don't share his youthful enthusiasm for outboard speed.

If there is one thing a teenager likes, it is action and excitement. After a particularly idyllic cruise marred only by one nasty squall, my crew of five young people voted instantly and unanimously that the best part of the entire cruise was the "storm."

So let's face it—there does exist a problem for the practical sailor: how can he live at sea with these exuberant young animals without losing his sanity and without suppressing their effervescent spirits? It can be done in most cases. As among more mature members of the species, there are some young people who, despite a dogged determination to like the life of the sailor, just plain don't: they may be timid or weak of stomach or too dependent on the comforts of home. Except for these obvious misfits, however, a reasonable *modus vivendi* is entirely possible if you will but heed the following tested suggestions.

Rule No. 1. *Treat them like people.*

Share with them your concerns, ask their advice, and listen to it. Give them responsibility, and expect them to live up to it. They will. Ask for their judgment about changing weather conditions as you would ask a grown-up contemporary. Let them decide when to shorten sail or where to drop the hook in a crowded anchorage. Put them in charge of preparing supper. Let them keep the ship's log. These are tricks that we "professionals" find bring out the best in our young charges.

These are the very things that their boat-owning fathers forget to do. No wonder the kids get bored cruising in the family boat if daddy hogs all the action and responsibility. Fathers, heed the all-too-common teenage lament, "When I go sailing with my dad, all I do is sit."

In addition to the routine chores of deck swabbing, trash disposal, polishing, and sweeping, assign the whole crew to watches and require them to determine on the chart the exact location of the ship every hour on the hour, to monitor Channel 16, to check the weather report, and, of course, to take a regular trick at the helm. These things are easier said than done. It is hard for the skipper to sit calmly watching incompetents bungle jobs he is accustomed to doing with alacrity, but a little patience will be rewarded sooner than you expect. If they know they are being trusted as mature people, your teenagers will cease being incompetents. They will become responsible sailing companions—real people.

Rule No. 2.　Keep them busy.

This is another way of saying, "Don't let them become bored." There is a lot of quiet sameness on board a cruising boat. That's one of the things we find so delightful. But teenagers don't. When they start eating candy, asking for coke, wondering five minutes after breakfast how long it will be till lunch, you know you have a bored ship and should introduce some energy-consuming activity. How about a Man Overboard drill, or a trip to the masthead by bosun's chair? Or break out the ship's kite, or trail a line in hope that a bluefish may be passing?

For those not on watch there should be games and other activities. It is up to the captain to assume the role of cruise director and to generate enthusiasm for a chess tournament or a baseball league. Excitement over the outcome of a baseball game played with a deck of cards, pencil and paper has caused a group of five thirteen-year-olds to forget lunch for half an hour! Although you should certainly have an interesting shelf of sailing books and magazines on board, don't count on reading to en-

tertain all your young charges. With over half the young people who have sailed with me, reading has not been a preferred occupation. Action is better than words.

Rule No. 3.　Get them off the ship.

You may want to keep sailing nonstop as long as the weather holds, but the kids will be happier, and in the long run so will you, if you anchor off an uninhabited island and send the gang ashore for lunch while you tend ship in welcome solitude. Send along a Frisbee or a whiffle ball. These items are vital ship's equipment if you have teenagers along.

When evening finds you in a quiet harbor, you need a sailing dinghy to work off some more energy. A clam rake may serve the extra function of supplementing the larder. Judicious exploration is sometimes in order. A shore party this summer out of Somes Sound proved immensely successful as it climbed 869-foot Mt. St. Sauveur and swam in fresh-water Echo Lake. Crew morale soared and we vowed to repeat the venture or try to duplicate it. A walk to town for rations or a movie can be rewarding, although the latter is expensive and often unsuitable. Since they need to release so much energy, give your young ones a chance to swim a long distance with you rowing along in the dinghy; or send them off in the dinghy to list the names of all the boats in the harbor, later to be looked up in Lloyd's. They love to sleep ashore, on their own, in a pup tent. A couple of air mattresses make a good addition; so does insect repellent.

Rule No. 4.　Develop group pride.

On preparing to enter a harbor where you know there will be many eyes watching, carefully assign a responsible job to each member of the crew. Then SAIL to your anchor, blatantly showing off that you are *real* sailors. For the sake of the ship and the skipper's nerves it is suggested that for this maneuver the skipper be at the helm. But the sense of teamwork that comes with all having a part in rounding up smartly, dropping sail at just the right moment, getting sails furled quickly and neatly, dropping the anchor at just the right time and place, keeping the dinghy out of trouble, and so on is a great morale booster. In fact, the captain may swell with pardonable pride as onlookers comment favorably on the show. He may indeed come to the conclusion that sailing with teenagers is pretty good fun after all.

How to Get Asked Again

The least expensive way to sail is as a guest. However, it is not entirely a free ride. To be successful as a sea-going guest, there are skills and qualities of personality one must cultivate.

The skills are the easiest. Like any good AB, you must be able to hand, reef, and steer. You must be a good helmsman. This involves principally the self-discipline to pay attention consistently to what you are doing, however tempting may be the conversation. Sailing by the wind involves simply keeping a sharp eye on the luff of the jib and the tell-tales, coordinating that eye with a light but steady hand on the helm. Nothing burns an owner-skipper so much as a helmsman who abuses his yacht by sailing her alternately ramping full and then pinched up too close to the wind, bobbing up and down in the same hole twice. Steering by compass also requires attention, for 150 degrees and 130 degrees can look much alike and west-northwest can be confused by an inattentive helmsman with north-northwest. A good helmsman should keep within one-quarter point (three degrees) of the course either way.

Second, develop your talents as a high-speed, short-order cook. Take as your model the cook in Conrad's *Nigger of the Narcissus*. With the vessel on her beam ends in a gale off the Cape of Good Hope, the galley washed out and all hands clinging to the poop half frozen, he made coffee to the defiant slogan, "While she swims, I cook." This is not to say that you will prepare every meal, but that under pressure which may force the regular cook into retirement, you can come through with a hot drink and a sandwich apiece for all hands. A knowledge of stoves, ability to boil water, and a copper-riveted digestion capable of keeping its balance in a battened-down cabin are the essentials.

A good rigger is much in demand. One who can tuck in a wire splice at short notice, or strap a block or run a snug tight serving so it need not be taken off and done again by an expensive boat-yard employee will earn the respect of the owner—and will deserve it.

The same is true of a good mechanic. A recalcitrant engine is a dead and stubborn chunk of cold iron, smelling faintly of gasoline and incurring the curses of the frustrated owner, embarrassed because he cannot show his guests the good time he has promised them. The guest who knows that most motor failure is due to the devils of dirt, rust, and dampness and who knows how to exorcise them from distributor, coil, and plugs so the engine will leap merrily into action once more is respected, admired, and asked again.

Similarly, any other skill the guest may possess will be welcome. The photographer, artist, musician, or poet can always find a place for himself.

I have omitted the art of the navigator. Most skippers like to do their own navigating and piloting, but certainly there are cases where the guest who can take over the task will be frequently invited. This is especially true in ocean cruising where celestial navigation is required.

More important than the skills that the guest can bring, however, is the atmosphere that surrounds him. Regardless of his ability to rebuild the engine or rerig the vessel, if he is a know-it-all, if he is always talking of how much better it was in another vessel, if he is always talking about any one subject, he will be left ashore. Let him who would be asked again keep still unless he has something pleasant to say of general interest. He must let the skipper command the vessel, offering advice when asked for it. He will be asked for it if he does not volunteer it too soon. He should avoid taking sides, particularly in family arguments, and should quietly enjoy everything enjoyable. The result will be that for the price of transportation and a bottle, a book, or a loaf of homemade bread, he can enjoy many a cruise as a valued and trusted AB on a variety of yachts.

Tables Aboard

The Chart Table

The navigator deserves a chart table that is not the dining table, the kitchen table, or the top of the icebox or sink. He needs a well-lighted place out of the fore-and-aft traffic where he can lay out a chart folded in half on a smooth surface over which a parallel rule can travel undisturbed. He should have ready at hand where they cannot slide into the lee corner of the cabin floor these same parallel rules, his dividers, pencil, logbook, and glasses. Within reach should be a shelf for storing a block of paper, tide tables, cruising guide, *Coast Pilot,* Eldridge, Bowditch, the *Nautical Almanac,* and those big books of navigational tables like H.O. 214. Within easy view should be the depthfinder and within reach the RDF, stopwatch, and sextant. Are we asking too much? You may have to compromise, but one yacht did it thus.

The forward side of the cabin bulkhead next to the companionway is flat and vertical. A piece of plywood as large as needed is hinged to this at its lower edge and a hinged leg provided to support the inboard corner when the table is lowered. The outboard corner is supported by a light chain to the overhead or the shelf. The table is set high enough and the bunk low enough so a sleeper's feet can lie under the table. An oak rail about an inch high is screwed to the edge of the table to stiffen the plywood and to prevent charts and tools from sliding off. However, the corners of the rail are left open to make cleaning easier.

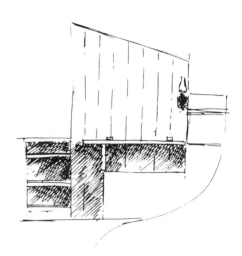

The shelf outboard of the table is wide enough for the navigation books and RDF. These are held in place by a high rail on the front of the shelf and a length of shock cord above it. Thus books are easily accessible and firmly restrained. Cup hooks carry some of the tools that have holes or can be drilled. However, each will soon wear its arc in the paint unless it is restrained as the boat rolls. A block with three-eighths-inch holes drilled in it will accommodate pencils and dividers. A light over the table can be fitted with a red bulb for night chartwork or with a regular bulb so the occupant of the bunk can see to read comfortably.

Located as it is next to the hatch, the navigator has good light by day, is in close touch with helmsman and lookout, and can easily pop his head out to see for himself. He is out of the cook's way and does not interfere with dining arrangements either on deck or below. When the anchor is down, the table can be hinged up with the chart still on it and secured with a hook. Thus it is out of the way of sleepers and bunk sitters, while other books on the shelf and the radio are still accessible.

Further refinements are possible, adding convenience and elegance. The plywood can be covered with Formica and can be made of a hard wood and attractively varnished. It also can be made in two layers with a couple of inches between them for chart storage. However, even in its rough form, it works out very well.

The table in position

A Successful Cabin Table

A cabin table in a small boat is both a necessity and a nuisance. It must be noncapsizable, rigid, and easy to stow. Tables with folding legs meet none of these requirements and bite one's fingers viciously.

The forward end of the table pictured here is braced against the mast and supported by a frame nailed to the bunks. Through table and frame drop two bolts, set up below on wing nuts, thus making the table rigid. The after end is supported on a rope bridle from the deck beam. There are no legs.

The table can be folded lengthwise on a piano hinge and stowed easily behind a bunk.

Clothing Aboard

Foul Weather Gear

Summer sailors don't need as much foul weather gear as most of them wear. Seldom do we get more than a day of rain at a time in the summer, and seldom does a skipper drive his crew through more than a day of hard windward work. The elaborate efforts to keep dry that are necessary for the offshore mariner are more trouble than they are worth for the weekender. For the passing shower or the dash of spray a good ski jacket will do very well.

For the really rainy day, pants and jacket are the minimum. It is useless to count on a raincoat; even the long slicker or frock some lobstermen use is not good enough even for a sharp shower. The Sailor used to favor the pull-over jacket with a hood, on the theory that it was less likely to leak in front. However, the last time he bought oil clothes, only the button-up type was available, and it has worked very well. It has a double row of buttons on the front—doubtless that makes a big difference. Also, the button-up type is much easier to get into.

The pants come either with a bib and suspenders or with a drawstring around the waist. Unless they are adjusted perfectly, one suspender will slip off your shoulder when you have the anchor halfway to the surface and when there is no time to readjust. The drawstring or elastic around the waist is good, but you may find it hard to get a wet, cold hand by the waistband and into an inner pocket for your knife. Some suits have a handy pocket in the front of the pants.

A hood is better than the conventional sou'wester because it doesn't leak around the neck, but the hood tends to flop over your eyes. A cap with a visor will keep the water off your face and the hood out of the way. The cap will get wet, of course, but it will dry out.

In the old days, oil clothes were literally oiled coats and pants. They were sticky,

The table stowed. Note the permanent support between the bunks.

smelly, and of little more than psychological value, and they lasted a season at best. Nowadays a good suit of oil clothes lasts so long that it is hard to tell which good suit is the best. In general, avoid the inexpensive nylon types. These either are not waterproof for long or sweat on the inside. Also, they tear very easily when caught on a projection. The sheet plastic kind is even worse. Just start a small tear and it is all gone. The kind made of cloth impregnated or coated with plastic is heavier, stronger, and is usually ventilated so it sweats less. The Sailor's own Canor Plarex suit has lasted a long time, but there are doubtless other good types too.

Some sailors favor a towel around the neck for warmth and defense against drips. In the short run, this is good. If there is a great deal of water about, or if it is a long watch on deck, the towel begins to act like a wick, conducting the cold wet outside to the inside, where it is most unwelcome. A wool shirt is most comforting under the oil coat, for even if wet, it is warm. A nylon shirt is clammy.

If you want to keep your feet dry, you will have to wear boots with the legs of the pants coming down outside them. Some sailors object to boots unless the weather is really cold, because to fall overboard with boots on is nearly fatal and ordinary rubber boots are both clumsy and slippery. If you must have boots, top-sider boots with squeegee soles and loose flexible uppers are probably the best kind. However, the worst part of wet feet is getting them wet. Sneakers with wool socks are quite tolerable in the summer time, once they are thoroughly soaked. One can get by thus for a day.

When wearing oil clothes, take particular and special care not to fall overboard. If you do, try to keep the air trapped in the back of your jacket by leaning forward as far as possible and breathing only at intervals. If you lose that bubble, you will have to get the oil clothes off, for you cannot swim in them. Hope you are picked up quickly.

The offshore sailors are now recommending wet suits as a far safer and more practical answer to the problem of foul weather. A wet suit is flexible and plenty warm enough for summer sailing. Furthermore, it has some buoyancy, and should you fall overboard, you can swim in it. Lands' End Yacht Stores, Box 66244, Chicago, Illinois 60666 sells a yachting wet suit, jacket, and long johns, cut looser than a diver's suit, lined and coated with nylon for extra strength.

Clothes

What clothes does one bring on a small boat for a coastal cruise, and how does one care for them? In the first place, the fewer the

174

better. Fundamentally, one must provide for warm weather, cool weather, and wet weather. Also, some provision must be made for minimum elegance ashore.

Few people need much guidance on warm weather clothes. Be sure to include slacks and a long-sleeved shirt in case of sunburn and a hat to shade the eyes, nose, and lips. It is not necessary to bring more than two changes of warm weather clothes, as laundry machines are available at almost every port and work quickly enough to do a wash before it is time to get under way.

For cooler weather, the first step is a T-shirt or light turtleneck worn under a regular cotton work shirt. It is surprising how much warmth it provides on a chilly day. A windbreaker or ski parka that cuts the wind and shelters the neck and wrists is the next step. Wool socks, a flannel shirt, and light windproof pants will keep you warm on almost any summer night. You will not need two flannel shirts or a heavy sweater. Keep the wardrobe to a minimum.

For elegance ashore, you may need pants, shirt, coat and tie, or a dress. Hang the gear on a wooden or plastic hanger, cover with a plastic shield that comes down over the shoulders, and hang in the locker. The shield will protect the clothes from chafe as the boat rolls. One can spoil a good sport coat in a day. Be sure the locker is well ventilated.

Other clothes should be brought aboard in a duffel bag, preferably with a zipper of heavy plastic up its side. If your skipper can provide a locker or drawer for your clothes, by all means use it, for it keeps them dry and well ventilated. If not, at least have a laundry bag so wet clothes and dirty clothes can be kept quarantined from clean ones. Wet clothes should be in a plastic bag separate even from the dirty ones. Once wet with salt water, clothes never dry out and on a foggy day will get positively slimy.

After you have added bathing suit, pajamas, toilet articles, underwear, camera, and so on, fill any cracks and crannies left with extra athletic socks. One can never have too many, and they keep girls' feet warm as well as boys'.

What clothes do you wear aboard your yacht? Whatever you like! It's your yacht! Writing about forty years ago, Francis Herreshoff insisted on gray flannel trousers, a double-breasted blue jacket with black buttons, cut high in front, white rubber-soled shoes that leave no marks, and a watch cap or beret. That seems rather elaborate today. The people in magazine ads wear dark glasses and very little else. Marine outfitters recommend short pants of Breton Red or fashionably faded blue with all manner of stripes above the belt. Whatever you wear for style ashore, protect yourself from sun and wind at sea with long pants, a shirt with sleeves, and a cap with a short visor you can pull down over your eyes on a bright day. A stout ski jacket will keep you warm enough south of Cape Sable in the summertime.

Peaceful Coexistence with an Engine

One yachtsman resolved to sail his boat to England. He found that the engine interfered badly with the stowage of stores, so he took it out and sailed without it. On his return, he had managed so well without the engine that he never replaced it.

Most of us, however, particularly coastwise cruisers with limited vacations, find that we can't live with an engine and we can't live without one.

One method is containment. Isolate the engine in its own part of the boat and ignore it. Strenuous efforts here will achieve some success. A bulkhead running right down to the keel must be built between engine space and cabin. This will prevent the oily bilgewater and associated smells from working forward into the cabin, but it will require a separate bilge pump on each side of the bulkhead and snugly fitting gaskets where necessary pipes and wires must pass through.

The engine side of the bulkhead should be insulated with fireproof insulation that cannot absorb water or oil. Then the engine room must be provided with a hatch from the deck and the hatch must be where it can be reasonably protected against spray and loose water, and must not be close to electrical components. Salt water on an active generator produces very quickly a greenish crust of horrible aspect and leads to the immediate demise of the generator.

Because the batteries should be as close as possible to the generator, thorough ventilation must be provided. Batteries give off hydrogen, a highly explosive gas lighter than air, and gasoline vapors produce a highly explosive mixture heavier than air. The minimum is a blower sucking from the lowest point in the engine room on the same side as the carburetor and a cowl ventilator drawing from under the deck. Obviously, the switch and blower should be nonsparking.

One advantage of this installation is the possibility of installing a fire control system that at the pull of a handle will flood the engine room with CO_2. However, a separate engine room is expensive in both space and money, for it takes up a large part of a small boat. A compromise omits the bulkhead but contains the engine behind removable cabin steps, lockers, and quarterberth liners. These, of course, are not air-tight and permit the subtle odors of hot oil and bilge to come forward under the sole and through the cracks. Although the panels enclosing the engine may be insulated against noise, it won't be long before they begin to rattle, unless they are firmly fastened or swell so tightly as to become immovable.

This method is generally the compromise adopted, for it gives more cabin room. However, the man who wants to close a sea cock, install a new impeller in the water pump, or take up a half turn on the needle valve had better be a professional contortionist. One boat the Sailor saw at a boat show had a six-inch hole in the quarterberth liner through which

one could shine a flashlight and see the engine. Then one removed eye and flashlight, ran in tool, hand, and arm and did the work by feel. The alternative was to dismantle galley and quarterberths, a half-day's work.

Access through a flush hatch in the cockpit floor is little better. The hatch is seldom big enough to more than reach through, head down. If it is big enough to climb down through, there is but little room to work under it. Furthermore, in hard weather you cannot lift it without taking in a good deal of water.

The third solution to the problem, also involving compromise, is to learn to love the machine. Lavish every care upon it. Conciliate it. Bring it into the cabin and make it one of the crew. Put an insulated box over it for a table if you like, or use the box as one of the companionway steps, but don't shut it in with a complex of lockers. Acknowledge its presence.

Keep it scrupulously clean. This means wiping off any oil or grease that may have gathered on it after running. It means cleaning the drip pan under it before much gurry accumulates therein. Some drip pans are installed before the engine is set on the beds and the pan simply cannot be cleaned. Be absolutely certain that, gasoline or diesel, the fuel line is a single length of tubing from tank to strainer, that it is as straight a run as possible, and that there is an easily accessible shut-off at the tank. The fuel line should come out through the top of the tank, leaving no holes whatever in the bottom, and the shut-off should always be closed when the engine is stopped. Thorough ventilation is necessary, of course; but with the engine exposed, this is easier to effect, and any foul odors caused by its running are quickly dissipated. With all wiring and piping exposed, also any leaks, overheating, or unusual noises are more quickly noticed, identified, and cured. Furthermore, the machine is likely to be kept drier and cleaner and to be used less often, for its noise is certainly more evident and insistent. However, the ease of maintenance and the extra room available in the cabin is to many of us worth the noise under way. It is a matter of attitude. Learn to love it and you can live with it.

Sleeping Aboard

The Fore Peak

Conventionally, the fore peak is devoted to tourist class accommodations. Two V-berths are built right into the eyes of the boat. These must be built as close under the deck as possible to provide adequate width for the sleepers' feet at the forward end and to afford a place in the after end for one to stand when he puts on his clothes.

The narrow space under the bunks is often used for rectangular drawers, a wasteful way in which to use triangular space, or for bins or lockers. These are necessarily deep and narrow so the smallest and most wanted hardware sifts to the bottom. Spill a handful of tacks in one of these bins and remember the carpenter shop in Conrad's *Nigger of the Narcissus!*

A door opens forward into this same narrow cave of a fore peak because it is better thus than opening aft into the head or the main cabin. A hatch is provided overhead for ventilation and escape.

The result is a combination of inconveniences. The hatch is used first as a place through which to dispose of anchor and rode, perforce on the narrow floor. Anchors have hard and sharp projections! Next the hatch is used to dispose of spare headsails, occasionally neatly bagged, but often just stuffed down wet. These fill the space between the bunks, jam the door, and render the fore peak uninhabitable and inaccessible. Before the space can be useful, sails and anchor must be moved on deck.

If one must sleep under way with any sea running, the fore peak is the worst place in which to do it. The motion may be enough to leave your insides up under the deck as the bow crashes down into a trough with the rest of you. Wet sails have an oppressive odor, especially obvious with the hatch battened down.

Consider an alternative. Tear out the bunks. Substitute a stout curtain for the hinged door. Build a stout bin under the hatch dedicated to the stowage of ground tackle. Roding can be coiled in large loose coils for good ventilation and chain dumped in the middle of the coil. The anchor can be laid on top where a long arm from the deck can reach it. Heavy hooks can be located along one side for sail bags. Along the other side can be built shelves and lockers of convenient size and shape to contain such bosun's stores as needed.

With this arrangement, the bulkhead need not be the length of a sleeper from the bow but may be moved forward several feet, making it possible to move the sleepers aft. A certain amount of privacy is lost, but there are ways of achieving it further aft, especially as some space in the best part of the boat has been released by providing stowage forward.

The writer, having crossed a considerable portion of the Gulf Stream in a fore-peak bunk with a wet Terylene jib, feels strongly about the subject.

Night Noises

Once you are moored in a quiet harbor after a long day in the sun and wind, sleep should come easily, yet how often has the skipper crawled out of the sack to hunt noises by the light of a flashlight! What is that bump? The dinghy? The mooring buoy drifted alongside? A log floating by on the tide? Wait a bit and see if it comes again. Silence. All is well. Bump. If it happens once more, I will get up and hunt it down. Now all senses are on the *qui vive*. Sleep is out of the question. There it is. Up and after it!

The dinghy is floating innocently on the end of its painter. The mooring buoy is clear. Stand shivering in the moonlight and listen. It is aft, in the wheel box. The rudder head is gently bumping the pin that engages the steering gear. Lift out the pin and go back to the sack—but don't forget to replace it in the morning!

Next it may be in the galley, where someone has hung a knife where it can tap against a bulkhead, instead of putting it in its box. A loose screw holding a lamp chimney permits a tiny clink—not on every roll but only occasionally. Those very faint noises are devilishly hard to find. I hunted one for half an hour and finally traced it to a loose piece of fire-brick in the stove.

Yet when the vessel is at sea with the bow wave rushing by the planking, the boom jaws squeaking, the staysail sheet slamming on its traveler, and decibels of every description bouncing around the cabin, one drops asleep like a rock down a well.

Early Start

Once in a while one must turn the crew out early to catch a tide or a fair wind. The important thing appears to be to get under way at once. Wait only long enough to dress. It is interesting and rather exciting, seeing the harbor in the gray dawn, anchor lights still burning, the streetlights ashore still bright. The wind is cold and fresh. The reef points patter. We break out the anchor, set the jib, coil down halyards wet with dew.

Outside, the sea turns from gray to the pinkish color of the dawn. The bright spot in the east grows, brightens, and suddenly a crumb of sun breaks over the horizon. The sea is blue black, the ripples edged in silver. Then it is day and the anticlimax sets in. When do we eat?

The cook has trouble lighting the stove, for the wind blows down the hatch as it never does at anchor. The motion of the boat, heaving the empty stomach about, is not quite nauseating but just disturbing. Exclamations of delight and wonder at the beauty of the dawn soon die away.

In due course breakfast is served, the crew on the lee bunks among the touseled sleeping bags eating with plates on knees, coffee mugs against the fiddle on the table splashing a little at first. The man at the helm eats and steers as the bacon grease congeals in the dawn wind.

Washing up is at length finished. The vessel is on her way, the fair tide helping her along. Faces are shaved, the cabin cleaned up, and what feels like 9:30 is only 8:00 on the cabin clock. It looks like a long day!

Some of us, accustomed to coastal rather than deep-water cruising, make a point of turning out a strong half hour early and seeing that all hands are fed, coffeed, and cleaned before hauling the anchor. The dawn will be more beautiful, the leisurely second breakfast, when it comes in the cook's good time, will be better appreciated, and the day, although longer in hours, will seem not so long.

Health and First Aid

Carbon Monoxide

A party of arctic explorers pitched their tent in the lee of a cliff during a gentle snowstorm. They started their Primus stove to boil the kettle and were found a year later in attitudes of pleasant relaxation. The snow on the outside of the tent prevented the escape of carbon monoxide through the canvas. You can achieve the same result in your cozy cabin.

Kerosene, gasoline, and diesel oil consist essentially of hydrogen and carbon. When they burn, the oxygen in the air combines readily with the hydrogen to form water vapor and with the carbon to form dioxide, CO_2. However, if there is insufficient oxygen present to form CO_2, the carbon combines with only one atom of oxygen to form carbon monoxide, CO. This is a colorless, odorless gas that combines with the iron in the red corpuscles of the blood and prevents the blood from picking up oxygen from the lungs and releasing it to muscles and brain. It is as if coal cars were filled with liquid concrete at the mine instead of loose coal. The result is painless asphyxiation from oxygen starvation.

A kerosene lamp, a kerosene stove, a Coleman lantern, a charcoal fire all give off carbon monoxide. This need occasion no concern if there is sufficient ventilation. An open companionway and ventilators turned to the wind will do the job. A charcoal or coal fire in stove or fireplace is safe as long as the smoke goes up the stovepipe. Fortunately, if it blows back you will know about it, for there are other gases given off whose odors are sufficiently noxious to drive the crew on deck. Turning the smoke head or putting a bucket over it will often solve the problem. Once the draft is well established, there is no danger. However, a charcoal grill that has burned down to glowing coals will emit monoxide with very little accompanying odor and is extremely dangerous in the cabin. Cook the steak on deck.

Propane gas usually has something added to it to give it a strong odor so you can tell if the system is leaking, but it too gives off odorless carbon monoxide when it burns.

An alcohol flame is much less likely to give off carbon monoxide because alcohol has oxygen in it as well as carbon and hydrogen. It has many other things in it too, including a denaturant to make it too poisonous to drink, so it is just as well not to be friendly with its fumes.

Sometimes carbon monoxide poisoning occurs in unexpected places. In a power cruiser the ventilation intake for the head was located just aft of the exhaust for the generator. Ordinarily the generator was not used when the boat was under way and the arrangement had caused no problem. On one occasion, however, the generator was left running and the forward motion of the boat carried the fumes into the intake and asphyxiated a boy in the head. Jacques Cousteau nearly died in the early days of scuba diving when the exhaust from a gasoline motor used to drive the compressor was drawn into his air tanks.

There is little warning of the onset of monoxide poisoning. Sometimes a headache or numbness will precede collapse. If you see people getting drowsy over the cards, get all hands on deck at once and open hatches. If a shipmate is overcome, get him to fresh air at once and call the Coast Guard or local police for a respirator to restore oxygen to his blood as soon as possible. If he is still breathing, keep him warm and watch him carefully. If he stops breathing, apply artificial respiration at once.

Coastal First Aid

A big genoa jib can be a brutal antagonist on a windy day, and someone can get sprained, strained, or badly beaten about the head with the snap shackle on the clew. A riding turn on the winch endangers hands and fingers. The block on the quarter leading the spinnaker sheet to the winch pulled out of the deck on one yacht and killed a man. Carelessly putting the winch handle in place before releasing the brake on the main halyard winch can knock cold the foredeck hand. Anchor lines, engines, wires under strain, and hot pots in the galley are always sources of danger; and the whole scene is floating in deep water too thin for a man to walk on and too thick to breathe.

What can the coastwise skipper do in the event of sudden accident? His best resource, of course, is the VHF radio. A call to the Coast Guard on Channel 16 will almost certainly get a response, if not from the Coast Guard at least from some interested listener. A call to the nearest marine operator can be plugged into the telephone system and help sought thus, although in the writer's experience the marine operators themselves are very helpful.

If the emergency is severe, the Coast Guard will probably dispatch a helicopter or fast picket boat to your relief. If not, you will doubtless head for the nearest civilized port under forced draft. In the meantime, what can you do to prevent further damage, to ease the sufferer's pain, and to reassure his tortured spirit?

Don't move him any more than absolutely necessary. He will probably have been hurt on deck. Not much good can be accomplished by maneuvering him down a hatch, and he will have to be maneuvered out of it again later, possibly at the expense of pain and effort. Let him lie on the cockpit floor or across the bridge deck. Cover him up with a blanket and oil clothes if necessary. Ordinarily one would keep the head of the sufferer low unless there is a head wound. Reassure him. Tell him how soon he can expect help, using the outside figure to avoid disappointment. Don't feed him. Don't give him a healthy tot of rum. Don't do anything at all that is not necessary. But what is necessary?

Watch him closely. Air is the most immediate necessity of life. Be sure he does not stop breathing. If he does, be sure his tongue has not fallen back to clog his throat and that the airway is otherwise clear. Tipping his head back will pull the tongue forward. Then administer mouth-to-mouth resuscitation at once. Keep at it.

Second, he must not bleed unduly. Direct pressure on the site of the wound is recommended treatment. A tourniquet should be the last resort, used only *in extremis* and then not twisted any tighter than absolutely necessary and slacked off frequently.

If sprain, strain, fracture, or dislocation appears to be the problem, simply immobilize the injured part and support it as best you can. Almost any stiff thing will do for a splint. A sail batten would be ideal. However, a magazine or newspaper will do very well. Whatever you use, pad it so it won't dig into the already tender flesh and lash it around the damaged part on both sides of where the pain is. Tie it just tight enough to hold it still.

In the event of food poisoning, possible on a cruise as a result of inadequate refrigeration, you will probably have everyone aboard suffering at once. There isn't much you can do but clean out the stomachs and digestive tracts and hope for the best until medical help arrives.

Small wounds always suggest the danger of infection. They should be disinfected as a matter of routine never to be neglected and the wound should be covered with a Band-Aid or dressing. This is especially true in cases like blisters and rope burns where the surface layer of skin is gone and the wound does not bleed enough to clean itself out. There is not much you can do about tetanus but have the injured man see a doctor as soon as he gets ashore. Everyone should have a booster shot as often as his doctor recommends it. There are not likely to be tetanus germs around a boat, but you never know.

Choking is a danger seldom considered seriously. A hungry man can die in a minute from a piece of steak or a fishbone, and in the really serious cases, he cannot tell you what is the matter with him although he may clutch his throat. A whack between the shoulder blades may help to dislodge the offending material. If this fails, get behind him, clasp your fists under his breastbone, and yank in and upward hard. As a last resort put your finger in the side of his mouth and sweep it across the back, but be careful not to push the object further down the throat.

If you as skipper get your hurt friend to a doctor, alive, and in the most comfortable sit-uation possible, you deserve for yourself the tot of rum you did not give him earlier.

As winter preparation for summer emergencies, the best thing you can do is to take the Red Cross First Aid Course. This will give you at least an understanding of what kinds of problems you may face. This course includes mouth-to-mouth resuscitation. The second best thing is to buy the textbook for the course and study it. Dr. Paul B. Sheldon's *First Aid Afloat,* published by Yachting Publishing Corp. in 1968, will probably scare you to death, for it covers not only the short-range problems faced by the coastal skipper but also some of the more difficult emergencies faced by the ocean cruiser. Nevertheless, it is a most useful book to have aboard.

While you are thinking in this gloomy vein about next summer's misfortunes, overhaul your first-aid kit. Someone has probably lifted the Band-Aids and sunburn lotion and used the adhesive tape for first aid to the rigging rather than the crew. Be sure you have at least the necessities, such as disinfectant, Band-Aids, dressings, adhesive tape, splinter forceps, scissors, ace bandages, and so on. If your doctor will give you a prescription for a few tablets of an effective painkiller, it might help a great deal in the event of a bad burn or a fracture, but it would be as well to get medical advice by radio before using it.

You better have your radio set checked out as well.

A First-Aid Kit
for the Afternoon Sailor
Robert C. Duncan

Several years ago I observed the absence of an adequate first-aid kit aboard my small boat. We had a box of Band-Aids and a roll of tape, supplemented by an empty aspirin bottle and a pair of rusty tweezers. By rebuilding the kit, thinking of possible emergencies, and noting missing items during small accidents, we have assembled a useful kit that has been most satisfactory so far.

The first assumption was that the kit should be designed for small emergencies that occur frequently. Massive injuries that require specialized equipment cannot be handled without a medicine chest and expert medical consultation. What we needed were useful items to stop children's tears and relieve adult discomfort until either a doctor could be consulted or a rum bottle could be broached before dinner.

The following items we consider basic, and may be useful as a checklist. Their uses are obvious.

Aspirin: Put nine in one of the small tins available from a drugstore. As they are used up, replace them from the larger bottle in the bathroom cabinet at home.

Band-Aids: The small box of five spots, five patches, and fifteen three-quarter-inch strips is adequate for stopping a veritable ocean of children's tears as well as covering small cuts.

Disinfectant: Any general disinfectant will do, and personal preference is your best guide. We use the 3.8-ounce bottle of hydrogen peroxide. It is not painful, and children's attention is quickly drawn to the fuzzy bubbles produced when it is applied to cuts and scrapes. With these three, many irritating small injuries can be made comfortable. Yet there is room for much more, which may not seem essential until you find yourself in the situation where someone says "Is there a first-aid kit aboard?"

I have added the following useful items: one roll of one-inch adhesive tape, six four-inch-square Steri-Pads, and one roll of two-inch by five-yard flexible gauze bandage. They have seldom been used, but they are most helpful for the larger cuts and scrapes that must be kept clean, dry, and padded until they stop bleeding or a doctor can be reached. As accidents do not always happen in daylight, I included a small flashlight and an extra set of batteries. The light itself has resolved many an "emergency" of a nonmedical nature, and the first-aid kit is as good a place as any to store it. Label it with your name and designate its home as the first-aid kit, or it will be used and never returned. I have been fighting this battle for several years, and the flashlight has been in the first-aid kit when I needed

it on most occasions. I also added a two-inch by three-foot elastic ace bandage. The little clips have long since been lost, but a short strip of adhesive tape will keep it in place just as easily. The uses for the ace bandage are obvious, yet in a more severe emergency it could be helpful in a variety of unconventional ways. I found the presence of an elastic knee brace similar to the ones used by skiers another useful addition that could be adapted to solve a variety of problems.

As for nonemergency items that are used to relieve common pains, I have a small package of ten antacid Gelusil tablets for a guest who ate too much ravioli. A box of Sucrets can relieve the sudden onslaught of the summer cold and sore throat. The four-ounce can of Solarcaine spray is a balm to those prone to wearing bikinis too long on the foredeck. The one-ounce container of Cutter's insect repellent is an effective defense against the "fighter planes" that attack as soon as you are comfortably seated in the corner of the cockpit on a quiet night with a tall drink.

The question of a motion sickness medication raises a valid point that should be given serious consideration. I will not offer or administer pills to anyone. Yet I do carry Marezine and Bucladin-S (a prescription drug) for my own occasional use. If another person chooses to take a motion sickness medicine, I feel he must make that decision for himself before he leaves the dock. Although seasickness is extremely unpleasant and can put a real damper on an afternoon sail, it is always cured by placing the recumbent form of the sufferer on a solid pier. The alternative of dealing with an allergic reaction to motion sickness medicine while under way could be serious. Therefore, I do not offer or administer it to anyone except myself or my immediate family after consultation with our family doctor.

Enough of this rather uneasy subject. I have included a few more items that have proven to be useful and prudent.

Vaseline: I don't know why it's there. I have never used it, but I like it there.

Children's aspirin: Half an adult dose would do, but children are used to the taste and take it more readily.

A thermometer: I had an extra one, it fit, so it was added.

A whistle: In a serious emergency, this might be very useful to call for help. It takes up very little room and a child could use it while your attention is on a victim.

At my wife's insistence, in a place of obvious residence is a Pamper, a cloth diaper, two safety pins, and a two-ounce container of baby powder. While running short of a diaper is not a real emergency, I have been extremely grateful for its presence on more than one occasion. It also occurs to me that the highly absorbent quality of a Pamper or diaper could be of real use in the event of a serious cut.

A few dollars in coins take up no room but might be very helpful for the emergency call from the inevitable pay phone found at the head of most runways. Tweezers, scissors, a pencil, and a few Q-tips were likewise thrown in because I might need them some day, and I have used them frequently. Finally, most drugstores carry small brochures or pamphlets with basic first-aid information about wounds, bleeding, animal bites, nosebleed, splinters, burns, shock, fainting, and artificial respiration. I keep this in the kit; for although all this information should be part of one's general knowledge, it is not always. During an emergency is not the best time to start reading up on first-aid facts, but if you can't remember the treatment and the pamphlet is there, you are better off than without it.

In conclusion, this kit is a waterproof steel box, nine by thirteen by three inches. Like the insurance salesman, each reader can point out numerous calamities that could happen and think of other items that should be included "if . . ." Someday I may find out what those things are. In the meantime I have a medical kit that has solved numerous problems for a variety of people and provided reasonable insurance for meeting emergencies and soothing physical discomfort.

On the theory that a spoonful of sugar helps the medicine go down, I included three small peppermint candy canes for those passengers who—after small pain, tears, a Band-Aid, and a big kiss from mother—still needed a boost from the practical sailor for being a brave mate and a needed hand on the main sheet.

Winter Aboard
Edward H. Simmons

With boats so expensive and rents ashore so high, some yachtsmen fortunate enough to work near saltwater live aboard all winter. During the past five years my wife and I have spent more time living aboard various boats than we have living ashore. We have found the experience enjoyable, challenging, and, at times, frustrating.

Several questions must be considered when one is planning to spend the winter aboard. First of all, where is safe and convenient winter dockage available? Second, how does one keep the cabin warm and dry? Finally, how does one provide for water, fuel, and electricity?

Consider location first. With the increasing number of thefts aboard private yachts, operators of many marinas welcome people living aboard full time. What better way could a marina be protected than by full-time residents who come to know owners of other boats and who would recognize interlopers?

Seek a berth likely to be free of ice. In Maine harbors in normal winters there is little problem with ice because the swift tidal flow keeps the water stirred up, but if you are in the mouth of a river, moor on the downstream side of the wharf to protect yourself from the hardpans of fresh-water ice coming down the river on the ebb tides in the spring. The mooring system we used is shown in the accompanying diagram. The float was built around the two piles and moved up and down them with the tide. We dropped a heavy tire over each pile and made our dock lines fast to these so our lines too moved with the tide and did not have to be tended twice a day. The anchors had each a short length of chain and ample scope of heavy nylon line. During ugly weather we slacked the dock lines and hauled the boat away from the float. We were particularly concerned lest a very high tide and rough sea raise the float above the piles and let the

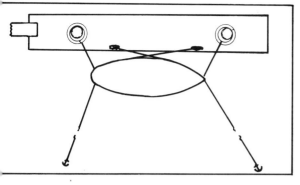

Winter mooring

boat come down on a pile. This remote possibility never developed, but the anchors would have held us off anyway, and certainly the vessel rode easier in rough weather away from the float. Of course, adequate fenders must be provided and every line must be wrapped in canvas, burlap, rubber hose, or some sort of chafing gear where it runs through chocks or over the rail.

Another important point neglected by some who winter aboard is the mast. Take it out. Not only is it better for the mast to be out of the weather, but if you leave it in the boat, she will want to sail. The spars and rigging make very considerable wind resistance in a winter gale and add measurably to the strain on mooring gear.

The first consideration on keeping winter weather out is a cover. We built a frame of two-by-fours, supporting the ridge on posts through the mast holes and laying rafters across to the life lines. Then we covered the frame with canvas, arranging it at bow and stern so the canvas could be unlaced along the top and opened up on sunny days to air things out. The canvas was carried down over the rail cap and nailed under battens above the scuppers. This leaves the scuppers open for ventilation and also permits one to throw a bucket of water down each side of the deck every day. If this washing down is neglected, the decks dry out badly from the heat of the cabin. After our first winter aboard, during which we neglected this practice, it rained for a week after we removed the cover and there was no dry spot in the boat.

We built a door frame and door into the

cover by making a dormer from the ridge pole, and we covered this with clear plastic to let in light and also so we could feel less like bears hibernating in a cave.

We kept our home warm with a small apartment-size gas heater. It had a thermostatically controlled fan and was vented to the outdoors. As we had a gas cooking stove, we were familiar with the substance on boats. A local company agreed to install the unit and deliver gas to the dock. We were charged a minimal installation charge plus the cost of the copper tubing and end fittings. This heating system was sufficiently powerful so that we could leave our deck ventilators open all winter. We were provided with a continuous change of air and suffered little or no heat loss.

The only place that condensation seemed to be a problem was under our mattresses, warmed at night by body heat and cooled during the day. This was solved by raising the mattresses off the bunk boards during the day. A few cans or bottles under the mattress by day did the trick. Also, we took every opportunity to air out on good days, opening up the cover and taking damp gear on deck.

We used the boat's own twelve-volt electrical system and kept it connected to a small trickle charger. If this method is used, keep a careful check on the water level in the batteries and provide adequate ventilation for them. The system was sufficient for our needs, as we used kerosene lamps to supplement electric lights and had no electric refrigeration. Instead, we kept perishables in the cockpit, where the temperatures seldom fell below 25 degrees F.

We always carried enough water in our tanks to last for several months, and because the tank was below the waterline, our fresh-water supply did not freeze. We supplemented this supply with water carried in jerry cans, which we emptied into the tank or used directly. Water in these did not freeze in the cabin. We used water conservatively for cooking, washing dishes, and brushing teeth. Laundry we did at the laundromat, and we took showers at the local YMCA.

There are a number of further incidental

considerations. Be sure to select a marina with storage lockers ashore. We stored all unnecessary gear there, allowing room enough aboard for our work clothing. (We are both teachers.)

Check with your insurance agent. Many policies do not provide coverage for a boat in the water all winter with heat aboard.

On boats under fifty feet, avoid working on your boat while living aboard. The dust, confusion, and space requirements make this difficult except for small jobs on deck.

Keep a checklist of things to be done to your boat; thus you can be more systematic in the spring.

Lay up the engine in the usual way and knock a soft pine plug into the exhaust pipe to prevent circulation of air and condensation in the exhaust pipe, muffler, and manifold.

The total cost for us to live aboard from October to May 1973–74 at a float was as follows:

Dockage at $3.00/foot including electricity, garbage collection, and water (when available)	$159.00
Propane gas	93.00
Heater installation	23.19
	$275.19

Of course this does not include the cover, but that would have been necessary whether the boat was occupied or not.

8

Watch Below

Photography Afloat
T. T. Gray

Sailing is an addiction. So is photography. Combine the two and you are really hooked. More than that, the two are complementary. The pleasure afforded to the sailor who can record the visual riches of the sport and to the photographer who can pursue his art under sail is without equal in the world of recreation.

The basics of photography, like the basics of sailing, are not as difficult to master as it would seem to the outsider. Furthermore, photographers and sailors alike are fortunate to live in a time when the quality of the equipment generally available is excellent.

But photography, like sailing, is a way of life—a way of seeing things. Sailing is not all boat and gear, and photography is not all cameras, lenses, and film. The following guidelines are by a man who is more photographer than sailor but happy to have a foot in both camps. We assume a rudimentary knowledge of photography on the part of the reader. This is quite fair today. Modern cameras, even those moderately priced, can turn out technically adequate (even excellent) photos in the hands of a person with less than an hour's instruction.

SO YOU'RE A SAILOR who wants to record some of the excitement and beauty of your chosen sport. What makes a good sailing photo? How can you avoid the disappointment of snapping a beautiful scene and coming up with a dull print?

To my mind, the answer in all photography is to select, to concentrate. The human eye—a lens far superior to the best products of Germany or Japan—takes in a broad and breath-taking vista of sail, sea, and sky. The photographer has to "fake" a little, to be selective in what he records in the relatively limited area of the photograph.

How can you apply this to photography on your boat? The first thing that distinguishes photography there from photography on your front lawn is the limited area of action. Aboard the average boat, stepping back for a more comprehensive view can result in a dunking. You really have three choices:

- Pictures of the boat itself and its crew—made from the boat
- Pictures of another boat or scenery—made from your boat
- Pictures of your boat—made from another boat or from a shore vantage point such as a bridge or dock

Most people go on for quite a while making pictures that somehow don't quite satisfy before they realize that the third option yields the best photos of the boat. A dinghy or other low-freeboard boat is the best platform for this, as discussed later.

185

In my view the guaranteed best shot made aboard your sailboat, the one that you will treasure long after many others have been discarded, is the one made while she is reaching or beating up in fairly lively weather—say ten-to-twenty-knot winds for a good-sized boat.

This shot requires that you get on the lee side, fairly well aft, with the camera as low to the water as safety permits, and shoot forward. The boat should have her rail well down and you should try to catch her as she punches into a wave and throws back some spray. You will be rewarded with a photo that will keep you warm all winter. It's almost failure-proof if you don't lose the camera and if you somehow manage to keep the horizon level.

Light

Light is the great controlling element in photography. I have seen professionals wait a day or two until the light is right. It always pays off. There is a general consensus that the light is best before about 10:00 A.M. and after about 3:00 or 4:00 P.M. It has a tendency at those times to define subjects better, to dramatize them and make them stand out. Remember, too, that bright sunlight is no longer an absolute requirement with today's lenses and films in both black-and-white and color.

The relative position of the sun to the subject is also of utmost importance. Most of us are taught incorrectly in this area. We tend to put the sun over the photographer's shoulder—and flat on to the subject's face. In the lee-rail photo described, try violating this old rule—as the professionals do all the time. Try heading the boat toward the sun; the sun will catch the spray from behind and, if you are lucky, turn it into diamonds on your film.

The lighting situation described above is called backlighting. One of the fundamentals of good photography is to learn how to apply it to dramatize a subject. Of course, you can never have the camera facing directly into the sun, but you can have the helmsman steer in such a way that the sun is hidden behind a mast or sail.

A good alternative to the photo described, particularly if the going is rough, is to station yourself in the hatchway and try catching the spray as the boat digs her bow in. With a little practice you can time the exposure so that you duck the camera and yourself into the shelter of the hatchway before the spray gets to you. Here, again, backlighting will catch the spray and make it more dramatic.

Camera Care

This is a good point at which to emphasize that cameras and water, particularly salt water, are highly incompatible. If you want to buy a waterproof enclosure for your camera, go ahead, but it will probably cost more than the camera. Here's a far less costly trick that will help you in rain or spray. Get a plastic bag of the kind used to enclose freshly laundered shirts. Put the camera in the bottom of the bag and screw the lens cap on the lens from the outside of the bag. The cap will act like a cookie-cutter and leave a clean round hole in the bag. Put a rubber band around the lens just behind the outer end to hold the bag tight to the lens. You have a shield against rain and spray that still permits reasonably easy focusing and adjustment.

If you do dunk your camera, all is not necessarily lost. Open it immediately, remove the film, and flush the camera with *fresh* water. Dry it as best you can. NEVER touch the mirror behind the lens with anything. Send it off to the manufacturer or to a good camera repair company with a note explaining what happened.

ALWAYS use a sturdy neck strap with your camera. It's also a good idea to have a harness that keeps the camera close to your chest. Otherwise it swings out of control like a pendulum as you work your way along a steeply canted deck using both hands.

Put a haze filter on your lens and leave it there. This filter helps to cut the haze often found at sea and has no effect on exposure or the fidelity of color photographs. More importantly, it serves as an excellent shield for the lens. It costs only a few dollars, and the filter will take the shock of a hard bump that might damage the more valuable lens. Also, I never hesitate to wipe from the filter the salt spray that accumulates even on relatively calm days, using a handkerchief or shirt cuff that I would never use on the lens itself. Your camera manual will tell you how to clean the lens.

What to Shoot

Probably most important to you are pictures of your family and friends aboard the boat. Shots at the tiller are always good, but remember to have the subject look elsewhere than directly at the camera. This is probably the first rule of photographing people. Have your subject at the tiller look in the direction in which he would be steering. Sometimes a profile of the helmsman looking aloft with the boom or main sheet in the background is a good way to put a little action and interest in a shot. Try using backlighting here too. A newspaper held off-camera will reflect some light into the shadowy side of a subject's face. Pros use "fill-in" flash in daylight for a shot like this; you should experiment with this type of lighting as you go along. If the glare of the sun

Rule Number One for photographing people aboard a boat is to have them doing something natural, as in this photo of the editor's wife putting the topsail to bed, not staring at the camera. Note the backlighting of the subject.

is a problem, ask someone to hold a hat so that it will cast a shadow on the lens but will not show in the picture.

When photographing people, avoid the "posed" look. Staging pictures is one of photography's highest and most difficult arts. A good picture of a person is almost always carefully posed and never looks it. The subject seems to be unaware of the photographer, and doing something you would expect him or her to be doing under the circumstances. Try the skipper raising the mainsail, laying a course on the chart, pointing to the compass as the children learn to box it or giving a lesson in tying a bowline. Work in close. All that matters in a knot-tying photo are the intent faces of the instructor and students concentrating on the knot and the instructor's hands. No need for seagulls or a lighthouse in this one.

In shooting scenery or other boats from your boat, try to get close enough to what is important so that it fills the picture. A hard-and-fast rule among photographers and artists says that you should never put the horizon in the middle of your picture. If you want to show a beautiful sunset or impressive clouds, put the horizon near the bottom and fill the picture with sky. If you want to show beautiful reflections of boats moored in a pleasant harbor, put the horizon high and get the camera as near the water as possible. A respected professional has rigged his camera, normally used at eye level, with a viewing screen seen from the top. He puts the camera almost in the water for a shot like this, and the results are breathtaking.

If you are shooting your boat under sail from another boat, use a low platform such as a float or skiff. ALWAYS shoot from the lee side of the subject boat, with the boat pretty well heeled. Shoot from a position off the bow, giving the impression that the boat is about to run you down or at least pass very close. Try to get backlighting in this picture as well. It gives the sails more life, more detail, when they are lighted from the far side. You will have to devote some time to this photo. You will find that the boat will have to sail by you several times before you get the picture pretty well filled with boat, even if you are fortunate enough to have a variety of lenses. On this one, of course, the horizon will have to be below the center line of the photo. When successful, this technique can provide a thrilling picture of a sailboat in action.

You can also get some good results from shooting the boat from a higher angle, such as from a raised dock, perhaps in the early morning or late afternoon with the sun behind the boat but still high enough to avoid glare.

You should always give the boat plenty of room to "sail into the picture," just as you should give a person room to "look into the picture." For example, if the boat is sailing from right to left across your view, locate the boat toward the right side of the picture with a little space in front of it rather than having the bow going out of the left side of the photo. The same with people. Don't have a man looking to your left jammed up against the left side of the frame.

Sometimes the best photos of people on your boat are made from alongside. Try getting in the skiff to get a shot of the crew wrestling with the anchor, or get them grouped at the stern, showing the boat's name on the counter. I've even been towed around in a dinghy while I got this picture.

Equipment

Although I firmly believe that perception, knowing what to look for, the ability to zero in on what is important, and the imagination and firmness to stage manage a picture are the essentials of photography, technical knowledge and the selection of good equipment are important.

What camera should you get? Unquestionably, the 33mm single-lens reflex (SLR). One reason I recommend this camera is that it is so widely sold that tremendous improvements and developments have been lavished on it in relation to its unit selling price. Get one that has a built-in light meter, and above all else, get one with interchangeable lenses. Start with a "normal" lens of about 50mm focal length. This lens sees about what the eye does and also has the greatest ability in dim light. As you advance, you may want a wide-angle lens of 25 to 35mm focal length and a

Get low to the water, shoot from leeward with the boat heeled toward you, and keep the boat between you and the sun so the sails are backlighted.

telephoto of 135 to 200mm. An additional feature of the 35mm SLR camera is that it produces the popular slide transparency—the means by which you are going to get the most enjoyment out of your photography. If you become really serious, you are going to graduate to black-and-white photography and to processing your own films and prints. But wait on this one. You can get a lifetime of pleasure from your photography and become a first-rate photographer without ever going into a darkroom.

Just as you can manage people to get maximum results in photography, you can also manage light to a certain extent. This is done with filters. Assuming that you will be using color film, I suggest that you get a polarizing filter fairly early in the game. This filter comes in a ring mount that attaches to the lens and permits the filter to be rotated. As you turn the filter, you will notice that the sky darkens and becomes very dramatic and that glare from the water, glass, or brilliant white sand or buildings is reduced. A polarizing filter will often save the day when you have to shoot in the sun for dramatic backlighting. Filters steal some light from the film, so each filter is assigned what is known as a "factor," which indicates how much you should compensate for the loss. If you have a single-lens-reflex camera with a built-in exposure meter, the meter itself will usually compensate for the loss of light, but you should always compensate anyway by "bracketing." You make one shot at the indicated exposure and one at the next stop (lens opening) above and at the next stop below. This is primarily insurance, but you will be surprised at how slight underexposure or overexposure will dramatize a part of the photo that you want to highlight. You have to realize that any subject presents highlights, middle areas, and shadows, and that even the best exposure meter will usually "read" the brighter areas of the subject.

Filters for black-and-white film are far more extensive than those for color. I suggest that you pick up one of the excellent and inexpensive booklets on the subject.

Film

Start with color film. My preference is for transparency film (slides), from which excellent prints can be made. For one thing, this is cheaper, because "negative" or color print film, designed for prints only, requires that you accept prints of each frame—like it or not. With slide film, you select the ones you want printed. Also, slide film is the only kind that can be projected. But perhaps the best idea is to start with color print film until you get the hang of it and then move on to transparencies. In this way you won't need to undertake the expense of a projector at the start—when you're bleeding from the cost of the camera and suddenly discover that you need a new jib.

There is one thing that photography will teach you that you can never learn as a sailor: you will learn to love fog.

Fog to the photographer is like snow; it beautifies everything—even though it's a pain to the pilot.

Filters help you manage light for dramatic effect or emphasis. Dark sky and highlighted rigging in this shot was achieved with a polarizing filter.

That's the great thing about marine photography. When you can't sail, you can shoot great pictures.

To Ship a Ship
Edward H. Simmons

We were confronted with the problem of how to return our yacht safely to the United States from Roadtown, Tortola. The following represents our experience plus information gleaned from others who have shipped sailing craft.

Our yacht is a heavy-displacement ketch thirty-three feet four inches on deck, ten-foot beam, and in sailing trim she displaces about twelve tons.

Our cruise terminated at the end of August. A sailing delivery of the yacht on her own bottom was discarded due to the approaching hurricane season. Several hurried phone calls to Puerto Rico established that there was regular freighter service to Baltimore and New York. Because the ships return to the States empty, the yacht could be taken aboard on any scheduled trip.

We then sailed the yacht to San Juan, Puerto Rico. There we found that shipping charges are based not upon weight but on the number of cubic feet in the package. The price for a 34- x 11- x 11-foot package was quoted at $2,400 for the trip to Baltimore. Just as we were leaving the office, I thought of our fifty-foot main mast. Could that be laid along the cradle?

"Of course," I was told, "but then the charges will be computed on a 50- x 11- x 11-foot package and the cost will be $3,780." We sat down again, and I attempted to show that it would only cost $300 to ship the mast separately as a package 50 feet x 6 x 6 inches. A compromise was reached and for an additional $100 the mast was carried alongside the keel on the cradle.

In a local shipyard we found a steel cradle that could be modified to fit the boat. Quotations for new cradles ranged from $900 to $1,700. Our cradle, fitted to our boat, cost $550.

A mobile crane was arranged for, and at the appointed hour our masts were removed. Our floating home was plucked from the warm waters of the Caribbean and placed on its cradle. Four by four timbers were padded and laid across the fore deck and cockpit coamings. Four pad eyes were welded to the cradle abreast the timbers. Stainless-steel wires were led over the timbers and set up with turnbuckles to the pad eyes. The entire package was lifted onto a low-bed trailer supplied by the shipping authority. We had to arrange for an independent trucker to deliver the cradle to the dock for loading aboard the steamer. From this time forward, no one except steamship personnel, not even the owner, was allowed to board the yacht.

We then flew to Baltimore to make arrangements for refloating the boat. We located a private trucker who would deliver our yacht to a small marina where she could be launched and her masts stepped. We then waited for the steamship to arrive. When we got to the docks, we found our little ketch atop a trailer in a dusty parking lot while tractor-trailer rigs weaved around her. The hull had received some minor damage where the pads on the timbers supporting the hull proved to be too small to support her weight. Upon boarding her, we found the main companion had been broken in and much of our equipment stolen out of the cabin. We had arranged for "all risk" insurance through the steamship authority and were told that our losses would be covered. After completing an inventory of missing items, we signed the necessary papers and accepted delivery of our yacht. Subsequently, we were launched, the masts stepped, and we headed east for a brief Maine cruise.

ANYONE SHIPPING A BOAT should keep the following in mind: First, allow plenty of time to complete the arrangements. Serious mistakes have been made under the pressure of time. Next, get a firm written quotation on the cost of shipping and the insurance coverage. Our insurance claim has yet to be settled, as the shipping company's "all risk" policy covered neither items contained within the yacht nor items not essential to its operation and navigation. For instance, our six-horsepower outboard motor stolen from the lazarette was not covered. However, our regular insurance company covered these losses and they have instituted suit against the steamship company. Check your own insurance policy before shipping your boat.

Finally, see that a proper cradle is constructed. The jockeying around that a yacht receives is excessive in the loading and off-loading areas. Bilge supports extending the length of the cradle are much to be preferred over the conventional post-supported pads.

A friend who recently shipped his sixty-foot ketch to the West Coast found what I consider to be the ideal solution to the loading and off-loading problems. He had his yacht hauled, a cradle built under her, and the yacht relaunched. The cradle was then delivered to the steamship and placed aboard. The yacht was sailed alongside the steamer and loaded directly aboard with a cargo boom. On the

West Coast the process was reversed, thus eliminating much rough handling on derricks and trailers.

Life Saving

How much of your life is it worth spending to save your life? One who had sailed in last summer's single-handed transatlantic race and spent all winter in Martha's Vineyard improving his boat struck out for England in March. He was capsized and dismasted in a gale off George's Bank and was picked up, serene and confident, after four stormy days in a life raft. He wore a wet suit, had food for a week, and had gotten off a radio message before he abandoned the yacht.

I saw a twenty-two-foot Folkbot in Auckland, New Zealand, her tiny staysail boom a stick with the bark on. Her rusty backstay was mended with links of heavy chain secured with wire clamps. Her owner squatted in the cockpit, viewing glumly pieces of his evil-smelling little diesel engine disposed upon the opposite seat. He seemed to have little confidence in its resuscitation. I saw no life raft, no ring buoy, no radio antenna. A tiny Danish flag hung from the end of the main boom. I suppose he valued his life as much as anyone does, but in the course of sailing halfway around the world, he had done less about protecting it.

Those who play rough games with big oceans sometimes get hurt. It is up to you to decide just how much protection you care to provide, just how much back-up equipment to carry to back up the spares. There is no such thing as "safe," but you must decide what you consider "safe enough." This should be a conscious intellectual judgment, not a decision made for you by ignorance, neglect, and a general unwillingness to face the unpleasant possibility of your own demise.

Sailing a Mile High
Harold Staddon

One doesn't usually think of masts being carried a mile high, but they can be and often are

carried up to two miles high on the high plains and in the Rocky Mountains. In fact, our boats are that high and so are our lakes. The area spoken of here is the Denver area to the Continental Divide.

Throughout this area there has been for several years a growing appetite for sailboats. To illustrate: when I bought my first cruising sailboat seven years ago, there was only one dealer in the whole Denver area who had any boats in stock one could see. He was a new dealer and had only the Venture line. I bought a V22, the largest boat he had ever sold. I found two other dealers who had only pictures to show. Now there are five dealers selling sailboats only. All these have several lines of boats up to thirty feet, stocked the year around, together with parts and accessories, and all the three dozen powerboat dealers have added sailboats to their lines.

Wind conditions on the high plains and in the Rocky Mountains differ considerably from winds at lower altitudes. Where you have hurricanes, we have tornados. We can plan every season on winds above 100 mph at least once, perhaps several times, and lasting from a few minutes to several hours. Usually our winds are very fickle; they don't stay in one direction very long. The wind will swing around a full 360° in fifteen minutes. This is no rare situation. No one hereabouts uses a spinnaker for just this reason. Recently I watched two sailors from somewhere else set spinnakers. Both were pulling beautifully until suddenly the wind changed to blow from exactly the opposite direction. One spinnaker fell into the lake and the other draped itself over the rigging. Two sailors learned quickly why we never use the beautiful balloons.

Another wind problem we have in and near the mountains is sudden and violent squalls. May I repeat SUDDEN, VIOLENT! These are usually small in area, but they come so fast! If one appears quite a distance away, you can let out sail or turn into it or both, but often they hit real close at seventy or eighty mph with no warning whatsoever, leaving not a second to prepare. There's no real danger involved; you've just had another knock-down. In a moment you're back on your keel sailing

191

merrily along. But if you have some nervous, half-scared person aboard, you have a moment of wild screaming and someone is forever cured of sailing. Others love it and wonder why you don't do it again. Sometimes you can oblige. I have a friend who was running before the wind when one of those squalls hit. It actually pitch-poled him.

Being on fresh, still water means that we freeze up easier. A mile above the sea, our season is from late April through October. Near the Continental Divide, two miles high, it is from mid-June through September.

Another problem we have is moss. You have barnacles; we have moss. To keep a boat's bottom in good condition it must be scraped off about every two weeks. This moss comes off easily with a rag or an old broom if it's not allowed to dry. I know of no way to prevent its growth. The method I use for cleaning is to beach the boat where there are no rocks and where I can get the car close. A line from the masthead to the car enables me to turn the boat on her side easily. The old broom does a fast, easy job of cleaning one side. Then I let the boat right herself, turn her around, and do the other side. The centerboard is up within the trunk when the boat is beached. There is not room for the broom to slide in beside the centerboard, so for this part I use the brush end of a windshield scraper. Working alone, I can clean my twenty-two-foot glass boat in an hour.

These may not be the only comparisons with saltwater sailing, but since I have never been privileged to sail on salt water, they are the only ones that come to my mind now except one, one indeed not to be overlooked.

Most of our lakes in this area are man-made. A dam is put across a stream, large or small, and a lake develops. Nine times out of ten the valley flooded was at least one farm, perhaps several. In recent years they have cleared debris such as trees, fences, and buildings before they have filled the reservoir—but if it's an old reservoir, all these obstructions may well be there. It is a real problem to retrieve an anchor that is well engangled in a farmer's old windmill or his barbed-wire fence.

Sailing without Sight
Joanne Jordan

Joanne Jordan was born without sight. She has learned to sail by the feel of the wind and the sound of the boat.

It was a fine day for an "ocean voyage." The sun was hot, the breeze steady enough, it seemed, to blow us all the way to the English coast, and I had made it safely across the gangplank without so much as a wet sneaker. I could hear smalltalk going on all around me as I settled myself comfortably on a seat in the cockpit. How like a rocking chair, I thought, as the boat rolled gently up and down over the small shore waves. The slapping of the water against the hull had a soothing, mantric quality. But I was too excited at the prospect of being under way to spend too much time in reverie. And under way we were in no time at all.

The sails caught the wind; the wind caught my hair; the temperature changed. I put on my sweater and drew it close around me. Freedom. Skimming over the water, I recalled the last time I had felt this way. It was when my brother took me flying. But this was better! There was nothing enclosing me, nothing separating me from the wind, the sun, and the water. The water was so close that I could almost touch it. It teased me occasionally with a tickle of spray. Conversations flowed more easily as people became more familiar with each other. The captain told stories. In the background I could hear the hum of motors, punctuated by the scream and cluck of seagulls.

"Trawlers," someone said.

"Hungry birds," I thought.

Although my voyage was only a four-hour sail around Boothbay Harbor, I had experienced the ocean. I had tasted the salt, turned the helm, and felt the boat respond to my direction. I had felt the sweet fatigue and ravenous hunger that only sea air can produce. I had enjoyed that special kinship of people who sail together.

Hearing a slight luffing of the sails, the air once again warm, we approached the mooring. It didn't take me long to master my land legs once on shore, knowing that there would be a beef stew dinner. It had been a fine day, indeed!

WE HAVE TAKEN other unsighted people sailing and found that the experience is so rich in its appeal to other senses that it provides perhaps greater enjoyment for them than it does for us who take so much for granted.

One very foggy day—we could not see the shore of the harbor from the mooring—we had planned to take a couple out. We assumed they would not want to go. When they hailed us from the wharf, however, we found that the gentleman was blind and was determined to go sailing if we could find our way. We felt our way out of the harbor and sailed a few short courses in the fog. Our guest enjoyed it immensely. He was very sensitive to changes in course from the feel of the wind, the sound of the waves, and the motion of the boat. He could hear surf on an invisible shore before we could hear it and identified islands by the sound of the gulls. It may be that the difficulty that we had in seeing anything in the choking fog added in a subtle way to his pleasure. He certainly enjoyed the trip.

Many times since then he has been with us. He has learned now the shape of the cockpit, the location of seats, wheel, and binnacle, and the height of rails and coamings so that he moves about on the boat remarkably well. Given an unobstructed course with the wind forward of the beam, he steers a steady course by facing the wind and turning the boat so his neck is always at the same angle. In puffy weather he adjusts the boat's course to the wind, not to the land, and hence steers very sensitively, although someone must stand a lookout and tell him when to tack.

If you are fortunate enough to have a boat, try taking along someone a lot less fortunate and enjoy the pleasure that he takes in using to the full the senses left to him.

Sea Dogs

Betsy Jones

"Does your dog really enjoy cruising and living on your schooner?" is a question we are often asked. The answer is certainly "yes." He is an enthusiastic member of our crew. Given his "druthers," he might opt for life ashore, but dogs don't understand druthers, so he adapts immediately when we put him aboard and adopts his sea dog habits without a backward thought.

One of the most interesting traits of dogs is their ability to adapt themselves to any situation fate hands them with speed, grace, and good cheer. There is an added advantage to his life afloat that he appreciates mightily, and that is "togetherness." The thing all dogs resent most in the world is to be left alone, and except for the occasional dinner we have ashore, he has us all to himself within the space of forty-one feet, twenty-four hours a day. He sleeps between our bunks, supervises all food preparation and consumption, goes on most shopping expeditions and sightseeing tours, barks at the same speedboats and water skiers we growl at, and can always find a warm lap to curl up in—his idea of heaven.

So much for the fun side. Now how about the problems? I've seen practically every breed of dog living happily on all sizes of boats—big hairy dogs on small sailboats to miniature poodles on palatial power yachts. Unless you had a dog you couldn't of course part with, it would make sense to choose a breed that fits your size boat. Big dogs need lots of exercise and just plain take up space. We cruised with a boxer who was marvelous, but on deck and below he needed more room than a person. If he chose to curl up in the galley, there wasn't enough room for even one of my feet. Also, when the boat heeled, he would start to slide and often scratched the deck trying to get traction. He learned to maneuver very well, but it was harder for him than for a smaller dog with a lower center of gravity. When he was gone, we chose a dachshund as the perfect sea-going dog. Such he has proved to be. Being so low, he hardly notices the motion and seems to have topsiders built right on to his big flat feet. He is clean, odorless, sheds very little, and hates to be wet. This latter is a great advantage, because he would never jump overboard for a swim and is extremely cautious about falling in the water.

His only close call in twelve years of cruising was the time he tried to jump ashore on a bulkhead where we tied up in the waterway. We scooped him up with the crab net we carry for this purpose, none the worse for his dousing—except for his dignity. He is theoretically trained not to jump onto docks or other boats just for this reason, but dachshunds will be dachshunds once in a while. He must have seen a cat.

The problem of shore trips is the major one, of course. It would be much simpler if dogs could be trained to relieve themselves on deck, but except in very rare instances this is just about impossible to achieve. A friend of ours trained a poodle puppy to a plastic dishpan, but from the time he first lived ashore for a few weeks, he would never use it again. A number of different vets have assured us that no dog will injure himself by waiting too long. Much as he hates to soil his boat, he will go aboard eventually, but he won't do it as a regular thing.

Dutchie, our dachshund, lasted about seventeen hours on a long Gulf Stream crossing without seeming to be in the least uncomfortable. On the other hand, he has made huge puddles on deck on some overnight runs. He tries to hide it, hangs his head, and looks away from us—then runs back to collect the biscuit he knows he's earned for his performance. A bucket of sea water takes care of the puddle quickly and easily, and we all feel better!

When cruising along shore, we take Dutchie ashore two or three times a day, depending on the weather and where we spend the night. Our skipper is an early riser, so he usually takes the morning run before rolling the rest of us out of our bunks. Unless we stop very early in the day, Dutchie expects to go ashore as soon as we anchor or tie up—more for the adventure than the relief. If it's convenient, he goes again before bedtime, and that's it. He expects no more, but he does know how long it might be before he gets another chance, so he takes care of his needs immediately, then goes in search of adventure if time and his chaperone allow. We now have our second dachshund, Ready About, who at

just seven months old was easily able to fit into this schedule.

Anyone who would consider taking a dog cruising is obviously a dog lover who happily accepts the responsibilities his friend demands ashore. The problems afloat are not that much greater, and the rewards are certainly worth a few wet dinghy trips ashore on rainy nights.

Coastal Whales
Bruce M. Wellman

A distant blow, pluming fifteen to twenty feet in the air before spreading on the wind, or a thin dorsal fin slicing the surface may be the cruising sailor's first indication that there are other mammals beside himself that inhabit the ocean. Written accounts or even films cannot fully prepare one for an encounter with a whale at sea. A dark glistening shape or glimpse of fin or tail might be all that you see. If you are lucky, you may view the tail rising out of the water as the whale dives, or see the whole animal slide alongside or beneath your boat. The majestic power and dignity of the greatest animals ever to live on earth is impressive.

The once numerous great whales have dwindled in numbers significantly because of the onslaught of modern whaling. Yet it is possible to view several species off the coasts during the cruising season.

The College of the Atlantic in Bar Harbor, Maine, sponsors the Gulf of Maine Whale Sighting Network to centralize reports of whale sightings by their own observers and by fishermen, freighter crews, and yachtsmen. Since 1973 the network has kept records and has maintained observers on Mt. Desert Rock and on frequent offshore patrols. Not only do they record sightings, but by means of photographers they even keep track of individual whales.

The humpback (*Megaptera novaenglia*) is probably the most easily identified of the large baleen whales and is certainly the whale with the most media exposure, from television films and articles in such magazines as *National Geographic* focusing on its "songs"

and other behavioral habits. Its most distinguishing characteristic is its habit of raising its flukes or tail clear of the water when it dives deeply. This does not occur every time, but it is frequent enough to look for. The flukes have a scalloped rear edge and are deeply notched in the center. The coloration of distinctive white and dark patterns on the underside of the flukes and flippers seems to vary with individual whales. Photographs of the undersides of flukes and flippers can help in determining the migration and behavioral habits of these animals. One hundred and twenty individual whales have been identified by these markings and something learned of their personal travels. Photos should be sent to Allied Whale at the College of the Atlantic, Bar Harbor, Maine 04609.

Humpback whales can reach a length of up to fifty feet. They are somewhat stockier than other baleen whales but are not as ballooned in shape as many drawings show them. They are usually dark in color above and light below. The head is distinctive, with many bumps or "knobs" randomly distributed. Another distinguishing mark is the long white side flipper with scalloped leading edges that can reach up to a third of the animal's length. These are sometimes raised out of the water to create a resounding smack. The slow-moving humpbacks often carry many barnacles and whale lice. The humpback probably gets its name from the hump or step just before the dorsal fin that is most visible when the animal arches to dive. The spout is low and bushy. Humpbacks are often acrobatic and will

breach clear of the water. There are some indications that this at times may be a sign of stress.

Humpbacks are found in the winter and early spring, in the Caribbean, off Bermuda on the banks north of the Dominican Republic, and in the Gulf of California. Courtship, mating, and calving probably occur at that time. As the spring progresses there is a northward and eastward movement toward colder, richer food-bearing waters, with whales arriving in the areas around Cape Cod in April and May and on into Maine and Canadian waters through the summer months. The pattern is reversed in the fall. Some animals may linger in one area for several days or weeks.

The relatively shallow waters over banks such as Georges Bank off Massachusetts, Stellwagen Bank north of Cape Cod, and Jeffrey's Ledge off the Maine–New Hampshire coast, and the West Coast at Point Conception and Point Sur are often good spots to see whales. Prominent land masses offshore, such as Matinicus Rock and Mt. Desert Rock, off the Maine coast, are also places where whales are present at times. The up-wellings in these areas stir and lift nutrient-rich waters, thereby attracting whales, which feed upon the organisms present.

According to the annual report of the Gulf of Maine Whale Sighting Network, the most frequently reported large whale last year in that region was the finback whale (*Balaenoptera physalus*). The finback is a large whale and can reach a length of up to seventy feet and a weight of fifty to sixty tons. The back of the animal is dark and the underside, including the flippers and flukes, is light. It is a baleen whale, as are all but one of the large cetaceans. Instead of teeth, these animals have a filtering apparatus consisting of large numbers of baleen plates, which hang down from the upper mouth. The outer edge is smooth and straight and the inner edge is fringed and hairy. The plates are used to trap and filter out small fish and large quantities of small marine organisms collectively known as krill. The finback has a prominent dorsal fin, but this by itself is not a good field mark for identification, since the size varies with individuals and it is easily confused with the dorsal fin of the sei (say) and minke whales. The best field marks of the finback are a pale colored V or chevron that starts behind the blowhole and opens toward the dorsal fin, the white coloration on the right side of the lower jaw, and the white or pale color of the first third of the right-side baleen. If possible you should try to maneuver to the right side of the animal to see if these marks are present. The chevron is not visible on all animals. The spout or blow of the finback on a windless day is somewhat V-shaped and can be from fifteen to twenty feet tall. It has been described as an inverted cone. When the whale is diving, the back and dorsal fin are arched high into the air. Fin whales do not show their flukes when diving.

Minke whales (*Balaenoptera acutorastrata*) are the smallest of the baleen whales to be seen off the Atlantic coast. They are in fact the smallest baleen whale species in the Northern Hemisphere. The minke is shaped like the finback and can be confused with it, but it is only fifteen to thirty feet long and relatively slender. The strongest field mark for this species is the wide white band running across each flipper.

The minke whale is quick moving. The head and sickle-shaped dorsal fin appear at the surface at about the same time. They are often curious about boats and may approach slow-moving or stationary vessels. They will also approach the shore closely and may even enter bays or inlets.

On diving, they will arch strongly like a finback, but will not show their tails above the surface. Minkes feed on small fish such as herring and capelin. The blow is low and inconspicuous.

Rarely seen and probably the most endangered of all the great whales in the North Atlantic, is the right whale (*Eubalaena glacialis*), still present in small numbers. There were sightings recently from Cape Cod and off Race Point. Traditionally, this was the "right" whale to hunt because it was slow moving and the carcass floated.

Right whales run in length from thirty-five to fifty feet. The body is fat and dark in color and lacks a dorsal fin. The skin is sometimes mottled with a light coloration.

The blow of the right is distinctive. The two blowholes are widely spaced, causing two distinct spouts when the animal is seen from the front or rear.

Like the humpback, the right whale will raise its flukes out of the water. The flukes are broad and smooth, with pointed tips and a curved rear edge.

Right whales also will approach boats and seem to display a curiosity about them.

The coastal cruising man may possibly meet a sei whale, a blue whale, a Bryde's whale, a sperm whale, or a pod of pilot whales. The killer whale with its tall dorsal fin and white markings running well up the sides suffers from a very bad press. Although there are many tales of its ferocity and although it has attacked and sunk small ships, the killer whale is an intelligent creature and under the proper conditions in captivity has proved to be docile and friendly to humans and a quick learner.

For further information and help with identification, there are two useful field guides. The first, published by the National Oceanic and Atmospheric Administration (NOAA), is *Whales, Dolphins, and Porpoises of the Western North Atlantic—A Guide to Their Identification,* by Stephen Leatherwood, David K. Caldwell, and Howard E. Winn. It can be obtained from the Superintendent of Documents, U.S. Government

Printing Office, Washington, D.C. 20402. The stock number is 003–020–00119–0. It is full of photographs and is a real bargain.

The other, a well-illustrated guide, is titled *A Field Guide to the Whales and Seals of the Gulf of Maine,* by Steven Katona, David Richardson, and Robin Hazard. It can be ordered from Allied Whale, College of the Atlantic, Bar Harbor, Maine 04609. The cost is about five dollars.

Whale-sighting forms to aid in ongoing data collection work are also obtainable from Allied Whale.

Shark Jaws

Jaws, the novel and the movie, triggered our instinctive horror of sharks, those silent, savage, irresistible shadows rising from the mysterious sea to eat us alive. The popularity of the book has stimulated a flood of reassuring articles by people who were not eaten by sharks. Yet beneath each article moves the possibility of sudden and fatal attack; for sharks, like all horrors, are unpredictable.

For a long time people have sought a shark repellent that would dispel the horror. The Knight News Service tells us that sharks will flee from a certain species of sea snake. "In fact, their apparent fear makes it very difficult to get the two creatures together long enough to test the theory." Dr. Roslansky, a marine biologist at Woods Hole, Massachusetts, adds, "'Fear' may only be a word—there could be a chemical basis. In insects we know chemical 'attractions' can function at infinitely low dilutions (10^{-7} to 10^{-9} molar concentrations)."

The navy tossed a dummy sea snake to the sharks. They ate it up. However, this snake inhabits the Pacific and these were Atlantic sharks, which perhaps did not know enough to be scared. The principal objection to this snake as a shark repellent, however, is that the snake is poisonous. So far as I know, only one person has made any real progress on shark repellents.

In the November 1974 *National Geographic Magazine,* Dr. Eugenie Clark, of the University of Maryland, wrote an article describing her research on the Moses sole, a flounderlike fish living in the Red Sea. This creature secretes a toxin from its skin that stops a shark even as the great fish with gaping jaws and razor teeth is about to engulf his unsuspecting prey (to overwrite the situation traditionally). A white film comes over the shark's eyes, he gags and backs off. When Dr. Clark wiped the toxin off the sole, he was gulped in an instant.

When asked whether any effort is being made to synthesize and manufacture this toxin for the protection of divers, castaways, and bathers, she was good enough to answer in part: "The U.S. Navy, Hebrew University, and the Israeli Navy are all interested in following up work on the shark repellent toxin. It will probably be undertaken, but on skimpier funds than necessary to synthesize and make it usable in the near future. But it may take years and maybe hundreds of thousands of dollars to produce. The need is not that pressing (except for psychological reasons), because actual shark attacks are so very few and the money funneled elsewhere might save so many more lives."

The statistical danger of shark attack as worked out by William Van Dorn in *Oceanography and Seamanship* is about one in three million for each exposure, based on the recorded average of twelve attacks per year. But how many attacks were unrecorded, for one very good reason? The horror remains.

February Visit

On a warm afternoon in February, take a run down to the yard and see how the vessel is making it. Throw back the cover along the sunny side. Open every hatch and port, every door, drawer, and locker. Take up the floor boards and let the air blow through. Unless she has been very well ventilated, she will sweat under the cover with every change in temperature. You may find her warm and damp as a greenhouse on a sunny day, yet with icicles hanging from the shelves.

Sit down in the cabin with a pad and pencil and list all those jobs you were going to do this winter but never got around to. If any of them concern health or safety, this may be the time to give up and ask the yard foreman to see to them.

While the boat airs out, see if you can find your spars in the spar shed without climbing over a dozen others. With a flashlight inspect the swagings for hairline cracks. Look at tangs, bolts, splices, shackles, spreader ends, spar iron work in general and in particular.

Before the sun gets low and the puddles begin to skim over, tie down the cover again, leaving blow holes at bow and stern for ventilation. It will freeze again and snow again, but the poet wrote, although with no reference to a boat yard, "If winter comes, can spring be far behind?"

The boat on the left with a double cover around her stern will sweat badly inside, but the boat on the right with ventilation at bow and stern should be all right.

Storing Your Battery
William H. Ashbaugh

One of the best places to store your boat battery is in your car, if the voltages are the same. Most automobiles now use twelve-volt batteries. The boat battery can stay in the same case that it sits in on the boat and be tied down with the same straps. Be sure it does not vibrate, or it will soon jiggle itself loose. Most cars ground the negative terminal of the battery. If this is the case, ground the negative terminal of the boat battery and connect the positive terminal of the boat battery to the positive terminal of the car battery. Be sure that you connect positive to positive or both batteries will probably explode. For connec-

tions use heavy battery cables. You can have them made up in any length and with either an eye or a battery fitting on the end. A smear of Vaseline will help to prevent corrosion.

Whenever your alternator charges your car battery, it will give the boat battery a boost too, producing the same result as an expensive trickle charger. Also, in cold weather, you will have the capacity of your boat battery added to that of your car to make starting easier. It is better for the boat battery to be used a little and kept up to full charge than it is for it to lie neglected in the shop.

The Pleasures of Power Boating
Hartley Lord

Friends often ask why I'm a power boater. I like sail and as a lad started in sail, but my life-style forced power on me and I have stuck, happily, with it ever since. I have a small sport fisherman, and what fun it brings me! Most important of all, it enables me to have a good ride in a relatively short time. Easily the times I most enjoy are those when I take a few friends for a picnic lunch or supper in a nearby harbor. Anchoring there in the lee of granite ledges and spruces is a treat beyond compare.

Being together in such a lovely spot with a few friends really gives us a chance to swap the news of our busy lives. Best of all, it seems to bring them as much pleasure as it does me. The trip each way is short, and three hours gives us a memorable reunion.

I love to explore new places, small coves, and inlets and the sort of thing that can't be done under sail. I enjoy cruising and know the coast from Cape Cod to Schoodic. My summer cruises, always within vacation limits, have brought me infinite pleasure, and my scrapbooks with color shots of our coast are sure proof.

My boat is too small to live comfortably aboard, so I have always made reservations ahead for accommodations ashore. Power keeps me on schedule except for days of thick fog or foul weather.

I remember heading east from Rockland a few years back; there was a fresh northwest wind and spray was cascading across the boat.

The wind was cool that late in August, but the spray made it feel *cold* in spite of foul weather gear and brilliant sunshine. We had planned to pass North Haven, but, chilled to the bone, turned in to Pulpit Harbor to catch our breaths. We secured to an empty dock and shut off the engine, making the most of that sunshine and our surrounding scenery. It wasn't long before we removed our foul weather gear, and soon thereafter our sweaters. Before lunch (this spot was too beautiful to leave!) some of the gang went for a swim. I coined a phrase that day with which I am sure all boatmen will agree: "Some of the best cruising is done at anchor."

I agree with sailors that the noise of a powerboat is unpleasant, but we make a point of not keeping under way for more than two and a half hours at a stretch. A rest and a chat and we're ready to go again.

The scope of your view as you conn high on the flybridge comes as a spectacular surprise. It "makes" boating for my wife, as she has often said. I love the excitement as the boat goes through the waves, snowy spray flying left and right in contrast to the blue of the sea. I love the security that my engine controls, supplemented by my VHF, give me.

I was born in a coastal Maine town, have a family heritage of the sea, and that my hours afloat are precious comes most naturally.

I have no quarrel with sailors, and the truth is, when I see a handsome sloop slicing quietly and so easily through the sea, I rather envy them. Talking in soft voices is a luxury they can enjoy, and the sound of the sea is far more theirs than mine. I suppose it's largely a question of how much time you have.

The main thing for us all is the relaxation boating brings, the stimulation of fresh air and magnificent scenery, the feeling of peace that comes with being in the expanse of the sea, the challenge that it brings, and the independence it develops. Whether under sail or power, stay afloat!

A Practical Look at the Sea

In spite of better engineered and more strongly built vessels than the world has ever known, in spite of electronic navigation systems, radar, depth sounders, and a vigilant Coast Guard ever ready to come to our aid, still ships are lost and men are drowned as they have been for ages. We account for these tragedies by anything from bad luck to the "treachery" of the sea. Let us take a careful look at disaster and see to what extent bad luck and treachery are involved.

Consider the following hypothetical but typical case, which could happen anywhere along our coasts.

Here is a man from up the river who likes to go fishing. He buys a fifteen-foot outboard from which he fishes at the mouth of the river. The river drains a large area, so on the ebb tide particularly a large volume of water must rush out between the jetties at its mouth. A bar has built up as the silt suspended in the river water settles outside the river mouth. Here is the best fishing and here our boatman frequently goes on weekends to hook a bluefish, bass, or mackerel. On a certain Saturday in May, however, he fails to return, his boat is found adrift, and no sign of him is ever found. Did he have bad luck? Was he set upon by a treacherous sea, which had lured him into a feeling of safety and then betrayed him?

Not at all. He was beset by a combination of purely physical forces. His death could have been predicted by computer had all the information been available. Consider the following facts: It was the time of the new moon with the sun and moon combining to cause exceptionally high and exceptionally low tides. This occurrence was predicted in the almanac and tide table. It had been a hard winter and ice was breaking up in the lakes, releasing a great deal of water into the river. The current ran hard. Third, a low-pressure area was approaching from the southwest, bringing pleasant spring weather followed by a shift of wind to the northeast. A heavy swell, as usual, ran ahead of the storm.

Our boatman, observing the pleasant conditions, took tackle box, bait, and a spring jacket, cranked up his outboard, and about two hours before high water, the best time for fish, roared down to the river mouth. The last of the flood was not making very strongly, partly because of the heavy river current running down above it. Outside, there was a long heave from the approaching storm, but at high water on the bar, nothing serious. Fishing was good.

Fishing was so good just outside the bar that he paid no attention to the shift of wind to the east, caused by no treachery or luck but by the heavy pressure gradient of the approaching storm. The sea increased, but outside the bar offered no serious problem. By two hours after the ebb had started to run, a very heavy current was running out over the bar, the sky had clouded up, and the easterly had picked up. Clearly it was time to go in.

However, not as a result of luck but of predictable physical forces, the increasing sea, driven by the increasing wind, and opposed by the ebb tide, was striking the shoal water on the bar. When a wave gets into shoal water, its bottom is slowed, it catches up with itself, becomes higher, steeper, and moves faster, until the crest falls forward and it breaks. Other waves, catching up, break close behind it in a smother of suds. From seaward, one sees only the backs of the breaking waves. They do not look very dangerous. They make no attempt to deceive anyone. They are simply water, affected by complex forces.

The fisherman, feeling from predictable psychological causes that safety lies upriver where the water is smooth—or always has been—pulls his anchor, stows it in the bow, guns his motor, and heads for home.

Predictably, his buoyant boat rides the crest of a sea, and plunges headfirst over the crest into the hollow below. The bow catches in the slowly moving water in front of the sea while the stern, driven by the motor, is then held high and rushed forward by the crest. The boat broaches in the trough, is rolled over by the advancing sea, and the fisherman is spilled overboard.

It is a law of physics that anything let down into a liquid will float if it displaces its own weight in that liquid before it goes under. A human body in saltwater will ordinarily float, especially if its owner swims strongly. However, the suds in which our fisherman swims are half air. Their density is not suffi-

cient to support the man. He falls right through them. Yet it is too wet to breathe and too cold to permit swimming. Drowned and frozen, our fisherman is finished.

The sea did not betray him. The sea is quite indifferent to him. It responds to the physical forces working upon it as it must respond. He had no "bad luck." Nothing that happened was the result of chance. Unfortunate circumstances did not "gang up on him." The whole situation could have been predicted by computer. He was lost because he did not observe the factors at work and use the computer inside his hat to take account of these forces and use the advantages he had.

Over and over again this story is told with variations. A scallop dragger sinks off Cape Cod. A sloop is found dismasted and abandoned. A catamaran is pitchpoled by a "rogue wave." It is always the same story of failure to make sufficient allowance for the tremendous forces of wind, tide, water, and weather.

Lest this sound arrogant, the Sailor must admit having got into a scrape last summer which with wit could have been avoided. As he rounded the end of a huge Canadian government wharf under power and headed out into a heavy on-shore southwester, smoke poured out of the hatch. A quick look showed several red-hot wires. Cut the switch. But seventy-five yards to leeward, the sea breaks against the massive wharf. Anchor! The water is deep and the anchor drags. Fend off with the boat hook as he drags down on the wharf! The butt of the boat hook catches in the furled mainsail with its point embedded in the wharf. She swings her bow and bowsprit down on the wharf. Shipwreck is imminent. Better burn for a few seconds and back off. The engine won't start, because the propeller wound up in the peapod painter at the engine's first turn. Fortunately, the boat hook does not break and the thrust of it pushes the stern by the wharf. Cut the painter and quickly row around the wharf, climb a ladder and get a line to the top of the wharf. Warp the vessel in into the lee. We are saved!

Analysis of the foul-up shows that it was inevitable. The wires running to the instrument panel were about fifteen years old and had been installed to serve a six-volt system. We were using a twelve-volt system in our newly installed engine. The wires carrying an unaccustomed voltage led very near the copper tube from the water temperature gauge to the engine block. The current found cracks in the old insulation and short-circuited through the tube, heating tube and wires to incandescence. This could have been calculated had the skipper's mind considered the problem.

The anchor failed to hold because the water was deep and the bottom hard. These were purely physical facts. The boat hook, the fouled painter, the escape from disaster, were all calculable. There was really no excuse for not calculating them.

Primitive man, unaware of the forces and their predictable operation, judged the winds to be let out of a bag at the whim of Aeolus and the sea to be disturbed at the call of Poseidon. Modern man should rely more heavily on Archimedes, Galileo, Bowditch and the National Ocean Survey.

Safety Is a State of Mind

To try to ensure our safety the Coast Guard requires that we carry life preservers, fire extinguishers, a horn, and a bell. This is somewhat less than the minimum equipment necessary to protect one's ship and crew. The responsible skipper would certainly carry an anchor and rode, a compass, chart and watch, but where does one stop? Radar? LORAN C? an EPIRB? Survival suits for all hands? Life rafts? Radio? There is no end to it all. Yet even with all the equipment, vessels are wrecked and people lost. When accidents happen, they happen not so much from lack of equipment as from defective attitudes, which lead to an error in judgment.

The man who is perfectly sure he is safe is the one who strikes the "uncharted" rock, whose boat blows up without any warning, who is overwhelmed by sudden fog or a squall.

A motor cruiser, well equipped and in top mechanical condition, was leaving New Inlet after an easterly storm. The skipper saw others sailing about outside. He wanted to go fishing so he went, following the line of nuns that marks the edge of the channel. However, one of the nuns was missing. He simply headed for the next one, got into shoal water, and took a breaking sea over the bow, which smashed in the pilothouse windows and flooded the engine. In seconds the yacht was swamped and sank. The three people aboard were rescued. It wasn't the skipper's "fault" the nun was missing. Nevertheless, he lost his boat and nearly lost three lives because he assumed that everything was all right.

A tug with a barge in tow made Manana whistle off the Maine Coast on a regular run down east. It was an early February morning, calm, thick, and snowing heavily. The skipper ran for the southern end of Monhegan about two miles away. He was steering a compass course and watching the fathometer for warning of the land. But right on the end of Monhegan the bottom drops off very steeply. Before he had time to turn, he was ashore on the Washerwoman, a rock on the end of the island. The remains of the wreck are still visible. He assumed that everything would be all right, had doubtless run on the fathometer many times before, and always had made it all right.

The writer nearly lost his father's boat by lying to a mooring consisting only of a chain attached to a flour barrel on one end and a big rock on the other. He passed a line from the bow chock around the chain under the barrel and back aboard, figuring that the big barrel would act like a button and prevent the line from coming off. Fortunately, a combination of an injudicious quantity of beans at dinner and a rolly night brought him awake at the right time to find the line clear of the chain and the barrel snuggled under the vessel's lee bow, held there by the tide. Again, a careless assumption was at the root of the trouble.

We like to think that in "the old days" the grizzled skipper, trained in sail, was a paragon of wisdom, one who never made a mistake because he could tell by some sixth sense when danger threatened. Yet a generation ago a three-masted schooner piled up all-standing

After sustaining punishment from the waves for six days, the Argo Merchant *broke in half, spilling most of her cargo—7.6 million gallons of heavy industrial heating oil—into the ocean.*
Courtesy Lawrence S. Millard, Providence Journal

on a very solid ledge because the skipper assumed that a certain black spar was marking the entrance channel to a harbor rather than the passage along shore. A quick look at the chart instead of the easy assumption would have saved him more than the embarrassment of waiting over a tide.

Equipment is no safeguard in itself. The *Titanic* was "unsinkable." The skipper was in a hurry, had been around ice before, and assumed that it would probably be all right to go ahead.

A yacht with radar picked up the buoy on the screen and headed for it, averting a collision only by virtue of an alert lookout who saw the "buoy" in time to identify it as another yacht with radar running for the same buoy that each assumed the other to be.

Almost every disaster, except for a few that seem to have been planned by a vengeful deity, has happened because a skipper assumed that "everything would be all right." There is nothing more conducive to this conviction than being cold, wet, and tired—unless it is two beers for lunch.

The insidious thing about it is that usually everything *is* all right. One cruising man on a weekend jaunt experienced an engine breakdown. He set his sails to a light air and enjoyed a sandwich and a beer for lunch while his wife sailed the boat. She was the worrying type.

"Why don't you fix the engine, Harvey?"

"I don't feel like it right now."

"But suppose you need it in a hurry?"

"Then I'll fix it in a hurry."

No disaster struck.

We have all seen people far offshore in outboard skiffs we wouldn't cross the harbor in. A dear friend cruised with a carburetor that had a chronic drip. He never blew up.

However, if you have any pretensions to being a responsible seaman, you will have to develop an aggressive attitude toward Misfortune. Instead of assuming, and hoping, that she will probably pass you by, attack! Forestall Misfortune. Assume not that she will ignore you but that she is malevolently bent on your destruction. As you approach a lee shore, try to guess what diabolical scheme she will adopt to cast you on the rocks. Will it be a failure of the steering gear? Will the gurry in the gas tank get stirred up and stop your engine at the crucial moment? Will it be a failure in spar or shroud, sheet or halyard? Have you the anchor ready bent on to a stout rode, cleanly coiled down and with the bitter end fast to the mast below decks?

If the kids are fooling and giggling on the foredeck, count on Misfortune's getting one of them to show off a notch too much and go overboard. Have a life ring handy and a man-overboard plan ready and rehearsed.

This attitude is not to be taken as one of whining submission, of avoidance of risk. On the contrary. Fog, lightning, gale, or squall are all to be regarded as opportunities for thwarting Misfortune. "Rock and tempest, fire and foe," as the old song goes, are chances to attack. The good skipper does not refuse to move because everything isn't just right. He does not decline to pull the anchor because he might hurt his back. He learns how to pull an anchor scientifically so he does not put unfair strain on his back. He does not stay home because the fog might shut down. He learns to travel in the fog and is ready to do it at short notice. The object of this game is to conduct one's vessel safely through the cruising season, to have a good time, to appreciate fully each dawn and noon and sunset, to face the difficulties and dangers with so resolute and well-prepared a mind that Misfortune will seek easier game.

> A little boy and his father were fishing from a skiff on a ledge where the chart showed twelve feet of water. As the tide dropped and the sea increased, the bigger waves began to hump up as they raced across the shoal. A passing lobsterman slipped alongside the skiff and, without stopping, gaffed up their anchor line and towed them into deep water without a word. "Some folks don't know when to be scared," he thought.

Yachts and Steamers

You must face the fact that as far as your yacht is concerned, a big steamer either cannot or will not make any response to your presence. She can run you down and grind you up without ever knowing she has hit something. This is not entirely the reflection of a heartless or irresponsible attitude on the part of the merchant marine officers. A big tanker's bridge is nearly a quarter of a mile from her bow and 150 feet from port to starboard. The mate cannot see you over the bow if you are close aboard, and you are too small to be noticed if you are within his vision. It takes about twenty minutes and three miles to stop a big tanker moving at sixteen knots. Furthermore, at slow speeds a big vessel loses steerageway. Her rudder is not big enough to control her reliably at five knots. Some of these vessels draw about fifty feet. In water less than seventy-five feet deep, their maneuverability is much impaired by the proximity of the bottom, even if they don't actually touch. Therefore, as the steamer approaches a harbor she may be scarcely under control at all, dependent on tugs that will come out to meet her. The law recognizes her helplessness by giving large vessels the right of way over small ones in narrow waters, regardless of their relative courses.

A steamer is usually moving a lot faster than she appears to be because the roll of foam at her bow is so small in proportion to her huge size. Of course, the cautious skipper would never try to cross the bow of a steamer, nor should he approach her course closely and plan to sheer off, for this could influence the steamer into an attempt to change course.

At night a steamer appears to approach very rapidly, perhaps because one does not see her until she is quite close anyway. Her navigation lights, although prominently displayed, may be masked by the blaze of cabin and deck lights. However, the two highest lights will probably be her range lights, the after one the highest, and from these and her side lights her course can be estimated and appropriate action taken.

If you are in doubt as to what her intentions may be, try to call her on the radio. All ships guard 2182 Hz, but few small yachts are still permitted to use this frequency. Some ships listen to Channel 16 on VHF, but you cannot count on it. You can, however, call the Coast Guard on 16 and they can communicate with the steamer. It is a roundabout way, but better than not trying.

In the fog, the long, deep blast of the big ship's whistle is frightening. Even with the radar reflector nailed aloft and horn in hand, a yachtsman feels blind and helpless. The radio may help, but probably your safest course, subject to local conditions, is to turn your stern to what appears to be the steamer's course and go for the shoal water, answering her deep blasts with the thin blast of your horn.

Thinking Out a Compass Error
Hugh G. Williams

"Your compass checks perfectly, captain. Dead right on every course!" The compass adjuster, rising to his feet on the foredeck, gave me a look across his pelorus—triumph mingled with just a touch of bewilderment. A year ago he had uttered almost the same words, after doing a superb job of compensating my compass, and given me the same look of assurance and satisfaction—but minus the bewilderment. What had happened over the winter to cause an error which amounted, on some courses, to as much as five degrees? Or did he suspect what the CAA calls "pilot error?"

Early in the season we were approaching the coast from an off-lying whistler. The course, 330 degrees magnetic, led just to windward of a bare rocky island and would finish at a nun buoy about eight miles distant that marked a string of sunken ledges. There was about twelve to fifteen knots of beautiful southerly, we were carrying the big, full-cut genoa, and were exhilarated at being able to start sheets a foot or two and still point the course. The speedometer settled down at just below seven knots. I settled down too, after saying with just the right intonation, "Well, it's lovely sailing and it sure was a long winter"—a sure-fire way of getting one's wife to relieve one at the helm.

Twenty minutes later I stretched, peered over the bow, and asked the helmsman, "Are you planning to cut Shark Island in two or just crawl over it?"

"You said 330—right?" Just one slightest breath of northerly in that voice.

We altered course to 325 and then to 320. It was slack water, so there had been no tidal set. We cleared the island but not by much, and in the fog we'd have gone right on to it. Fifty mintues later the nun buoy appeared way to port. Several other courses produced the same result, some of them easterly, some northerly. With each one, she sailed four or five degrees to the right of where she should have. Obviously, it was time to hunt up the compass adjuster and, at the very least, have a chat with him.

The adjuster, a seaman of many years' experience and a thorough and utterly competent professional, lived in a resort town seventy miles east of us, and on the trip down we made every effort to avoid thick weather.

The run was made mostly in light southerly airs with the wind either dead aft or over the quarter. On the way we made a table consisting of two columns—compass headings and actual chart courses. On most of these there was far less difference than what we'd noticed that afternoon in June. None were more than a couple of degrees apart; some coincided exactly.

When the adjuster had finished his work, which included headings made both under power and with the engine shut off, he pronounced us clean of any deviation and I gave him my table.

"How were these courses run?" he asked after deciphering my handwriting. "Were they sailed or run under power?"

I said they were all sailed and in a light breeze.

"Now last year when I got through with you, you made a large part of your return trip in thick fog and under engine, didn't you? And you wrote me a note to say you'd made all your marks right on the nose."

"Yes," I said, "that's how it happened."

One other consideration occurred to me. "On that shakedown sail in June, a number of tools usually carried in a cockpit locker—an axe, a saw, a clam fork, and my toolbox—had not yet been put aboard for the season. Was there enough iron there to make a difference?"

"No; all too far from the compass.

"I did notice one thing, though," he remarked thoughtfully. "Although we did our tests under engine this afternoon, there was a little chop in some places and there were some wakes from powerboats. When you called 'Mark' from your position back at the compass, I saw that if she were rolling a bit, she was a bit slow to come back on to the mark for me. Now put that together with the fact that your worst deviation occurred in a fairly fresh breeze, with less of it during light airs or on a run—with no error at all under power.

"What you're probably getting is heeling error. When your boat is listing, the compass remains level but the engine is in a different position relative to it. And of course I can't do anything about that."

The lesson, of course, is simply to make as many observations as you can about the difference between your heading as the compass gives it and your course as laid out on the chart. With us, it looks like an error of five degrees when the boat is noticeably heeled, which gradually lessens as she returns to an even keel. If a sizable number of your courses don't come out right, a good possibility to check may be heeling error. With us, it's constant on whatever course and can be corrected simply by sailing to the left of the course, the amount of correction according to the amount of wind. Certainly a fact about one's boat worth knowing.

The Closed Loop

The Sailor took his hand-held radio direction finder aboard a friend's Hinckley Pilot to help him in his position as navigator for an ocean race. Only five miles away from Halfway Rock and less than fifteen miles from the Monster Buoy off Portland, he found that, seated by the mast, he received nothing but static.

Then he moved to the quarter and found less interference. It occurred to him that closed loops of wire can induce electric current. Therefore, he opened the gate in the life lines, tried again, and received both stations "loud and clear"—at any rate, better than before.

It seems that the problem is the closed loop. Sitting at the base of the mast, the Sailor was within the influence of a great number of loops. The shrouds were grounded to keel bolts and met at the masthead to form an athwartships vertical loop, divided into two loops by the aluminum mast. The forestay met the backstay at the masthead and both were grounded, forming a fore-and-aft vertical loop, also divided into two loops by the mast. Then the wire life lines encircled the boat, joined to bow and stern pulpits and grounded. Each loop was of a different length and orientation.

When radio waves hit these loops, their energy is absorbed, changed into induced current, and grounded. The extent of the interference depends on the wave length and frequency of the signal and on the length of the loop. Apparently, the loops on a Hinckley Pilot are just wrong for radio beacon signals.

However, one can avoid much of the effect by taking bearings from the quarter, outside the fore-and-aft loop, and by opening the gate in the life line, thus breaking the horizontal loop.

To the Owner of a New Power Cruiser

Dear Joe:

I am sure that you will enjoy your new *Alice*. At twelve knots you will see a lot of coast in a day and will enjoy the rush of water, the steady thrust of your big engine, and the sense of controlled power under your hand. However, you may be surprised at the attitudes of sailboat men, who will refer to *Alice* as a stinkpot and curse your passing.

They do not own the ocean, but they enjoy it in a different way. They move, not with the thrust and thrum of internal combustion but by presenting a curved surface to the wind, which converts it into power. This surface, the sail, maintains its shape by the same force of the wind that drives it, and to maintain the shape requires constant attention to helm and sheet, the rope that controls the sail.

As you pass close to windward, you disturb the air currents, especially when the wind is light. On such days, the momentum, the "way," that a sailboat builds up is particularly important, for the faster she goes, the more wind she makes for herself. When you pass at twelve knots, not only do you disturb the air flow but you leave behind a wake in which the sailboat rocks and lurches violently, shaking the wind out of the sails, destroying the boat's way, and bringing everything to a standstill. No wonder the sailor is enraged at your passing.

The problems raised by your wind and wake are multiplied by the heat of competition. To pass between two racing sailboats will hurt one more than the other and anger both.

There are other factors too. Just as you love the powerful thrust of your engine, the sailor hears the swish and rush of passing water and the subtle sound of the wind. Almost subconsciously he hears the creak of blocks, the strain of rope on winch and wood, the drum of taut canvas. He enjoys the rhythms of the boat's motion and the smell of air so different from air ashore. When you roar by to windward, you destroy this subtle compound of delight and leave a feeling of disgust.

You know from your Power Squadron course that operating a powerboat safely requires skill and judgment. However, the sailor, picking his way to float or mooring through a crowded anchorage, regards you as a bicyclist does a truck driver and wishes you would be gone.

To be sure, the law gives him the right of way over you in all cases except when you are not under control or when he is overtaking you, but he does not own the ocean by prior arrangement with Poseidon. You can each enjoy your own boat by understanding each other's pleasures.

Take it from an old "rag and rope" sailor. If you pass a sailboat to leeward, slow down a little to moderate your wake, move at dead slow speed through anchorages, and keep away from races. Instead of being damned for a stinkpot, in response to your cheery hail you may get a friendly wave.

Index